SEX, LOVE, MONEY, REVENGE AND RUIN

DIVORCE
CONFIDENTIAL

*The explosive confessions of
how the rich divorce*

**GERALD NISSENBAUM
& JOHN SEDGWICK**

D0784456

**EBURY
PRESS**

Published in 2010 by   , an imprint of   Publishing

A Random House Group company

First published in the US by Penguin as   and Money

Copyright © Gerald Nissenbaum and John Sedgwick

The Random House Group Limited Reg. No. 954009

Addresses for companies within the Random House Group can be found at
www.randomhouse.co.uk

A CIP catalogue record for this book is available from the British Library

The Random House Group Limited supports The Forest Stewardship Council (FSC),
the leading international forest certification organisation. All our titles that are
printed on Greenpeace approved FSC certified paper carry the FSC logo. Our paper
procurement policy can be found at www.rbooks.co.uk/environment

Mixed Sources

Product group from well-managed
forests and other controlled sources
www.fsc.org Cert no. TT-COC-2139
© 1996 Forest Stewardship Council

FSC

Printed in the UK by CPI Mackays, Chatham, ME5 8TD

ISBN 9780091933371

To buy books by your favourite authors and register for offers visit
www.rbooks.co.uk

To my amazing wife and law partner, Madeline Marie Celletti, with love
—G.N.

To A.G., with love and gratitude.
—J.S.

All the stories in this book are true. The characters existed. The events happened. Most of the information is in public records. Even so, to avoid disclosure of items that remain within the attorney-client privilege, I altered a variety of identifying details, including names, places, and merged facts from one case with another. In the complex cases, the legal procedures have been streamlined and other issues left on the cutting-room floor, lest they obscure the fundamental issues at hand. Aside from these cosmetic changes, the tales will unfold in this book exactly as they occurred, with all the quirks, mayhem, and drama that have made divorce law such a flavorful career for me for more than forty years. —G.N.

Part One

THE
SCENE

CHAPTER

ONE

SOME YEARS AGO, A CLIENT OF MINE, ARNOLD BURGHART, CALLED me in a panic. Arnold was an older man, nearing seventy, somewhat wizened with years, and I was afraid he might have a heart attack. He'd served in the army in World War II, and was one of the poor bastards sent to Nevada to witness the first atomic testing. He said the radiation never affected him, but it couldn't have felt good to know that the U.S. government had made him a human guinea pig. Now he ran a small ad agency here in Massachusetts. His wife, Cheri, was an ice dancer. A very fit, very lithe, very clever woman, maybe fifteen years younger than him, she had long, flowing blond hair that flapped behind her when she skated. He had shown me pictures. He was nuts about her. And I was afraid that was why he was so upset now.

"Arnie, calm down," I told him. "What's the matter?"

"She's moved out."

This was no huge surprise. Cheri had left him once before, maybe a year back, and she'd been talking divorce off and on since.

"What did she take this time?"

Last time, she'd drained their savings and checking accounts. I'd had to rush into court to tie up the rest of Arnold's money so she couldn't make off with everything. But then they reconciled a few weeks later, Cheri full of tears and apologies, and Arnold told me to forget about the courts. He was so besotted with Cheri, he simply couldn't see what she was about. I'd wanted to split their liquid assets fifty-fifty—half in his name, half in hers—just in case. That way, if she split again, she could only take her half, which she'd probably get in a divorce settlement anyway. But Arnold said no, no, no. She'd never do that. She loved him.

"Right," I said.

That was a year ago. Now he could hardly breathe.

"Arnie," I repeated. "What did she take this time?"

"Everything." He could barely speak.

"Everything? What do you mean, everything?"

"*Everything* everything. All my bank accounts are empty." He had four of them. "Even the home equity line. Maxed out."

"What'd she do with it?"

"She bought a fucking condo. Paid for it in cash, Jerry. My cash!"

"Okay," I said, trying to calm him down. "She bought a condo."

"And she took all the furniture!"

"You're kidding."

"I wish. I got home last night, and the whole house was empty. From the attic to the basement. Empty. The floors were bare, Jerry. The walls. Nothing! My art, my photographs. She didn't leave me so much as a soupspoon. Even my clothes are gone."

"Jesus—everything?" It was hard to imagine anyone going this far, even Cheri.

"Well, no, not everything. She did leave me something."

"And what's that?"

Arnie didn't speak for a second, and I thought that maybe there was something wrong with his heart.

"Arnie?" I asked.

4

"A spaghetti pot," he said. "She left me a spaghetti pot. One of those big black ones. She left it for me in the middle of the front hall. Couldn't miss it. It was the only thing in the whole goddamn house. And I looked in it, and guess what."

"What?"

"There was a penny. A single fucking solitary fucking penny."

So that's how it happened to Arnold. The love of his life left him a penny, and a pot to piss in.

☙

It CAN COME SUDDENLY, IN A TERRIFYING RUSH; OR IT CAN DAWN ON you slowly, over time. But for every divorcing couple there is a moment when the truth hits: the marriage is over. Whether you leave or are left, it's a shock. The life you built with your spouse—with the beautiful house, the children, the minivan, the dog, the vacations, the friends—is gone. Over. Done. It's like a death. Or, worse, a death in life. Because, after all, you are technically still alive. It's just that everything has been turned upside down and inside out, and now you don't know where— or who—you are. The person you considered your closest confidant and best friend has changed into an untrustworthy snake and your worst enemy.

It happened to my charming but frumpy client Gail Langer when she looked over the American Express bill while her husband, Philip, was off in Tokyo on an extended business trip. She noticed some charges that were made at Bloomingdale's in New York—lingerie—which was odd. So far as she knew, Philip hadn't been anywhere near New York, and he hadn't given her any lingerie. Convinced that it was some mistake, Gail called the store. The clerk assured her Philip Langer had purchased a pair of lacy bras and a camisole on the date listed on the bill. And while he was at it, they told Gail, he'd entered his name into the store's bridal registry. Gail started to say that was ridiculous—until the clerk told her the name of the bride. It was her husband's law partner.

5

That's how it goes, especially if you're on the receiving end. The best part of your life becomes the worst part of your life. Love turns to hate, the grinding, burning kind that has put more than a few of my clients in the hospital and placed their former mates at risk of serious injury or worse. Depressed and angry, Gail did not handle the situation well at all.

But she merely wanted to screw her husband to the wall financially. Another of my clients, Priscilla, wasn't so lucky. She ended up dead in her Mercedes, with a gun in her hand and a bullet in her temple. The cops called it a suicide; I call it murder. Her husband ran a cab company in Boston. He didn't like that she objected to his screwing around, and he didn't want to mess with a divorce settlement or risk her tipping off the IRS about the true state of his finances. And he knew the kind of people who could fix all that.

Of course, once you calm down, if you ever calm down, the real torture begins: dividing the assets, selling the house, pleading your case to some overworked thirty-year-old guardian ad litem who decides who gets your kids and on what terms, fighting over the pets (no joke: I worked for months on a custody fight over a Great Dane named Rajah), negotiating child support payments, making alimony payments, dragging yourself to a therapist and your kids to child psychiatrists, and allowing some black-robed judge to have the last word on your future.

I always make sure that I have a Kleenex box handy in my office.

So it's also a death—a death of just about everything you loved. Except there are no regular procedures to follow. You don't call 911, or summon a medical examiner, or send for an ambulance. You don't hire a funeral parlor, or pick out a casket, or dress up the body all nice for a final viewing. There is no sitting shivah. No wake. There is no priest, rabbi, or imam to comfort you with soft words about the hereafter and help you plan a crackerjack funeral. You don't summon relatives and friends to attend the service, or fortify yourself with booze at the reception afterward. You don't choose a cemetery plot, stand there stoically while the casket is lowered into the earth, and toss some dirt in. You don't have anywhere to go later, after dusk, when the grief settles in—not to a gravestone where you can leave some flowers, or a place where you can sob in private.

No, you don't do any of these things.

Instead, you call me.

I'm a divorce lawyer, and have been one for more than forty years. Yes, I know all the jokes. We're not the most loved members of the species. Fine. But if you're Arnold Burghart or Gail Langer, who else are you going to call? Your minister? Even my wife, Madeline Celletti, has very mixed feelings about our profession—and she's also my law partner. That's right. She's a divorce lawyer too, and a really good one. (She's also my second wife, so I know about divorce as a client too.) Call me a sick pup, but I love my work. I feel terrible witnessing such suffering—sure I do. But I'd be lying if I told you I didn't find it fascinating too: the things you learn about people, what they're capable of, how they act and react. I cannot wait to get into my office in the morning and hear the next installment of their stories.

This is a book of those stories. I have too many! My clients, thousands of them, are all buzzing around in my head. Forty years ago, last week—it doesn't matter. They are right here with me, like I met them this morning. They're just so interesting to me. It sometimes seems to me that I know better than anyone else in the entire world what people are really like.

I remember one guy, Paul, came to me after a waitress he'd known from high school got him plastered on champagne at a wedding, purred that she'd always had this huge crush on him, and, after one last slow dance, lured him into her Toyota. There she unzipped his fly, slid a condom on him, and blew him in the backseat. She saved the condom, complete with its contents. She brought the little love package home, carefully emptied the sperm into a turkey baster, and injected herself with it. Nine months later, she had a beautiful baby boy who looked . . . just like Paul. Now she was demanding child support. Paul was beside himself, ranting and pacing, when he came in to my office. But there wasn't much I could do. He was clearly the father, and the deception didn't matter. Someone would have to support the child, and that someone would be him.

One of my more paranoid clients, Marci, thought the CIA, FBI, and NSA were all sending her urgent messages through the comic strip *Zippy*. I started checking it myself, but I couldn't even make out the jokes, let alone any directives to Marci. When we talked about it, though, she insisted I whisper, because she was sure her husband had bugged her Rolex. I wrote on a sheet of paper: *Take off your watch so I can remove it from the room*. I'd never been so adored in my life. Finally, someone believed her.

Another of my paranoid clients, Francine, believed martians were beaming down into her bedroom at night to have sex with her and to steal the poetry she was writing in her mind so they could publish it themselves. (Hence my office policy: one paranoid at a time.)

I'll always remember the delightful Miss B, a tough woman from a bad part of town. When I told her the amount of the retainer she'd need to put up for me to take the case, she calmly replied: "Oh, well, shit. I can have him killed for less than that."

You also encounter people like the pathologist Alice. The pathological pathologist, I should say. When her wealthy husband, Alejandro, was diagnosed with ALS, and it was clear that he would face a long and expensive decline, Alice told him, straight out: "Do the right thing, and kill yourself." And she added that, as a doctor, she'd be happy to prescribe him the pills. "You don't want to be a burden to everyone, do you?" In case he missed the message, she had her brother repeat it to him. That's when Alejandro came to me. Horrified, I told him he should secretly build a separate home for himself several towns away and have it outfitted with all the special equipment he'd need, such as wheelchair ramps and elevators. Fortunately, he was able to move into his new home before his dear wife pressed a pillow over his face while he slept.

I also well remember Sam, a devoted husband who changed genders and became a devoted wife, renaming himself Sal. His wife was having none of it. She dumped him. And because Sal was out every night enjoying her new life and ignoring the family, the ex-wife demanded primary custody of the kids. I had a parade of beefy transvestites come through my office to testify to Sal's good character. No soap. It turned out that Sal was also a cocaine addict.

And I will always love the story of Patricia and Don, divorcing med students who'd been able to divide up all their property except for one item: a human skull, dubbed Yorick by my colleague here in the office, Stanley Cohen. Yorick had been in Patricia's family for at least two generations, although apparently he had not actually *been* anyone in the family. The skull stayed in their apartment after Patricia split. Then one day, Patricia came around to say hi and tried to make off with poor Yorick. Don tore after her, catching up to her in the subway station, where he screamed at her and ripped the skull out of her hands. The MBTA police called that assault and battery, as well as larceny. Don called it the recovery of stolen property. We had a helluva time straightening that one out. Yorick had to make an appearance in court, to the surprise of the security guards in charge of the X-ray machine he passed through on the way in. But in the end, in exchange for not pressing charges, Patricia walked out with Yorick's head in hand.

Well, I could go on. More than eight thousand cases, from more than forty years in the business. For each case, I have the full story, backed up by all the pertinent documents: the original case files, confidential client narratives, detective reports, psychological testing records, lie detector results, sworn depositions, trial transcripts, judicial opinions, and my own copious notes—not to mention my memories, which are remarkably extensive and detailed. Ask my wife! I now concentrate my practice on divorces of the rich, because only the rich can pay what I charge: $700 an hour, which is tops for this kind of work in Boston and in most places around the country. If I'm going to take them on, my clients need to have assets of at least $5 million, and usually a zero or two more. My fees on a case can run into the millions, or be as low as $3,500. Highly contested cases can easily take two years of discovery. Tracking down overseas money in shell companies, worming out trust income—it takes time. And there are expenses—for private investigators (there's a retired state police sergeant I really like), lie detector operators (one a former FBI agent, another a former army officer), forensic accountants, antiques and fine art appraisers, and other specialists like that. One case went on for seventeen years. My fee? A cool and hard-earned million. For a client who left happy. There's no shortage of divorces, God knows. But rich divorces are rarer.

I get my business by word of mouth and through Google searches, so I'm only as successful as my reputation. Lawyers who don't do divorce send me clients, and so will ones who do, if they can't handle some aspect of a case, like its financial complexity or its international reach. No referral fees, though. Why? Because any referral fee comes out of the award, and every penny of that is supposed to go to the deserving spouse. Here in the United States, contingency fees in divorce cases (by which another lawyer takes a portion of any award) are forbidden for the same reason. Imagine a lawyer getting a wife three hundred dollars a week in alimony or child support and then taking a third of it. The woman needs that money, and no court is going to allow any of it to be diverted to a lawyer—except in the great state of Texas, which thinks the practice is absolutely fine, and in Argentina, where they think allowing a lawyer to charge by the hour is an invitation to run up a bill, and a contingency fee encourages lawyers to work hard and more quickly bring the case to a good conclusion for the client.

Having been president of the American Academy of Matrimonial Lawyers, I get a lot of work outside my home state of Massachusetts, and I've had cases involving just about every state in the union by now. And as the founding president of the International Academy of Matrimonial Lawyers—an organization that for its first four years was headquartered in my office, with my Rolodex for its database—I've handled cases from dozens of countries around the world. I'm a sucker for cross-cultural issues. I've worked with clients in Turkey, Indonesia, Hong Kong, Singapore, various states of the United Arab Emirates, Taiwan, England, Israel, and many more.

Divorce work is a mix of law, money, and emotion. I like the dry stuff: monetary settlements, financial malfeasance, business valuations, exotic executive compensations, and all that. But it's not all numbers, that's for sure. Lots of times, I'm the shrink, or at least I do a lot of what a shrink does. I help people grieve. Unlike shrinks, I actually can do something to fix what's wrong. I can't revive marriages, but I can help restore some financial security, the absence of which can be the source of a lot of the anguish and grief people experience in a divorce. I can improve people's access to their kids and help create a sensible living arrangement for them, reducing another big source of stress. And I can ensure that children stay in their homes through high school, which can be a huge relief for them, giving their world a little more stability than there might otherwise be.

For me, the case is all about the story of the marriage. Before clients come into my office, I have them write down their story from beginning to end. The sex, the love, the money, the kids—everything. they would never tell anyone but me. The narrative, I call it: what happened before the marriage, in the marriage, to the marriage, and after the marriage. In one case, the narrative ran three hundred pages, but it's the Bible to me, and I go back to it again and again to try to understand what happened. I can't help with the divorce until I understand the marriage.

So I'm an ex post facto marriage counselor too, somebody who is brought in to understand the problems in the marriage, although it's too late to undo them. I try to learn about its interpersonal dynamics—did he bully her? did she cheat on him? how was the sex? was it frequent? were the in-laws intrusive? who made the money? who inherited it? who spent it? who raised the kids? and so on.

And I'm a statistician, specializing in litigation risk analysis. That's how we determine if it makes sense for us to take the case, and for the client to hire us. When it's all over is the client likely to come out ahead? This is a complicated calculation that involves determining the likely emotional strain on the client, total assets involved, our expenses in working the case, and the probability that the decision will go our client's way.

I'm also a forensic accountant, with a nose for money and the many places it might be hidden. I give a formal lecture at legal and accounting conferences called "How to Find the Cash." It is invariably well attended. I'm often astounded by the lengths some people will go to conceal their money—not just through the usual offshore bank accounts, which can often be traced (even the numbered accounts in Monaco), but by sliding assets over to business partners and relatives; hiding the money in foreign real estate; or converting the money to gold bricks or to bizarre "currencies," like supermarket coupons. I have to translate the values back into dollars so I can tally up the sum of the other side's holdings. Stock options, private offerings, royalties, royalty trusts, intellectual property—I need to be aware of all these assets and their value, or my client's screwed.

Unlike most divorce lawyers, I'm also a seasoned trial lawyer, and I live for depositions and trials, for direct and cross-examinations, those times when you really have to think on your feet and be prepared for anything. In court, I've had a few Perry Mason moments where I won the case with a single question. Boom.

I watched one husband, Louis, sob on the stand as he testified about how much he missed his kids and wanted to live with them, and even though judges have learned not to pay much attention to tears, the whole display seemed halfway convincing. But the truth was that he had a huge anger management problem. The guy could just snap, and then you'd better look out. On cross-examination, I wanted to establish this fact indelibly in the judge's mind.

Tears don't show up on a transcript, so I asked if he had been crying while testifying about missing his kids.

"Yes."

Then I took Louis back to the evening a year before when his wife told him that a suit he'd just picked out didn't look quite right on him, and he went ballistic.

My question: "Sir, were you crying then—as you were beating your wife to a pulp with a chair leg while your kids were cowering in the corner of the kitchen?"

He paused, stunned. The question hung in the air. Then he sighed. "No."

I had no further questions. His wife, my client, got sole custody.

ೞ

IN MY WORK, I'M RUTHLESS ABOUT ONE THING. MY CLIENTS CANNOT lie—to me, or under oath. If they do, they're no longer my clients. They can lie to their soon-to-be ex-wives, their children, their employers, their friends. But they cannot lie to me. If there is any doubt about whether they are being straight with me on a critical point in the case, I have them take a lie detector test in my office. They don't have to pass it, but they can't fail. Henry came to me when his visitation rights with his teenage daughter, Jarlene, were eliminated after Jarlene claimed he'd brutalized her. It was a complicated case because Jarlene also hit herself, making it difficult to tell who inflicted her injuries.

I told Henry he'd have to take a lie detector test to sort it all out.

"But I didn't hit her!" he insisted.

"Then you'll have no problem with the machine."

It took forever to get him in for the test. When it finally happened, Henry failed. But he insisted the result had nothing to do with him. "That lie detector examiner of yours—he asked all the wrong questions," he told me.

Henry wanted the examiner to ask only those questions that Henry had written out on cards for him. That was ridiculous, and I told him no way. But as a courtesy, I did let Henry take the test again. And once again he failed. I brought him into my office, and this time he made a confession, albeit a peculiar one. "Well, maybe my hand hit her. But I didn't."

That was too much. I gathered up the box with all his case files, and I handed it to him. "You're fired, Henry," I told him. "Go. Leave my office. Now. I'm done with you."

He was astonished. "But why?"

"Because you lied to me! Twice! First you said you didn't hit your daughter, when you did. And then you had this bullshit story about how it wasn't you who hit her but your hand. That's bullshit, Henry. That's just total, crazy, ridiculous bullshit."

Henry left my office like a dog that'd been smacked for shitting on the rug, but he only went as far as the waiting room, where he remained, morose, for nearly two hours until I threatened to call the cops to take him away. Then he finally boarded the elevator and left. That was the end of Henry.

୧୬

SURE, THESE ARE DIVORCE CASES, BUT REALLY THEY'RE LIFE STUDIES. Divorce reveals the full range of human behavior, from the good to the very, very bad. I sometimes think it shouldn't be part of domestic law, but should be put in with criminal law, because of the stuff that people do. Divorce rarely involves murder, but my cases have plenty of theft, battery, tax evasion, kidnapping, drug taking, verbal and physical and sexual abuse, willful destruction of property, and illicit sex of every sort, from the adulterous to the utterly perverse. Because divorce cases entail the love and betrayal that go into every marital meltdown, these stories have enough emotion for a century of soap operas—jealousy, rage, lust, passion, vengeance, mourning, spite, revulsion. That's just the short list! And in these high-end cases, you have to add in all the emotions that

14

surround money—greed, insecurity, fear, status lust, resentment. Divorce offers an inside look at the nature of commitment, with the tangle of conflicted feelings blown up, as big as a house, for all to see.

Divorce is not exactly an isolated phenomenon. It's the country we live in, the air we breathe. Forty-three percent of all marriages end in divorce. More than twenty million Americans are divorced and have not remarried, the highest number in history. Fifty-three million have been divorced at least once, and the million more Americans who get divorced every year only add to their ranks. I doubt there's one single American who isn't divorced or who isn't the child of divorce, the parent of a divorced kid, or the friend of someone who's divorced. And many people are several or even all of these. Divorce is as ubiquitous and impactful as gravity, and as little mentioned. But every divorce is a story, one couple's own private hellhole, each one different.

Most people shut up about it, or shrug. It's just too awful. People will talk about money, sex, religion, or any of the other big secrets far more easily than they do about divorce. Maybe it's because divorce covers money, sex, *and* religion. Not to mention failure, infidelity, anxiety, and status. So people say hardly anything about it to anybody—except to me. They tell me all about it.

When I'm at a party and somebody asks me what I do, I like to play it coy. "Actually, I do God's work," I say quietly.

They look at me a little funny. "Oh, so you're, like, a minister?"

"No," I say. "I put asunder what man has joined together."

That sort of language stops just about everybody. But I like the lofty sound of it, and I don't mind sparing myself the conversation that invariably ensues when I tell people my line of work straight-out. If they insist, I give it to them. "Some would call me a divorce lawyer."

"Really?" they ask, suspiciously.

"Really," I say.

A moment usually follows where they act like I have cancer and it might be catching. But then they realize that, no, I am more like the cancer doctor, and then they bend toward me like I'm in that old E. F. Hutton ad, and they're full of questions. A whole roomful of people will go quiet, fixating on every word of my answers.

Divorce is scary, a weird force field that moves in and takes over. A single divorcing couple in a plush suburb can cause a contagion. First the Jarvises go. Then the Wangs' marriage starts to wobble, and then the Feltsmans, who'd always seemed so stable, are in marriage counseling.

But that doesn't mean that, deep down, people don't want to know every last thing about it. Divorce may be a terrifying subject, but everyone wants to know what happens if . . . It's like asking what happens if you get rectal cancer, or audited by the IRS, or indicted for embezzlement. Scary, but people do want to know what it's like, and there are precious few places to get a sense of that.

Movies and TV shows never get it right. They don't register the desperation, the wildness, the shock. My clients are jumpy, edgy, crazy, freaked out, weirded out. Most need a few years of Valium to get through it. I'm not joking. I'm going to tell you what divorce is really like.

Remember: whacked-out as they are, all these stories really happened. They're as real as my fist. They contain the truths that make fiction jealous.

CHAPTER
TWO

I HAVE A BOUTIQUE FIRM IN DOWNTOWN BOSTON. NISSENBAUM Law Offices. It's located on the top floor of an elegant art deco building on Federal Street. It's a small suite with a little waiting area as you get off the elevator where clients can sit, or more likely pace, while they wait for me. Mindy, my law clerk, can give them a good look-over there, and I am always curious about her take on clients before I see them. That way I can be prepared if somebody's going to freak out on me. And, being young and attractive, Mindy is also, despite her engagement ring, likely to get a fair amount of attention from the soon-to-be-single guys, which makes me think there is hope for them.

It's a pretty normal office: conference room, offices, storage area. The thing that draws people's eyes is the artwork and antiques, which makes it seem more like a home than an office.

Stanley Cohen is of counsel, meaning he conducts his own practice inside my office. He has worked on a lot of my cases over the last twenty years. I've only worked on one of his: his divorce. It went as smoothly as these things can ever go, but it took forever. I've also got a senior associate, Wendy Hickey. She's in her early thirties and is a great person, really hardworking, smart, and has a gift for this kind of work. She came aboard as a paralegal and then, drawn to the work, went nights to Suffolk University Law School to get her degree. She's been what lawyers call second chair, or assistant, for me in court on many complex cases, and now is handling cases on her own. She's handled a number of unlawful "removals"—kidnappings, basically, where a spouse scoops up the kids and scrams to some foreign country. Like the Irish immigrant mother who flew off with her two boys back to Ireland and holed up there in a remote village, hours and hours from anywhere, claiming that she was protecting them from a drunken father. Which you might understand, except that she never produced a shred of evidence that our guy was a drinker.

My wife, Madeline, is also a partner in the firm, although these days she works from our home in West Boxford, where we live with our three children, Marleah, Nick, and Ben. She's great at settling cases and is a great resource, always coming up with ideas and approaches I wouldn't have thought of. But she doesn't like fighting in court over assets, visitation, custody—everything that can go on in divorce law. So when her cases need to go before a judge, she hands them to me.

We all have boxes of Kleenex handy, since the clients pour their hearts out to us. I keep a good supply of them in the storage room. Our office is a place to cry—and then to get busy making things right again.

One thing you won't find anywhere is my framed law degrees or certificates from the professional associations of which I am a member. I graduated from Boston University School of Law with both a JD and a Master of Laws in Taxation, but that was a long time ago. Hanging degrees on the walls won't help me get a client or win a case, so I leave that stuff at home.

೧೧

I HAVE A NEAR PHOTOGRAPHIC MEMORY FOR THE FACTS OF THE CASES I work on, which is useful in a line of work with so much paper. I know the law cold, but, more importantly, I know most of the judges and most of the attorneys on the other side. I wouldn't want to face me in a divorce case. I'm also a colorful dresser. At least, I think I am. I own maybe three hundred bow ties, more than a hundred shirts, and at least that many suspenders, more than enough for a new combination every day of the year. But I also have red-green color blindness, so I often ask Madeline for help when I choose the next morning's clothes before I go to bed. That way I avoid looking like I've gone through the Mixmaster when I show up for work at the office or in court.

I think of myself as being in the business of turning a crappy situation into something better. When clients come to me, their lives are a mess. There's money flying out the window; they're not seeing the kids; they're ready to kill. It's pretty awful. I can't fix everything, but I can make it better, so my clients can breathe again and not hurt so much.

It's in my blood, to tell you the truth. It's the family business to make something out of nothing. Seriously. I come from a long line of family junk dealers in Russia. It was a way to make a living in a country where it was illegal for Jews to own property. So Jews made sure their wealth was moveable. Either it was light and portable, like jewels or banknotes or a sewing machine, or it was in their heads, which is where my business is. When my grandpa, Joseph Nissenbaum, came to America around 1900, he was a ragman. He drove a horse and wagon around the streets of Somerville, advertising his wares. "Rags! Rags! Rags!" he'd shout. He sold other stuff too. He'd find things that were worn out or unwanted, then he'd clean them up, make them like new, and find a market for them. That's what I do. I take my clients' broken lives and turn them into something better—and take a piece of the action, just like my grandfather did.

My dad, David Nissenbaum, grew up with two brothers and two sisters in East Somerville's Brickbottom section, so called because nobody could afford to brick their houses past the first floor. The family didn't have much, but Dad was determined to move up from the rag business into something more respectable. He paid his way through law school by working as a page at the county courthouse in Cambridge and taking classes at night.

My dad set up a little one-man neighborhood law practice not far from his parents' house and was soon joined there by his brother Morris, after he finished his military service at the close of World War II. My father married a cheerful woman named Nettie Sugarman, who had also come up from nothing; her Russian father was in the slipcover business. They bought a house by the subway tracks, and all day the trolley cars went by. But the house quickly filled up with children—Eve, me, and then Janice—and with my dad's stories. That's what I remember best about my childhood. Stories about colorful judges, slippery lawyers, crooked cops. He'd tell them at dinner, in the living room, out on the porch. Whenever he started to tell those stories, the whole house went silent—except for the screeching of the trolley cars outside.

By the time I started law school in 1964, I had a wife to support, Barbara, and a son, Kent. She'd been a college girlfriend, and I'd gotten her pregnant junior year. We'd married while we both were still in school. We weren't perfectly suited for each other, but we tried hard to make it work. We committed ourselves to family life and had another son, Dion. Barbara was a great mom, and still is. She is also a wonderful grade school teacher and administrator. While I'd never say anything bad about her, I couldn't ignore my feelings. It was agonizing. I went to a therapist named Ed Daniels—to whom I had sent a number of my clients—so I could think through what I wanted to do and why. I started with a two-hour session because I had so much to say and then went three times a week the first year, two times the second, and just once a week the third, which I guess was progress. We discussed many issues, but at the heart of it there was just one: should I stay or should I go? Barbara knew why I was in therapy; for the two of us it was a very tense time. Finally, I admitted to myself that our marriage wasn't working for me. We'd lasted eighteen years, and I wanted out. It was sad all around.

Although my dad died during my first year of law school, when I graduated I joined his old firm of Nissenbaum and Nissenbaum as a junior associate. I did a little of everything: debt recovery, evictions, divorces, defending citizens accused of DUIs, assault and battery, kidnapping, and rape—all the cases nobody else in the office wanted to handle. A big turning point came when I was handling a case for an anxious sixteen-year-old named Jeannie. Her father was a top guy in the Winter Hill Gang, which was later run by James J. Bulger, better known as "Whitey," and now a longtime member of the FBI's Ten Most Wanted Fugitives list. Jeannie's dad has since done serious time in Walpole Penitentiary for a slew of different crimes, but the authorities never pinned a murder on him, and he never ratted anyone out. I'm not sure his time up the river has altered his temperament enough that I can safely use his name here, so let's call him the Mobster. He was a tough, scary guy, with lots of even scarier guys doing his bidding, but he looked mild enough to be an accountant. I never knew why, but he'd hired me to defend his daughter against charges brought by a Somerville cop who'd stopped Jeannie on the sidewalk and then gotten fresh with her, trying to fondle her breasts under her shirt, after she refused to answer his questions about her father's business. She'd tried to push him away, but the cop grabbed her and ripped her blouse. To defend herself, she scratched his face up pretty good and ripped his uniform. I found some witnesses, but lost the case in district court because the judge, an old nemesis of my father's, took the cop's word over everybody else's. I appealed to superior court, and I got the charges dismissed—so long as we gave the cop money for a new uniform. Fine. That was a small price to pay.

The outcome must have impressed the Mobster, because he started sending me some of his wiseguys who'd gotten in trouble. If the Mobster sent them, of course I had to take them. I won my share of the cases, but, no matter what the result was, after each case was over the Mobster always handled payment the exact same way. He'd walk right into my office. No appointment necessary for the Mobster. And no knocking either. If I had a client, that client stepped right out. The Mobster never sat down; he would loom over me at my desk and, with exaggerated politeness, insist I stay seated. "You did a good job," he'd say. "How much do I owe you?"

I'd tell him my fee, whatever it was. A thousand, fifteen hundred.

"That sounds right," he'd say. He never haggled. Never. He'd reach into his pocket, pull out a roll of cash—all hundreds—then he'd lick his thumb and peel off the bills and lay the money on my desk.

He'd thank me, step to the door, grab the handle, and then turn back to me. "You know," he'd say, "you don't have to put that money in the bank."

And I would always say, "If there is any money I'm ever going to put in the bank, this is it."

Then the Mobster would smile, a little half smile like he didn't really mean it, and I'd smile back at him because I did.

I wasn't going to hide the cash or let him think I would, because I didn't want the Mobster to have anything on me. If he knew I was not declaring that income, he had me by the balls. And if he had me by the balls, someday he'd squeeze them. So as soon as the Mobster was out of the office, I told my secretary to take the cash and deposit it in the Somerset Savings Bank across the street. Right away. I wanted her to either get there before the bank closed at three or, if it was too late, be the first one in line in the morning. I was sure the Mobster had people in the bank watching to see if that money came in. But even if he didn't, I didn't want anyone to have any reason to think I wasn't depositing it.

It was a bad time to be a gangster in Somerville, and a bad one to be a gangster's lawyer too. I never handled any gang-related activities. But I did do some stuff involving midlevel drug dealers that probably came to the gangsters' attention. Marijuana, mostly, but some heroin, and a few pills.

One of my clients was a heroin addict who dealt on the side to support his habit. The cops grabbed him for intending to distribute, and since they had him cold, they wanted him to turn state's evidence and rat out his supplier. But that would have been a death sentence. He was between a rock and a really, really hard place. If he flipped, the drug dealers would kill him. If he didn't flip, the cops would get pissed and say he had, and the drug dealers would kill him. If he went straight to jail, he said he'd die without his junk. Not a lot of good options there. I told my guy that the best he could do was to agree to be a rat, get the charges dropped, and then get the hell out of here. Move away. Way away. Another country away. He said he couldn't; he needed his heroin, his supplier. I said okay, it's your funeral. That was a Thursday. Monday's paper had a picture of his body. He'd been found the night before in a Boston back alley, with a bullet in his head.

In those days, the Winter Hill Gang was facing down a couple of rival gangs that were trying to muscle in on the Mobster's territory, and they were all killing each other at a pretty good clip. It seemed like another body turned up in the trunk of somebody's car every week or two. The cops didn't do much to stop it for fear they'd get killed. Besides, it was a lot easier for them to collect the bodies than to solve the crimes the dead men had been responsible for. But it was hard on the lawyers, because they became targets too. A lawyer named John Fitzgerald had represented a heavy-duty gangster named Joseph "the Animal" Barboza on some mob stuff. Fitzgerald went out to his car one morning and turned the ignition, and the car blew sky high. Incredibly, he wasn't killed. But he did lose a leg.

It was a lesson to me. As I said before, I didn't deal with gang-related crime, but I did deal with some of the stuff that gang members were involved with, and I thought I'd rather not get blown up after breakfast some morning. So I decided I'd had enough of criminal law.

Before I could get out, though, I had to go see the Mobster and explain myself. He worked out of the back room of a bar on a side street off Broadway. He had a guard out front, and I told him whom I was there to see. After the guard checked with someone inside, I was ushered to the back room. This time, the Mobster sat and I stood, but I didn't feel any more in control of the situation. I told him that I was getting out of criminal work to focus on divorce cases. I didn't say the reason was that I didn't want anyone to plant a bomb in my underwear.

"So you'll not be doing any criminal work except the stuff that is divorce related."

"Correct."

"I liked your work, you know. I might feel insulted if I heard you were handling somebody else and not my guys."

"I'd never ever insult you. I would never even think of it."

"Well then, best of luck."

"And to you, sir."

And that was it. His wise guys never called again.

∽∾

IN BOSTON, THE LAWYER WHO FIRST MADE DIVORCE WORK ACCEPTABLE for the nonwhite-shoe set was Monroe Inker. He started in back in the 1950s, and is dead now, but we had several run-ins. He was the grandson of a Russian Jewish immigrant, just like me; and he was a sharp dresser, just like me. But while I went to Boston University, he went to Harvard Law, and that was a big deal to him.

Inker was a very capable lawyer, and also a publicity hound. When I started to get a little ink of my own, he decided I was his nemesis. He wanted me off his turf. It bugged me the way he'd showboat around on cases, while leaving most of the work to beleaguered junior associates. And the guy would never negotiate, no matter how much it meant to his client in added legal fees. Inker would take their money, hungering for an out-and-out win that would make it clear to the world that he, Monroe Inker, was the better lawyer. It was for him that I developed my Turtle Defense, pulling in my legs, head, and tail whenever Monroe started lobbing legal hand grenades at me. When he was done with that round, we'd start lumbering toward the finish line again in order to finally get my client divorced.

One time, Inker represented a former "Golddigger" dancer from *The Dean Martin Show* who was divorcing a client of mine, a big-money heir named Hanley Jackson, of Lincoln, one of the swanky, woodsy towns west of Boston. The judge in the case was one of Inker's best friends. Just before the trial, they had gone rafting together down the Grand Canyon. Even so, I believed the judge respected me and I trusted him to be fair, and I ventured that I had a pretty good idea of what the final result would be. I called up Inker and offered to settle the case for five million dollars. He spat at the offer, calling it an insult and demanding nearly half of my client's four hundred million. Well, two years later, after each side had spent two million dollars in legal fees and gone through twenty-four days of trial, guess what. The judge awarded Inker's client exactly what I had offered Monroe in that first phone call. Five million dollars, *to the penny*. His client wasn't a bit happy thinking about the two million she'd paid him to get there. But that's the way Inker was. He didn't want to settle with me; he wanted to beat me. He never did.

ॐ

By the early seventies, I could see that society was loosening up; divorce wasn't so shameful anymore, and I figured it could be a growth industry. Plus, there weren't too many lawyers doing divorce full-time. That's when I followed Inker's lead and jumped in.

My first divorce case was in 1968. It involved a woman who wanted to leave her husband to shack up with a guy I knew from high school. He was a bully, actually, and the first thing I told her was that it was stupid to go with him. But she insisted. Back then, no-fault divorce didn't exist, so she needed her husband to divorce her. The only way he'd do that was if she gave him the house, waived alimony, and agreed to fifteen dollars a week in child support for their three-year-old. That shows you how long ago this was. Some six months later, the new guy started beating the crap out of her, like I'd figured he would, and she was out of there. On to welfare this time, since she'd waived alimony. She came back to see me, asking me to make a phony claim against her ex to try to get some money out of him. I told her what I have said to every client who has proposed I help them by doing something illegal or unethical. I said, sure. Fine. I'll be happy to help you with that. But you'll need to put twenty-five million dollars in a Swiss account for me, taxes paid. Because that's what I'll need to live on if I can't practice law anymore, and I won't be if I agree to help you with that shit. Then I show them out the door, saying, "Think about it."

She didn't take me up on my offer. They never do.

In those days, I dealt with a lot of questionable characters. In one case, I was so concerned about my client's soon-to-be ex-husband that I wore a bulletproof vest into court. He ran a chop shop with mob connections. Back then, they didn't have metal detectors to screen people coming into the courthouse. I was very concerned about what the guy might do when I told the court about the other set of books he kept, ones that revealed the true figures for his business income, not the fake ones he furnished to the IRS. The judge might be obliged to report the discrepancy to the IRS, and that would cost the ex big-time. I was afraid the man might pull out a gun and shoot me right there in court. Well, he wasn't packing that day, or at least he didn't shoot me. And then—the two reconciled! He offered his wife a pledge of undying fidelity, plus a few safe-deposit boxes, each one stuffed with a million dollars in cash, if she'd let him move back in with her. I told her not to, unless she wanted to put on a bulletproof vest every morning. But I'll be damned if she didn't take his offer. And I never heard from her again.

I haven't handled any mob cases in more than a decade now, which is fine with me. I've traded up for higher-end clients: the owner of a local sports franchise, a longtime TV news broadcaster, top executives at some of New England's largest corporations, dozens of international tycoons, globe-trotting megaconsultants, tons of money managers, three or four bank presidents, a few dozen real estate developers, a slew of entrepreneurs, major retailers. Picture all the rich in America, and in several other countries, and I've had a cross section of them in my waiting room, in my office, on the phone, telling me the most intimate details of their lives. I know how they behave in the shadows, when they are in bed with someone they are not married to, or while they're trying to find someplace to hide the money they're sure to lose if they leave it out in the open. And I know how they behave when these matters are brought to light.

Because I am the one who flips the switch.

Take Louise Bakersley. She was the artistic wife of a prominent software developer. They lived in Wellesley. Bored with her leisure, she decided to break with the crass commercial world her husband occupied and become a memoirist. She enrolled in a memoir-writing course at Bard College one summer, where she fell for her long-haired, twice-divorced instructor. They went on long walks, swam naked in a pond deep in the woods, and got it on in a big way. They then exchanged graphic e-mails exulting in all the positions and toys and techniques they'd used together, and how long he was, and how great she felt when he put it all the way up inside one orifice or another—e-mails that were read by Louise's nine-year-old son after she accidentally left them open on her computer at their summerhouse in Provincetown. The kid was stunned. Right in front of him was evidence that his mother had betrayed his dad, after any number of prissy, repressed lectures to him about sex. He told his father, Michael Bakersley. Enraged, Michael checked through the files on the computer's hard drive and discovered that there weren't just a handful of these e-mails, but hundreds of them. After consulting with the boy's school psychiatrist, he called me and insisted that such behavior posed a potential threat to his nine-year-old. I agreed to ask for a court order forcing Louise to vacate the house immediately.

When the constable showed up to serve the order, Louise stood there in the living room in front of him and, staring directly into the constable's eyes, stripped off her clothes piece by piece and placed them in a pile before her, with her bra and panties on top.

Now why would she do that? To seduce him? To make herself vulnerable? To play the victim? To say, "See? See who I am? What I am?"

I don't spend a lot of time pondering such moves, since there really is no way to understand them. The constable, who'd been in the business for almost thirty years, said this was a first for him, and he couldn't believe it either. To get her to vacate, the constable had to call the cops, who brought a matron to throw a sheet over her in case she refused to get dressed. Naked in her front hall, Louise finally put her clothes back on. She then climbed into her own car to leave the premises as ordered. She drove to a nearby hotel, where her instructor was waiting.

ಞ

I HANDLE THE FULL RANGE OF DIVORCE CASES, EVERYTHING FROM money cases to money cases. I say that because in my business everything comes back to money—the money that I'm paid, the money that one spouse is trying to get from the other. So money is at the heart of all these stories. And it's money to burn—enough to excite lust for it if you're on the short end, and enough that you'll fight like hell to hang on to it if you're on the long. But, either way, it's enough that you don't mind my fees and expenses. That's why, one way or another, all these stories end up being about money. But they don't start there, so I won't either. They start with sex. Marriages all start with sex, and they almost always end with it too although by then it's outside the marriage. Sex lights the fire, for good or ill. But sex also leads to children, who focus the passions in ways that are unimaginable to the childless. Often there's a dispute over who gets the kids and when, which is yet another focus of my work. And that is the subject I will end the book with: the kids.

So what follows is the life of a marriage that ends too soon. It starts with sex, becomes preoccupied with money, takes on children, and ends with sex with someone else. But it does start with sex—sugary, intoxicating, irresistible sex.

Part Two

———— ⚭ ————

SEX

———————————————

CHAPTER
THREE

L ET'S FACE IT: SEX CAN FUSE A COUPLE TOGETHER, AND IT CAN blow a couple apart.

When I think of the big ka-BOOM, I think of Sidney, a kindly, bald, fortyish anesthesiologist at one of Boston's larger hospitals. I knew him socially before he was a client, and he always struck me as a sane person—quiet, easy, methodical. Anesthesiologists aren't exactly known for going wild, right? He'd been married to his cute wife, Alyssa, for about a decade while he worked his way up the ladder at the hospital. Alyssa had been a physician's assistant, but she quit when they married, and then they turned their attention to having babies, which came fast. Three of them. All girls. It seemed like everything was going very nicely for Sidney.

Sidney had always dreamed of living in a log cabin, God knows why. And he was determined to build one for the family. Of course, these days log homes aren't really built; they are assembled from various logs that are sent, precut, from a factory. Sidney bought a lot for the cabin by a pond on the other side of town. He'd been so busy, he hadn't had a chance to see the builders put the house together; he'd left the supervision to Alyssa. One Saturday afternoon, Alyssa hired a babysitter for the kids while she ran some errands. Sidney had the afternoon shift at the hospital, but before heading downtown, he decided to take a few minutes to finally swing by the building site and see how things were going. There was a pickup truck in the drive, and his wife's Toyota. That was a surprise; she hadn't mentioned coming over.

Sidney didn't think about it; he was so happy to see that the walls were mostly up and that the roof was in place. It all seemed really solid and rustic, just what he'd wanted. As he stepped through the front doorway, he heard some rhythmic cries—oh! oh! And then he saw his wife. She was spread-eagled on a canvas sheet on the floor. Naked to the waist, with her skirt all bunched up, she was writhing under one of the carpenters, whose pants were down around his knees.

Sidney felt sick, and nearly fainted. He could not believe what he was seeing. Alyssa? This was his wife? With this guy? But Alyssa loved *him*. Right? Those were his thoughts, he told me. Basic thoughts, running over and over in his head. Their sex life had not been nearly as active since their last child was born, but he'd never imagined that she'd have sex with anyone else. He didn't say anything. He was pretty sure she didn't even see him. He staggered out of his new dream house, climbed back into his car, and shot out of there.

He had a licensed gun in his glove compartment. And it was loaded. As he bombed down the road, he popped the catch on the glove compartment and then groped inside for the gun. All he could think of was the carpenter on his wife—the guy's pale butt, and his wife's breasts shaking with each thrust. He had the gun in his hand, pointing toward his temple. He started crying, and yelling about how he couldn't believe that his wife would do it with another man, a fucking carpenter for Christ's sake, and he pounded the dashboard with his fist. "Shit!" he screamed; then threw the gun down on the seat beside him. Miraculously, it didn't go off. He wouldn't blow his head off. Fuck that. No, he'd drive the car into a goddamn tree, or a house, or another car. Just rev it up and let loose. Fuck them all! He unclipped his seat belt and prepared to launch himself through the windshield. But then he heard a siren behind him, and saw a flashing blue light, and a cop inside the cruiser was gesturing for him to pull over. When the policeman came to the side of the car, Sidney was still crying, and he was incoherent as he tried to explain what the hell was going on, about his wife, and the carpenter, and how fucking fucked up it all was. When the cop saw the gun on the seat, he undid the snap on his own gun and gripped the handle.

"Leave the gun right there, okay, pal?" he said to Sidney. "Just leave it and get out of the car real slow. With your hands out where I can see them."

"But I'm an anesthesiologist," Sidney said, coming out of his funk. "I've got—I've got to get to the hospital. They're expecting me."

"Not today they're not."

The cop put the silver cuffs on Sidney's hands, behind his back, then steered him to the back of the cruiser and pushed him inside.

"Wait—where are you taking me?"

"Don't you worry about that."

It proved to be the psychiatric wing of Quincy Medical Center, which made Sidney even crazier than he had been. "No!" he started shouting. "I'm not going in there! No!"

The cop told him to calm down, or he would only make matters worse. But Sidney couldn't calm down. Seeing his wife with another man, feeling panicky and suicidal, and now this. But the cop was not sympathetic, nor was the admitting department when the cop presented Sidney to them and described what he'd seen.

Sidney did not give a very good account of himself. To the psychiatrist on call, he must have seemed like a raving lunatic. Deciding Sidney was a danger to himself and others, the shrink pink-slipped Sidney for a ten-day stay. He was placed in the locked ward on the fourth floor, on a suicide watch.

He wasn't allowed to make a phone call until the next morning.

Father's Day—isn't that nice? That's when he called me and laid out what had happened to him in the last twenty-four hours. I'm often astounded by the things clients tell me, but I was absolutely staggered by the realization that Sidney, of all people, had turned up in a psychiatric ward.

After we hung up, I called Phil Aiken, a forensic psychologist I'd known for a long time, and told him I needed a big favor.

"Sure, Jerry, what's that?"

"I've got a situation here." I explained what was going on with Sidney. "I need you to drive right out to Quincy Medical Center and run some tests on Sidney to see if he really is a danger to himself, okay? Or see if everybody over there is overreacting?"

"Why, what's your read on the guy?"

"Well, he's sure had quite a jolt, but he's always seemed pretty stable to me. I really don't think something like that is going to put him permanently over the edge. But believe me, if Sidney doesn't get out of there soon, he'll be there for ten days—and then he probably *would* turn pretty buggy."

"I'm on my way."

Phil did what I asked. I stayed by the phone, and he called me back a few hours later.

"Well?" I asked.

"He's saner than I am," Phil said.

"That's not good, Phil," I deadpanned. "You don't set that high a standard."

He laughed. "Well, let's just say he's not a danger to himself."

"Terrific," I told him.

Phil wrote up a report, and first thing the next morning I took it in to Norfolk Superior Court. After filing a complaint, I secured a writ of habeas corpus, requiring the hospital to bring Sidney to court or explain to the judge why that was too dangerous. The court issued the order, requiring the hospital to produce Sidney by two o'clock that afternoon.

By one, Sidney called to say he was a free man, out of Quincy Medical and on the way to his afternoon shift at Boston City Hospital.

I started his divorce proceedings shortly after that. It was quite a battle, with a lot of acrimony and paperwork, and one not aided by Sidney's lingering fury about his wife's betrayal. Finally, we hammered out an agreement, both sides signed it, and the judge gave his okay. Everything was all set. I'd gotten my client out of a bad situation, one that was literally driving him crazy, and into a new life. A job well done.

Then, about three weeks later, I received an envelope from the court, containing copies of a motion to vacate both Sidney's divorce judgment and his separation agreement and to dismiss the complaint for divorce. Legal moves that had all been allowed by the court.

Looking at the documents, I thought, "What the heck is this?" Surely, there was some mistake. Was Sidney getting undivorced?

I called the court and got a clerk on the line, and I asked her why I'd received the dismissal of Sidney's divorce case. "You mean Sidney and Alyssa?" the clerk asked, very chatty.

"Yes, that's my case," I told her.

"Oh, my heavens, Mr. Nissenbaum, they were in here three days ago, all lovey-dovey. They were really cute together. They've reconciled! After all that stuff they went through! Isn't that funny? They went to the judge and put forward their motions to dismiss, and said that's what they really wanted. He asked them if they were sure about it several times. They said, 'Yes, we're absolutely sure.' So the judge said, 'Fine, all set; you're married again, and good luck.'"

Well, they were sure going to need it, I figured.

Their relationship had fallen apart and now revived so dramatically, I had to call Sidney to find out what happened. Well, he'd gone back to the house to pick some stuff up, and Alyssa was there, and they had some coffee together, and they got talking, and the next thing they knew they were in the sack going at it like never before. And they'd kept at it. All that anger turned into wild passion. Sidney wasn't just crazy anymore. He was crazy in love.

ೕ

IF YOU ASK ME TO NAME THE BIGGEST SINGLE CAUSE OF DIVORCE IN this country today, I'd have to say it's marriage. And the biggest single cause of marriage? That would be sex. From where I sit, sex explains everything people do, especially at the start of a relationship, and it's all they think about besides. Sex is a full-time preoccupation. When can I get it? How good can I make it? Who can give it to me? Where? It eats everyone up. It accounts for most of the feelings people have: worry, lust, obsession, boredom, fear, desire, heartache. It's the dynamo that pushes society along, causing people to do ridiculous stuff like what Sidney and Alyssa did: come together, then split up, only to come together again.

I'm not complaining. This unmating ritual has given me a pretty good living. I know that sex is the story behind all relationships, the one that accounts for the inside stuff my clients tell me about in their narratives. Contrary to public impression, in nearly all states extramarital affairs have no bearing on a divorce outcome. Now that no-fault divorces are the norm, the judge has little interest in any extramarital affairs, even the ones that end a marriage. So the days of private eyes lurching into hotel rooms to catch an errant spouse in the act are pretty much over, except in New York and a couple of other states where a spouse's adultery means no alimony. Some lawyers use such salacious material as a threat to get the other side to back down in the face of terminal embarrassment—although when you see how much of this stuff does come out, you have to think that it isn't used that way very much, or that if it is, it doesn't work. Here in Boston, a lawyer tried this tactic on a lecherous billionaire investor, threatening to go public with embarrassingly obscene letters he had written to some floozy. He said go right ahead, and they were all over the newspapers, but the billionaire never flinched. There's so much openness about sex now, I doubt an affair bears that much stigma. In some quarters, it is a point of pride.

It always surprises me how little shyness my clients have about their sex lives. In the private space of those narratives we always ask for, they'll let me know what positions they like, what times of day, what sorts of places, how often, who was wearing what. The narratives are like something John Updike might have cooked up, although they aren't so well written, and the grammar is a mess. From them, I can tell where the heat is, or was, in the marriage and what happened to it. It's important, because I'm convinced that sex is the single biggest predictor of marital outcomes. Happy couples are happy in bed. If the sex goes early, the marriage is likely to go early too. And I have yet to handle a divorce where the sex was still great. Great sex is like a combination of Velcro and superglue—you can't pull the two people apart.

Check that. There was one case where the sex was out of this world and the couple wanted to split up anyway. But it's the exception that proves the rule, an adage that otherwise perplexes me. Because—get this—even after they started divorce proceedings, the wife did not want to give up screwing my guy, and he felt the same way about her. She kept inviting him for dinner—and a little something extra after dessert. Until . . . she got pregnant. Thereupon she reversed course and wanted to keep the marriage going long enough so her child would be born in wedlock, which would mean that she'd be entitled to a portion of her husband's property, plus alimony and child support. My client didn't want his child to be a bastard, so he agreed to it, even though that meant much bigger payments. Nevertheless, that ended her sex appeal for him. Getting dunned will do that.

But the killer of it is, the sex is almost destined to go bad, because it is almost never as good in marriage as it was during the heavy romance that led up to it. Think about it: first you're having hot sex after gorgeous, candlelit dinners in fine European hotels. Then you're crammed together in some schlumpy apartment, dealing with each other's dirty dishes and bad habits. And then the children come along, and you might as well put your genitals in a drawer.

And that's when it hits: marriage is a birdcage. A gilded birdcage, perhaps, but a birdcage. There's nowhere to fly, and nothing but newspaper down below to catch the droppings.

But the sexual urge, the ache, never ends. That's the part that amazes me. It lasts and lasts. Over the years, I've had some randy old goats, with an emphasis on old. Egg-bald, well into his sixties, drugstore magnate Franklin was twice divorced when he fell in love with skinny Judy, two years his senior, and never married. They dated for a few months, but never went to bed together, and hardly touched. And that was fine with Judy. After one nice dinner at the restaurant on the top of the Prudential Tower, he pulled out an engagement ring and smiled, and she tearfully said yes.

The wedding was modest—a justice of the peace followed by a dinner at a restaurant. That night Judy was in for a big surprise. A really big surprise. A penile implant. Without her knowing, Franklin had gone to the hospital for a hydraulic pump that would make him erect pretty much forever. A boy with a toy, Franklin wanted to put his thing in every hole he could find. Judy was horrified. But they worked out an arrangement that brought Franklin satisfaction without making Judy too miserable. Then, for their first anniversary, Franklin went and got a new, sturdier version that produced an erection that might have been made of metal.

Judy wanted out.

She didn't tell Franklin, though. Knowing what he wanted, she decided to take a few things in trade. A nice condo in Steam Boat Key, Florida, for starters, one that she had him give her daughter, knowing it could not then be part of any divorce settlement. A Lexus. Diamond jewelry. Some swell vacations. All of which he cheerfully provided as long as she would come to bed with him and lie still. After Judy had loaded up on all the goodies she wanted, she served him with divorce papers.

I represented her, and she did well, mostly because I found out that

Franklin was not reporting a substantial amount of cash income to the IRS. But I'll admit I felt a little badly for Franklin. He only wanted what all guys want. He just chose the wrong partner. No, I'm not too proud of sticking it to him, but the law was on Judy's side, and she got what was coming to her.

The sex does not always stay within the confines of marriage, needless to say, and it is most destructive when it does not. The most common scenario is the eternal triangle—a boy, a girl, and another boy (or girl). It is fair to say that there would be many fewer novels, movies, and TV shows but for the many possibilities of this arrangement. Something about it—maybe it's the conflict between the sex that's socially okay and the sex that's not socially okay—makes it particularly interesting to read about or see. And I have certainly had more than my fair share of cases, like Sidney's, that feature the triangle. But the love triangles that wreck marriages aren't always conventional ones where the husband or the wife is banging somebody on the side. No, it's often a lot weirder than that, with the guy—and it more often is the guy—putting his dick someplace he *really* shouldn't.

Or two places. Or five. We had a New England Patriots football player here in town who couldn't stop knocking girls up. I represented one of them. Cheryl. A Barbie doll—very shapely, but dumb as plastic. She wanted the Pat to marry her, and figured the best way to catch him was to bear his child, which wasn't hard since he considered it unmanly to use a condom. He preferred to buy his way out, so we arranged for him to provide some generous child support, get her an SUV and a cushy condo, and put away a quarter million in an educational trust fund for the kid. All that was fine with our Patriot. He knew the drill. He had several other relationships I don't know much about, and then he married one of these gals, to everyone's surprise, and got her pregnant, probably not in that order. But when he came up to Boston for the next football season, he picked right back up where he left off with Cheryl—and knocked her up again! Or so she told me. When I called the Pat's lawyer to open negotiations, he insisted on a pregnancy test. Almost immediately Cheryl miscarried. Or so she said. But by then, I'd checked into our Patriot's love life and discovered that, at that particular point in time, our Patriot's missile had impregnated two other women, as well as his wife. If he had concentrated as hard on the football as he did on his dick, he'd still be playing.

Or sticking it in the future mother-in-law. *And* the future father-in-law. Both. The penis in question belonged to a prominent but weaselly Seattle psychiatrist named Roger Stone who entered into the life of his future wife, Kathleen, by taking as patients first her mother and then her father. Stone started screwing them on his psychiatrist's couch. It was all part of treatment, he said. I suspect that neither the husband nor the wife had any idea that Roger was doing the other. I think they believed he loved each of them exclusively. Still, it makes me ill to think how each of them, after they'd repeatedly done the deed, sent their tender, musically inclined daughter, Kathleen, to him to work on some personality issues at age sixteen. In her innocence, Kathleen became captivated by this snake too. Desperately so. She hung on him. He was her first and her everything. And in contravention of every law, convention, and code of behavior, Roger married Kathleen a couple of years later, before she was even twenty. He was fifty-three.

Wretched as he was as a psychiatrist and human being, Roger was a brilliant investor. He'd made millions by investing in gold shortly before the United States went off the gold standard and prices exploded just as he had predicted. He retired with his young bride to Costa Rica to live in paradise. Unfortunately for him, it was there that, poking around in the closet off his office, Kathleen happened upon some videotapes he had recorded of himself having sex with a number of his patients, including her parents. God knows why he'd made them, let alone kept them and brought them with him. She nearly gagged at the sight of her former psychiatrist, and current husband, gently stroking the bare breast of her mother, asking how that felt, moving his hands down her body, getting naked with her, and then going on to do things that I need not list here, although Kathleen did for me in a riot of tears, doubled over, quaking. In another tape, Roger did similar things to— or was it with?—her father. Kathleen saw the two of them entwined on the psychiatrist's couch, nearly every part of them revealed, and then she could watch no more.

By then, Kathleen and Roger had a nine-year-old daughter, Juliet, and Kathleen was terrified that her husband would try something with her too. She fled with her daughter back to the United States that very day, to Boston, where she rushed into my office first thing the next morning. She was in the waiting room when I arrived. As soon as we started to talk, she told me she didn't want to be married to Stone a minute longer.

When he got word of Kathleen's intentions, Stone didn't put up any fight. Kathleen had taken the tapes, and he knew what she could do with them. The guy was loaded, and he gave her a hefty settlement, plus a good chunk in trust for young Juliet.

Thinking it important to allow Juliet to maintain some contact with her father, creep that he was, Kathleen agreed to some visitation. But she was terrified, sleepless, every time her daughter went to visit Roger. All went fine until a few years later, when Juliet was thirteen. She was with her father in Costa Rica, and they were driving on a narrow road when Roger sideswiped a small boy on a bicycle, sending him into a ditch. Juliet screamed at him to stop and check on the kid, who looked badly hurt and was barely moving, the bicycle twisted around him. Stone insisted everything was fine—he'd not struck anyone, nothing had happened— and he just kept driving. Juliet was frantic with distress.

When Kathleen heard the story, she decided the visitation had to stop. Roger was plainly out of his mind, and she feared for her daughter if she spent any more time with him.

We took the matter to a judge, and this time Dr. Stone showed up to defend himself pro se; that is, without a lawyer. He was a scrawny lit-

tle guy with thinning hair and a ruddy complexion. I'd expected someone far more handsome. His defense to the judge was even more of a
mess. It went every which way and made little sense. The judge stopped
Stone before he even finished and passed a note to the courtroom clerk,
requesting the court psychiatrist to come and evaluate Roger's sanity.

The doctor looked stunned to learn that he would be on the receiving end of a psychiatric evaluation. But everything stopped while we
waited for the court's shrink to examine this shrink. While we were
waiting, Stone started humming to himself, really loud, producing a
deeply bizarre sound in a courtroom that echoes so. Then he lurched up,
looked all around the room, and shouted out: "Wait—what am I doing
here? *What am I doing here?*"

"What do you mean, sir?" the judge asked from the bench.

Roger continued to act all bewildered. "Where am I?"

"You're in the Probate and Family Court," the judge growled.

"But why?" He was still loud. And a breathless sort of crazy. "Why
am I here? Why here?"

"You're here on a complaint for modification."

"What's that?" he asked, as if he really didn't know. "What are you
talking about?"

The judge's patience was wearing thin. "You were married, divorced,
and now we're here to determine your rights of visitation. Now be quiet
please, or I will cite you for contempt."

"Well, I must have been in an amnesia fugue," Roger declared in a
strangely calculating voice. The guy was faking. He was both crazy and
not crazy.

"You can discuss the diagnosis with the court's psychiatrist," the
judge told him sternly, obviously bothered by his antics. "He'll be here
in few minutes. I've ordered you to have a consultation with him. You
remember that?"

"Oh no!" he shouted. "No!" Then Stone jumped up and dashed
out of the courtroom at full speed. I followed him. When I reached

the front door, he had rushed into the street, flagged down a cab, and jumped in.

And then he was gone. Back to South America, as far as I know. Kathleen and I never saw him again. Nor did Juliet.

That's one of my frustrations. I see all these crazy things. But unless the participants pursue a legal case, I never get the explanation. I never learn why—or what happened next. So I'll never know why Roger decided to have sex with Kathleen's parents, and why they went along with it. And I don't know what became of Dr. Roger Stone. Nothing, I hope.

൚

THINGS GOT MORE COMPLICATED ONCE, WHEN A SEX-CRAZED HUSBAND turned lustfully toward his sister-in-law.

My client was Elise, the daughter of a wealthy Boston family. She was a real beauty, fair skinned with delicate hands, and one of the nicest young women I've ever met. Really gentle and sweet. She was in her early twenties, and she worked as a nurse in a hospital where she met a Brazilian medical student, Jorge, who was training to be an ear, nose, and throat specialist. Dark and suave, Jorge had a lot of Latin flair, and some Latin hotheadedness too. He'd been convicted of assault and battery for smacking a previous girlfriend around. But Elise was taken by his Latin charm, and, foolishly, she believed him when he said he was simply defending himself. The INS saw it differently and, after months and months of legal procedures, deported him to Brazil.

Jorge had proposed by then. Elise had accepted, and she went to Brazil with him as his wife, even though she'd never been there before and spoke less Portuguese than I do, which is none, and she wouldn't know anybody in all of Brazil except for her husband. They settled into his condo in his home city of São Paulo, where he worked in a local hospital, and he did okay.

Elise wasn't so happy, since she didn't have any friends, and Jorge wouldn't let her work. But she got pregnant, and that was exciting. Her sister, Andrea, flew there to help out with the birth. She was just as pretty as her sister, with dark eyes, but a little more slim, and shyer. Elise stayed alone in the hospital for the early labor, leaving Jorge in the apartment with Andrea. He cooked for her, played the stereo, and turned on the charm. He was drinking, and wanted her to try this fancy liqueur he liked to bring out for special occasions. Andrea didn't like to drink, but Jorge insisted, and she took a few sips, and immediately started feeling ill and light-headed. She told him she had to lie down on the couch or she'd faint. As soon as her head hit the pillow, everything went black. Andrea claimed that while she was unconscious, Jorge raped her.

Andrea was groggy when she came to, but from the state of her clothes and the way she felt, she knew what had happened. She was furious and disgusted, but she didn't dare do anything drastic like call the police and claim her Brazilian brother-in-law had raped her. Not in a country where she couldn't speak the language. Plus, she didn't want to ruin her sister's excitement over the baby. For the next few days, Andrea carried on as though everything was fine.

It wasn't until Elise returned to the apartment with the newborn that Andrea broke down and told her sister what had happened. Elise knew in her bones that it was true.

Elise confronted Jorge, who angrily denied raping her sister. Andrea had seduced *him*. He screamed and raged, threw things, but he didn't change his wife's mind. Elise called the police. When they showed up, Elise could scarcely find the words in Portuguese to describe what had happened, and Jorge denied everything. He couldn't believe he was being persecuted by his own wife and her sister.

As far as the police were concerned, there was no reason to investigate further. They didn't want to look at, or photograph, the red marks and bruises on Andrea's pelvis. Andrea flew home in disgust. Elise wanted to leave too, but Jorge got a court order forcing her to deposit her passport with the court and legally prohibiting her from taking their baby out of Brazil.

There was no way Elise would leave without her baby.

A day or two later, Elise's mother, Margaret, called me. She was a very proper woman from Beverly Farms on the North Shore. The moment Andrea got home, she had told her mother everything. Margaret was outraged at what Jorge had done to Andrea, and furious that he had kept Elise a "prisoner"—as she said—in his apartment in São Paulo.

"Mr. Nissenbaum, what can I do?" she pleaded.

I asked her to let me speak to Elise. She gave me the number, and I got through to Elise the next morning when Jorge was out. I explained who I was, then had her tell me the story again, to make sure I had it right. She wept into the receiver as she went through it.

"I'm trapped here in an apartment with the man who raped my sister!" she told me. "She could be pregnant by him for all I know. He makes me sick. I want to *kill* him! I swear to God. I need to get out. But I can't leave my baby!" She broke down.

"Well, you can't fly out," I told her. "Your passport is impounded in the courthouse. And if you're caught trying to leave with the baby, the authorities will arrest you for kidnapping. Then the court would award custody to Jorge."

"So what can I do?" she asked, sniffling.

"There's only one thing you can do."

"What's that?"

I'd researched it the previous afternoon and much of the night: "You need to take a bus. South to the city of Foz do Iguaçu, where Brazil, Paraguay, and Argentina meet."

"Down there? I don't know if I can!" she told me. She knew about the reputation of that part of Brazil. It was supposedly one of the loosest and most dangerous parts of the world. Drug runners move through there all the time, crime is out of control, and the poverty is horrendous, with hundreds of beggars roaming the streets.

"You're going to have to," I told her. "Look, the dangers will make it easier. Believe me."

"*How?*"

"The border is poorly controlled," I assured her. "You can bribe your way across."

"But I don't speak any Portuguese," she protested, panicky. "My husband will send people after me. And everybody will know it's me."

"Look, Elise, listen to me. I've called around, and you don't have too many good options right now."

"Okay," she said. There was silence on the line. "I'll do it."

"Good," I told her. I left it to Margaret to go through the drill. She told Elise not to wear anything nice or fancy, nothing to call attention to herself. That she should dress like a peasant and wrap the baby in some grungy old blanket. Since she couldn't speak Portuguese, she should avoid speaking with anyone. Margaret would visit São Paulo to deliver the money to Elise and visit for a week. Then she'd fly across to Paraguay to greet Elise when—or if—she got across the border.

With her baby—a tiny little thing named Antonia—tucked under a light coat, Elise snuck out of the apartment one morning right after Jorge left for work and found her way to the bus. She bought a ticket with her mother's money. It was a long ride, several days and several bus rides to the border, and it was hell to keep the baby quiet. Somewhere along the way she must have fallen asleep, because she woke up to find all her money gone. Stolen. Any of the passengers could have taken it. The thief could be sitting on the bus with her still, or he could have gotten off while she slept. Perfect. So she arrived with Antonia at this outlaw town without a single centavo—or any papers to say who she was.

The plan was for her to get lost in all the chaotic comings and goings. Migrant workers went back and forth across the border every day, no one bothering to check their papers very carefully, if they checked them at all. It was her only hope for getting out.

At the border, she found a road where a crowd of migrant workers was crossing into Brazil from Paraguay. She watched the guards wave them all through. This was the right place. She spent the night on the street, nursing Antonia in the shadows. In the morning, just after sunup, she returned to the border crossing and slipped in with the other workers shuffling across into Paraguay. By then, her own clothes were so soiled that she didn't stick out. She tucked the baby under her shirt, threw the blanket over her shoulder, and prayed that no one would pay her any extra attention.

She made it across.

On the far side, her mother was waiting with a car and driver. After a tearful reunion, they went together to the American consulate, which issued a new passport for her and Antonia. This was long before the security crackdown that would follow 9/11. After a quick meal and a bath, Elise and Antonia flew back with Margaret to Boston.

Jorge was enraged that his wife and baby daughter had fled his apartment, and he intended to follow them to the United States. He sent blistering letters to Elise through her mother, threatening to come for his daughter. Maybe not today, maybe not this year, but someday he would grab her and bring her back with him to Brazil.

Too bad for him, the INS had flagged him as a violent offender after his assault on his previous girlfriend and refused him entry into the country. Even before 9/11, the INS took violent misconduct very seriously. And now, of course, forget it.

Still, I insisted that Elise take every possible precaution. After all, Elise wasn't supposed to kidnap Antonia, but she did. So Jorge could as well. And if he didn't do it himself, he could dispatch a friend or family member to do it. So I encouraged Elise to move away, and she relocated to a small town in the Midwest where the sudden appearance of some Brazilians would be noticeable. Elise had to make sure that Antonia was never alone, and that doors were locked at all times when they were home. Antonia was taught never to believe anyone who claimed that her mother had died suddenly, which can stun a child into accepting the other parent and make her think there is no reason to ever try to call home. Elise gave photographs of Jorge to all of Antonia's child care personnel, and, later, to her school's staff, in case he showed up to attempt an abduction. And when Antonia learned to speak, I told Elise she needed to have a particular word—like *potato* or *butterfly*—to serve as code for "I'm being kidnapped."

Antonia has never had to use any of these measures, thank God. She is an adult now, getting a medical degree. Jorge has remained in Brazil. Elise has returned to the Northeast, and her nursing career is thriving, but she has never dated again. Her sister Andrea suffers from psychological problems that she dates to the rape. But Margaret has carried on, hardy as ever.

ᏋᎪᏋ

BESIDES CREATING MAYHEM, SEX ALSO HAS, OF COURSE, A PROCREATIVE role. It's not just sex; it's also sperm seeking to crack an egg. And many is the time that I have had to mop up after the sperm goes somewhere it shouldn't. Remember the waitress who put her turkey baster to good use with the jism of the guy she'd had a crush on in high school? There are plenty more like her. The women who thought it might be fun to have sex with the guy who'd drunk himself legless at a house party and now was out cold in an upstairs bedroom. Well, one leg still worked. Nine months later, he was a father. And a few months after that, he had to pay child support.

And then there was the waitress at Logan Airport who had a thing for bachelor Delta Air Lines pilots. Single, childless, and not earning as much as she'd like, she lured one pilot after another into the sack, dreaming of their pay checks as she pulled on their joysticks. She assured each of them that she was on the pill. Not exactly. Before too long, she had three little Delta kids and a total of $75,000 a year in child support, tax free, to raise them with, courtesy of three Delta pilots and the generous child support guidelines of the Commonwealth of Massachusetts.

I know because the third pilot asked me to represent him and make everything better. I told him I didn't see how I could. He was the one who chose to have unprotected sex, and now that the baby existed, whom did he expect to support it? The court would not punish the child for the mother's deceit. He saw the logic to none of these arguments, but got increasingly angry and resentful that he had to give $25,000 of his $125,000 salary to support this child. My suggestion that he get involved with the child fell on deaf ears. Finally, he grew so frustrated and belligerent that I had to kick him out of my office.

☙❧

But the sperm I'll always remember belonged to Franz, a world-class German orthopedic surgeon, who lived with his wife and three children in a castle in Bavaria that he claimed had once been owned by Ludwig II, the so-called Mad King. Dashing to the point of being impulsive, he was also a consultant to a firm in Massachusetts that made disposable casts, and on one trip he had a fling with one of its senior executives, the svelte, athletic, and scheming Martha. At thirty-one, she was nineteen years younger than Franz, which was fine with him. They screwed their brains out.

The torrid ones tend to burn out. And the affair fizzled after a year. Franz would have never thought about it again, if it hadn't been for . . . the car crash that happened three years later. His oldest daughter was driving Franz to a scientific meeting in Switzerland, and on the twisting mountain roads the car skidded off the pavement and smashed into a rock face. She died instantly. Franz had multiple injuries—both legs were broken in several places, and a blow to his head left him in a coma for weeks. But he eventually recovered enough to go back to work.

His wife, Karina, blamed Franz for the death of their daughter. More than blamed, she raged at him, pounding her fists against his chest. Physically weakened by the accident, he gave way emotionally too. He fell into a deep depression, and he struggled at work. His legs

49

had not fully healed, and it was torture sometimes to perform surgery on patient after patient. In all the acrimony and emotional frenzy, the marriage just drained away, and after about a year, Franz and his wife decided to go their separate ways. He gave her a generous settlement, sole possession of the house, and much more. Determined to start over, he took a position as head of the University of Bern's orthopedic surgical faculty. Despite the physical agony it put him in, Franz continued to perform his own surgeries at the affiliated hospital.

He was attending a medical conference in Geneva when he met Martha again. She'd married since they had last seen each other—and divorced. She laughed about it; the man had been so wrong for her. "Not like you, Franz," she said.

She was as attractive as ever. That night, they picked right back up where they'd left off and proceeded to screw their way through a dozen conferences in Europe and the United States. Breathless in their eagerness for each other, they decided to marry, but Franz needed to get divorced first. In Germany, divorce proceedings can't begin until an official notice of intention to divorce is delivered by one spouse to the other and followed by a full year of physical separation. The end of that year was still months away, and, nearing forty, Martha was desperate to get pregnant. Franz was game. She went at conception like a science project, taking her temperature almost hourly to determine the time of peak fertility—the exact moment of ovulation.

They had tons of sex, but nothing came of it. No pregnancy. Martha persuaded Franz to go with her for tests at a Massachusetts infertility clinic. She checked out fine, but Franz did not. His sperm were slow swimmers apparently. The brilliant, accomplished Franz, father of three, couldn't believe it, and he insisted on retesting his sperm on his own turf, in Switzerland. He flew home to Bern and dropped off a sample. Since he wasn't too far from the German border, he thought he might take the occasion to see his two daughters at the family castle in Bavaria. His wife was home too, but he was okay with that. While he was there, the couple talked for the first time in months. They cried over their deceased daughter. They drank a good deal of wine. They enjoyed being together. They had sex. And they thought maybe they should start over.

Two months passed, and then it was definite. They would give their marriage another go. He was soon to be given an award at his hospital during an elaborate ceremony, rich with pomp and ritual. He wanted his wife and their two surviving daughters to attend. Not Martha. It would be like a second wedding, but with the girls there.

Martha had no idea. None. They hadn't seen each other, but they had chatted gaily on the phone almost daily for months. As far as she knew, Franz was still all hers. He let her know that his sperm didn't get any higher marks in Bern, but he attributed any deficiency to a virus he'd had over the summer. At her request, he express mailed a new sperm sample for her to test back in Massachusetts. Excited at the thought that the new stuff was good, Martha decided to skip a step and go straight to insemination. The clinic where she was going to do this gave her the forms that Franz had to sign to give his permission for her to use his sperm.

Here the stories diverge. Martha claims that she reached Franz by cell on the train that was, unbeknownst to her, bearing him, his wife, and two kids to the induction ceremony and pseudo remarriage in Bern. And that, in the course of the conversation, he told her he was fine with her signing his name on the permission form. Franz agrees they spoke while he was on the train but insists they talked only in general terms about her wanting kids. According to him, they agreed that if it was so important to her to get pregnant, she should go ahead with sperm from an anonymous donor. He says he never agreed to let her use his sperm. In fact, he claims that she never even asked.

Whatever actually was said, she went ahead and signed his name on the form. Although the in vitro fertilization clinic's doctor is ethically required to speak to both of the potential parents before an insemination, this clinic's doctor failed to do that, assuming that Martha was free to speak for Franz. Martha went through with the procedure. Two weeks later, she received great news: she was pregnant. Franz's sperm did work. She passed word of the pregnancy on to Franz.

Franz was happy for her. He claimed he had no reason to feel otherwise, because Martha had left out the tiny little detail that she'd used his sperm for the procedure, making him the dad.

Wanting to seal their remarriage with new honesty, Franz told his wife all about Martha, about how they'd met, and then remet. But he assured Karina that he loved her more than ever and that it was all over between him and Martha—who, by the way, was now pregnant by an anonymous sperm donor, Franz added, as casually as he could. That was good for everyone, he felt compelled to add. Martha would finally have the child she wanted. Franz would be free of her since the child absolutely was not his, and Franz and Karina could rededicate themselves to each other.

Despite's Franz's certainty, Karina wasn't so sure that Martha's child wasn't his, given how much of his sperm Martha had had in her possession. She made Franz fly to Massachusetts to get the truth—with their seventeen-year-old daughter Erika along as chaperone to make sure the visit wouldn't bring any worse problems for them. Karina's idea was to build a wall between Franz and Martha, and to gain assurances that her child wasn't his. The unstated idea was to make sure that the conniving Martha had no chance of marrying her Franz.

Franz said yes, yes, yes. But once he got to Boston, he didn't stick with the program. He told Erika he needed to see Martha by himself to figure out where things stood. So he left Erika at the hotel one evening while he met Martha at the waterfront restaurant where they'd dined many times during the heady days of their affair. Martha was waiting for him at the table when he arrived. Three months pregnant now, she looked radiant. Franz—out of chivalry, he always insisted, nothing more—gave her a necklace with a large, heart-shaped diamond that he'd brought her from Bern. He wanted to let her know that she would always have his heart.

He skipped over the part about how he'd returned to his wife. She looked so happy, he couldn't bear to hurt her. But finally he brought the conversation back around to it, and just after the waiter had cleared away their entrées, he told Martha the truth.

"I'm going to go back to my wife."

Stunned, her face went slack. Then Martha reached back and unclasped the necklace, flung it at his face, and started to sob. Her eyes streaming, she said that she'd told her parents about the baby and how she and Franz were going to get married as soon as his divorce was final, and—

"But I never agreed to that!" Franz interrupted.

"I know, I know!" she assured him. "But everybody is thinking it."

Martha cried some more, and he tried to soothe her. And then she told him, sniffling, that there was a big family gathering coming up that weekend. All her relatives would be there, and they'd all want to congratulate both of them and find out what was going on with her pregnancy and their wedding. She wanted—needed—Franz to come. She reached across the table and grasped his hand. "Please?" The way she looked at him!

"But why do you want *me* there?"

"Why, Franz, I want everybody to meet the father of my child."

"But I'm not!"

"Oh, I know, Franz," he later claimed she said, piling on the lies as she smoothed out the tablecloth. "But they don't know that. They all think—well, you know what they think."

She pleaded with him and said he owed it to her.

"Okay," he said. "I'll go."

He brought Erika. Had to. He wanted her to see that things were fine with him and Martha. They were friends, and as a friend he had to be there for this occasion.

I can't imagine this sounded quite right to Erika. It certainly didn't sound right to me when I came onto the case. But Franz was her dad, and she was inclined to believe the things he said, which was a big mistake.

The event was a horror. Three hours of wild, drunken greetings from people Franz devoutly hoped he would never see again, all of them complimenting him on his virility. Erika spent the evening with her knees together on the couch, watching.

That night, Franz and Erika were to stay over at Martha's house, and she whispered in Franz's ear that she wanted him to sleep with her. No sex, she purred. It was just that there wasn't a bed for him anywhere else.

Erika could sleep on the single bed in the guest room. There was no other way.

Franz said okay.

Martha and Franz slept in the same bed. They had sex.

But he used a condom. Too little, too late.

In the morning, when they were having breakfast with Erika, Franz finally steeled himself to ask the questions.

"Martha, I have to know: am I the father of your child?"

"No."

"You swear?"

"Yes, Franz. Of course. You are not the father."

"And you know I can never marry you."

"Yes, of course. I know that."

"You swear?"

"Yes, I swear."

"There." Franz turned to Erika. "You see? It's just as I said."

Relieved, Franz returned with Erika to Germany. Mission accomplished.

Two months later, Martha gave birth to her daughter, four months early. She was the size of her mother's fist. Born so early, she was at serious risk for a host of cognitive impairments, as well as blindness and other defects. Raising her could cost a fortune. To figure out where that money might come from, Martha did the genetic testing necessary to prove what she already knew. Franz was the father.

Martha asked him for money.

Outraged, he refused to pay a deutschemark—and he didn't relent when Martha got a temporary order from a Massachusetts judge requiring him to pay temporary child support plus $25,000 to cover her legal fees.

Martha attached stock that Erika and her sister owned and forced some of it to be sold immediately even though the stock market was tanking. Martha claimed that Franz was hiding his assets in his kids' names, even though she knew perfectly well that he had given stock to his kids as part of his initial divorce agreement with Karina.

Then Franz called me.

I got an order to stop any future sales until Martha could prove that he had created these accounts after she got pregnant. Then I went after the doctor at the fertility clinic and, in a deposition, got him to acknowledge that he did not secure the proper informed consent from Franz to do the insemination.

Next, we went to trial to determine if Martha had improperly signed Franz's name on the form permitting his sperm to be used by the IVF doctor. The trial was a disaster. It wasn't the genetic evidence that nailed my client. We were prepared for that. It was Martha's testimony, particularly the bit about the diamond necklace. Franz had not alerted me to that little morsel, and it killed him. Nor did he give a believable account of that critical cell phone conversation from the train. He was muddled and evasive and totally unconvincing, even to me, and I was inclined to believe him. By contrast, Martha was crisp and compelling and sympathetic.

The judge was completely candid afterward: "I believe her. I don't believe him." The court was scheduled to reconvene in three months to set the amount for child support. But Franz didn't hang around for that hearing. He left the country and refused to come back for the trial.

It was a Mexican standoff, and it went on for years. Franz wouldn't pay any money or provide any info; Martha wouldn't release him from the case. Finally, at year four or five, I convinced Franz to pay a relatively modest sum just to end the case. The money would not be for child support. Rather, it would go into a trust for the daughter, and Martha could be the trustee. Martha said fine; Franz said fine; the court said fine. And it was done. Franz remained in Bern with his wife. And Martha raised her daughter here in Boston. The girl has never met her biological father, and most likely never will.

CHAPTER
FOUR

WHEN YOU GO THROUGH A CASE LIKE FRANZ'S, DESCRIBING how this happened, then that happened, and then another thing happened, it can seem sketchy, as though the characters were made up of nothing but their mad passions—for sex and money, primarily. And those are definitely powerful impulses in anyone's life. But once you live with a case like that for a while—and it can go on for months or years—the more you see the subtleties of it. Sure, time and again, I see my clients involved in the Big Swap, of sex for money and vice versa. Let's face it: at its crudest, that is what many relationships are. One side offers money; the other responds with sex. But you hang in with a case long enough, and you see there is more to it. I love peeling back the layers that cover this exchange.

And the characters who pass through my office—there is nothing simple about them. On the surface, they may be very principled and proper. But go a few levels down, and you see that they are anything but. Go further, and you see something different still, often something scary. And the divorces I see happen more than a few levels down.

In the case I call "The Madam and the Millionaire," the whole thing was nominally about the exchange of money for sex. The madam of the title was just what you'd think: a hooker. There are a hundred words for it, probably because, as the world's oldest profession, it's picked up so many from all its customers along the way. I like to say that my madam was simply a hooker who went into management. She'd made a decent living on her back, and then she made a better one on her ass in the executive chair, running everything. My millionaire was actually a multimillionaire, but who's counting? You can probably guess the relationship between them.

Actually, you can't, because you can't guess all the permutations of need and longing and desire that go into it. And the twists in the case! Every day, I couldn't wait to go home and tell Madeline the latest revelations. The murder scheme; the jailhouse lesbian romance; the madam telling me she wasn't gay but that "even in jail, everyone needs a little love"; a hooker convention; bail jumping. And all that was just Act One. Even while I was working like a pile driver to make things right for my client, I had to marvel at the drama of it all and to tip my hat to God for making a creature of such bewitching mendacity as the woman on the other side of the case, the madam of this tale. I wanted to strangle her sometimes, but I had to hand it to her too.

Her name was Tonya Steele, or Tonya Steele Pryce once she married her millionaire, as, incredibly enough, she did. That was Augustus Pryce Sr., a tall, slender, slow-talking seventy-three-year-old businessman from Dallas who was worth just shy of seven million dollars when Tonya first got her hooks into him. Gus was a kindly, unpretentious gent with few close friends and a hunger for all the Viagra-aided sex a wild filly like Tonya could give him. It must have got him off pretty good, because as soon as she gave it to him, he couldn't think about anything else. His career, his family, his reputation—all of it went into the garbage disposal, he was so focused on that lithe little body of hers and what it felt like to have sex with her. Or so I figured.

By the time I got into the case, about three years into the marriage, his lifelong alcoholism had given him liver disease, and he was in a nursing home, straining to breathe. Before all that, he'd been a pretty straight, fairly sensible guy. Not the kind of person you'd think would put an engagement ring on a C-note whore. You can't be too flaky and run an $850 million business, as he'd done in Texas. By then, Tonya, at forty-eight, had lived several hard lives, but there was still a crackling energy to her that held a man's attention. Or was it her smell? Sometimes I think there must be a musk to certain women that makes guys so crazy they throw over their entire lives for them. How else could Tonya hold Gus in such thrall that he'd wait out her multiyear prison hitch for prostitution and then greet her with open arms when she got out? He'd been married twice by then, and he had a grown son and daughter and seven grandchildren. There had to be some musk, didn't there? That's the only way I can figure it. Some pheromone that drove Gus wild.

Tonya had a checkered past, needless to say, but it took a while for me to figure all that out. By the time she got to Gus, she'd had two husbands, one of whom had tried to murder her. We'll get into that. But the thing that always interested me was why she was so warped. Sex was her only profitable business before the marriage, during the marriage, and after the marriage. Even so, it seemed to me she could have gone straight. With her ingenuity, her energy, and her salesmanship, she could have done very well in a legitimate business, running a clothing store, perhaps, or even a good-sized company. She didn't have to make her money on her back. Tonya once said she'd been adopted and then abused by her adoptive dad. But that sounded to me like something she'd say to win sympathy from a judge. She would say anything for sympathy from a judge. It seemed just as likely that she'd grown up solidly middle class, with piano lessons and a bedroom full of dolls. She said she had a college degree, but she said a lot of things. I don't know for sure if she'd even finished high school. But she knew her way around the English language, and she knew which words worked, regardless of the truth behind them.

As such, she was everything I wasn't. I'm a truth addict. But Tonya takes whatever path will get her where she wants to go. That made her about the shrewdest, canniest, and most maddening adversary I have ever faced.

But I am getting ahead of myself.

It was August of 2005 when the call came in. I was in my office on Federal Street. It was one of those steamy Boston afternoons that makes most people wish they were at the beach, but I just cranked up the air-conditioning. Mindy picked up. It's her job to screen all the calls, figure out which ones are worth my time, and then get the basics of what's going on.

This time, Mindy buzzed me right away. "I think you'd better take this one, Jerry," she told me.

I told her okay and picked up the receiver. "Jerry Nissenbaum," I said. "How can I help you?"

The caller was Augustus Pryce Jr., or Gusty. Early fifties, he was a senior executive at the Boston office of a global insurance firm and lived out in one of the ritzy suburbs. He sounded stressed.

Once we got through the preliminaries, he cleared his throat and began: "It's about my father." Augustus Pryce Sr., he meant. "He's in the Far Oaks nursing home up in Manchester-by-the-Sea."

"I'm sorry to hear that."

"Well, he isn't doing well. But that isn't why I'm calling. It's . . . it's his wife." He paused. "His third wife." That was Tonya. "He married her three years ago." He paused for a moment, then gave out an audible sigh. "Just after she got out of prison."

I made a note: *wife—ex-con*. Then, neutrality in my voice, I asked, "What was she in for?"

"Running a house of prostitution and solicitation."

He paused, waiting to see how that went down.

"Did six years in Framingham," he added.

"I see." Another note: *6 yrs. F-ham.* That was Framingham State Prison, the women's correctional facility. Not the most cheerful place.

"Dad used to visit her there just about every week."

Once again, I could tell that Gusty was waiting for some reaction, but I just listened.

"Believe me, when he told us he wanted to marry this woman, we were not thrilled. I'm the oldest. Well older. There's just me and my sister, Patricia. We were both pretty livid. We actually hired a detective agency to check her out."

"What did you find out?"

"Nothing reassuring, I'll tell you that. My wife—that's Lorie—she can . . . well . . . she can take a strict view of these things. She was very upset that my father would even think of marrying such a woman. Let's not mince words here. Tonya Steele is a whore. A whore, Mr. Nissenbaum. A lying, thieving whore. My sister and I aren't happy to have her as a stepmother. I'll send you the detective report. It's pretty long. There is a lot of ugly stuff in it—death threats involving a previous husband, drug dealing, a son who's been imprisoned for armed robbery.

"All of this stuff. Mr. Nissenbaum, you have to understand. My sister and I, we're professional people. This is embarrassing to us, to have a hooker in the family.

"We showed Dad the detective report, but he scarcely read it. It didn't matter to him what Tonya Steele was. He was completely committed to her. She convinced him she'd been falsely accused and wrongfully convicted. He was sure we'd like her, and he wanted us to meet her and give her a chance. But that wasn't going to happen as far as I was concerned. Lorie wouldn't be caught dead with her. And so he went right ahead and married the woman. The wedding was on the lawn of his house on Wingaersheek Beach in Gloucester."

I knew the area. A lot of expensive houses there.

"None of us went," Gusty went on. "Couldn't dignify that wedding, if you want to know the truth."

"So how can I help you now?"

"I'm worried about my father. I'm afraid he isn't getting the care he needs."

"What makes you say that?" That particular nursing home had a good reputation.

"She hasn't been paying the bills! That's how I found out Dad was there—the nursing home called me about it. Tonya didn't tell me—didn't tell anyone—that she was putting him in! She just did it. Just put him in there. That's what she does. She just does these things. I haven't been able to reach him for over a month. She's incredible. She changed their phone number at the house, and the one for his cell phone. When I figured out what had happened, she changed it again! I used to talk to my dad once a day. But once he . . ." His voice trailed off. "Oh, what's the use.

"He hadn't been well, I knew that. He has a drinking problem, always has. For years. Long before Tonya. He'd sit outside in a lawn chair and drink manhattans. All afternoon. Once, the lawn sprinkler came on—it drenched him, but he didn't move! He was so stewed, I'm not sure he even noticed. He stayed right there, staring out across the water toward Crane Beach, drinking and drinking. But I didn't know he was so sick. I saw him just this morning at the nursing home. He looked *awful*! His skin was this waxy yellow color. Just lying there, barely breathing. He was hooked up to some oxygen tank. His stomach was all bloated, like this big mountain under the covers. He didn't recognize me, hardly even turned toward me when I spoke to him. It was horrible."

"Did you speak to the physician in charge?"

"Yes, Dr. Sullivan."

"And what was his assessment?"

"He said that Dad was pretty badly impaired. 'Legally incompetent' was his term."

"Unable to manage his affairs."

"Right. And that's the thing. When I found out that the nursing home hadn't been paid, I called Dad's stockbroker to see if a check had gone out, and the manager said no, that none had. But when he looked over the account, he could see there'd been an increase in the money flow. I asked by how much. And he checked and said he'd have to run the numbers to get it exact, but maybe six hundred thousand dollars had gone out in a margin loan."

A margin loan is made against the stock holdings, sort of like a home equity line against a house.

"That's a lot, obviously. That account used to have four million dollars or so with no margin loans. So I said, 'Since when?' And he told me, 'Over the last few years.' Meaning since Dad married Tonya."

"I asked the man to pull up the canceled checks on his screen. He said that they all had my father's signature, every one of them."

"Your father's signature?" I interrupted, needing to be clear about that. "Every one?"

"Right. My dad's. But the money moved out in a strange way. No stocks were sold. It was all just margin loans."

"That is a strange way to go," I agreed. The interest is much higher than a regular bank loan, maybe two points above prime.

"Yes, especially for someone in business. Dad knew better than that."

I waited a second. "But Tonya wouldn't—that's what you're thinking?"

"Right."

"But the signatures? You think they might be forgeries?"

"It had crossed my mind."

"Did you ask the broker to compare the signatures on the checks to the signature on file?"

"No."

"We can do that," I told him. "If there is a discrepancy, they can refuse payment without a court order. But you don't want to claim forgery without proof. That's a serious charge."

"Yes, I know. But read the detective report, Mr. Nissenbaum. She has done worse." He picked up again. "Another thing. After I saw Dad, I drove to the Wingaersheek Beach house to make sure everything was okay. Well, guess what? There were some workmen there installing new hardwood flooring on the first floor. They said they'd torn out the kitchen and were ready to buy new granite countertops and appliances. Now, someone else had already put in a new back porch and a massive hot tub. A hot tub—can you imagine? That was the last thing Dad needed. So I called Dad's contractor, Lou Casavecchia, to see if he'd talked to Dad about any of this. And he said no, everybody dealt only with Tonya. Get this: she was going to put on a three-hundred-thousand-dollar addition. She'd had Lou draw up the plans, but Lou backed out because the whole thing seemed too weird. Which it does."

"Does Tonya have title to the house?"

"God, no. At least, I don't think so. Do you think my dad would give her that?"

"I don't know. Let's find out." I yelled for Patty, one of our paralegals. She used to be a bar manager, and I figured if she could handle drunks, she could deal with our opposing lawyers. I asked her to check the Essex County Registry of Deeds Web site for any changes in the title on Gus Sr.'s house. All that stuff is online these days. She said she'd get right on it.

Gusty took a deep breath and let it out into the receiver. "Look, Mr. Nissenbaum, Dad's obviously in no condition to make any financial decisions. Given the stuff at the stockbroker's, I don't want Tonya taking charge of his house."

"Absolutely," I said. "I can file a petition to the court to get a guardian to protect his interests." There'd probably be some other work to do too—motions for trustee process and for a real estate attachment, and maybe some restraining orders.

We went over a few more details, and a few minutes later Patty came back with a printout of the deed off the registry's Web site.

With the receiver in my ear, I glanced over it. "Well, looks like Tonya has beaten you to it," I told Gusty.

"To what?"

"Your father and Tonya own the beach house as tenants by the entirety. That means that if your dad dies, the house is all hers."

"Shit!" Gusty said.

The whole conversation ran almost two hours. I used up maybe fifteen pages of my legal pad, notes that I'd have to type up right away while I could still remember what the little squiggles might mean. Before we hung up, I laid out the terms of our own agreement, detailing my fee schedule and likely expenses.

But Gusty interrupted me. "Yes, yes," he said. "I know all about that. It's fine. We've checked around, Mr. Nissenbaum, and my sister and I want to go with you. You're worth it."

That was heartening. There can be price resistance. I asked him to wire a fifty-thousand-dollar deposit into our clients' trust account, with another fifty thousand to follow, and we'd get started. Gusty said that sounded fine to him.

The first fifty thousand came in about an hour later. When I told the staff about the new case, it was like a tornado had hit. Everything had to happen, and all at once. Mindy, Patty, and our senior associate, Wendy Hickey, all scrambled into action. I could have recruited Madeline, up at our house in Boxford, but we agreed it was better to leave her out of the case so we weren't both consumed by it. All the same, papers flew, and everybody pounded keyboards and dashed around. Collecting financial information, background, legal precedent, forms, procedures—a million things, all right away. I've usually got twenty to thirty cases going, but they all came to a screeching halt when the madam's case hit my office.

One of the first things I did was call Dr. Sullivan at the nursing home to confirm what Gus Jr. had told me: that Gus Sr. really was incompetent. That was key. Luckily, I got right through, and Dr. Sullivan indicated that his patient did not know where he was, why he was there, his home address, or the name of the president. "I'd think that would indicate incompetence, wouldn't you, Mr. Nissenbaum?" I had to agree.

"Tonya been there much?" I asked. If she'd come every day, that would suggest she was indeed a loving wife. But if she just dumped him there, that meant something else.

"I'm not around enough to say," Dr. Sullivan told me. But he passed me on to a member of the nursing staff who was in a better position to know. I asked her how many times Tonya had come by in the month that her husband had been in the facility.

"Once," she told me. "Maybe twice. But definitely no more than that. I'd have remembered. Very striking woman, you know. Wore flaming red one time, like she was out on a date. Long dress. To a nursing home! We couldn't get over it."

"Has her husband been sick this whole time?"

"When she brought him in, he was alert, reasonably talkative, not too bad. But he is now."

"Could he recognize people?"

"At first."

"Does he ask about his wife?"

"He used to all the time. 'When's Tonya coming?' 'She coming?' 'Any message from Tonya?' All that type of thing."

"But she hardly ever comes?"

"Just once or twice, like I say. And that was for legal stuff, trying to get him to sign things. Didn't help his mood any. That can mess up your immune system. Of course, I'm no doctor. But that's what I think. He seems like such a nice man, Mr. Pryce. I really feel bad for him."

ॐ

I HAD WENDY PREPARE A CERTIFICATE FOR DR. SULLIVAN TO SIGN, certifying to Gus Sr.'s incompetence, along with papers asking the court to terminate any power of attorney or health care proxy that Gus Sr. may have signed over to Tonya. I didn't want her pulling the plug on her husband.

I also started in on the affidavit that Gus Jr. and his sister would have to sign and file in court, making their claim against Tonya. An affidavit is serious business. Every claim in it has to be rock solid, or the other side will blow it up and the judge will never believe you again. When I did criminal defense, the case was all about the jury, the twelve peers who were sitting in judgment in the jury box. In divorce law, it is all about one juror: the Judge. Lose the judge and you've lost the case.

ॐ

I'D FOUND OUT FROM GUS JR. THAT HIS FATHER HAD BEEN REPREsented by a lawyer named Russell Towers back in Dallas at the time of the marriage. As a matter of professional courtesy, one lawyer will reveal to another some important details about a client's legal affairs, so long as it doesn't breach confidentiality. Towers was a good ol' Texas boy, and he spoke in a noticeable drawl on the phone. Before I pressed any questions on him, I played a little lawyer geography, running through some of the lawyers I know in Dallas, showing that I knew some of the more important ones pretty well. "You know Willy Henkell?" I asked him.

"Why, Willy's a good friend."

"He stop drinking?"

Towers started to laugh. "When his wife took sick, Willy took the pledge."

"You know what they say about Willy, don't you?" I went on. I was starting to enjoy myself. "That the second-best divorce trial lawyer in Dallas is Willy Henkell, sober. The best is Willy Henkell, drunk!"

He got a good laugh out of that, and I joined in, and we were the best of friends there for a little while. So I took the opportunity to ask him if there was a prenuptial agreement.

"Sure there was," he said. "We worked like the dickens on that thing."

"It's in effect?"

"Hell no." Towers chuckled. "You know, funny thing was, she didn't use a divorce lawyer to negotiate it. She had a *criminal* lawyer. Now, what the hell kinda message does that send?"

"Not a good one."

"Not a good one at all. In the end, she didn't sign it. Never went into effect."

"But he married her anyway."

"That's right. Sure did. Up there in Massachusetts." He paused a second. "I was there for that. My wife and I stayed at the Four Seasons in Boston, and Gus brought Tonya by for tea a few days before the wedding. One look at her, and I could tell this was a disaster. I tried to pull him aside, but all he could say was, 'Wouldja look at that body on her?' I figured it was hopeless. So, that's all the questions you got for me?"

"One more. Any will?"

"Yep. Signed it the day before the wedding. I drew it up for him down here myself. He signed it up there."

"And how'd Tonya come out?"

"You know I can't tell you that till someone's appointed guardian. But let's just say she won't be left out in the cold."

He paused for a second, and his voice changed a little. "Okay, now I have a question on my end." But for this one, he had to shut the door to his office first. "There," he said somewhat breathlessly when he came back on the line. "Nobody else needs to know about this." He spoke in little more than a whisper. "I should tell you that about a year ago, I received a tape from an unknown source."

"What sort of tape?"

"An audiotape. A cassette." It was a recording of a conversation that Tonya Pryce had had with a friend of hers named Marcia. "I forget her last name right now," Towers went on. "You can get it easy enough. Marcia served time with her in prison. You do know that Tonya was in prison?"

I said I did.

"You'll understand that I can't describe the contents of that tape to you, but under the circumstances I would strongly recommend you give it a listen."

"It's serious, I take it."

"Hell yes! I thought so. But Gus laughed off the contents. Just laughed it off. But I think he should have taken it a bit more seriously, especially now, in light of what you are describing to me."

I'd told him how Gus had ended up in a nursing home, with the strong possibility that his wife was plundering his assets.

"Yours is not the only copy of the tape?" I asked.

"There are a couple of others around. You shouldn't have much trouble finding one, if you look in the right place."

"Where might that be?"

"You'll have to figure that out on your own, good buddy."

℘

It was in the middle of my call to Russell Towers that Mindy came in lugging a big box full of materials that Gus Jr. had sent over by messenger. Soon as I was off the phone, I dived into it. I love documents. Just love them. People will tell you anything, and then they'll tell you other things that are completely different from what they just said. But while documents may not be the absolute truth, they never change their story. They are true to themselves. I love the clarity of them, and the fact that you can stack them into perfectly squared-off stacks on the conference room table. You can organize them by name, by date, or by time and index them to pull up whatever you're looking for, and they always remain exactly where you put them. You can keep PDFs of the documents on your computer and do word searches on them. I've got close to a photographic memory for things I read about for my cases, but these documents have me beat. They never forget.

This time, when I popped open the flaps of the cardboard box, I found staring up at me a thick, plastic-covered report from an investigative firm called Precision Analysis, Inc. Bound like this, it was a good deal fancier than the reports I get from the private eye I use, a retired state police sergeant named Ted McCallum who used to do undercover work hunting drug dealers along the Boston waterfront until the stress got to him. On the surface, Ted is the most forgettable guy you'll ever see. He is so average—medium height, medium weight, medium everything—he becomes invisible. There is nothing to notice. But inside, he has definitely got his quirks. McCallum's reports are just a few sheets bound with a staple; everything you need to know and not one word more. But this Precision Analysis report went on for about a hundred pages, starting with a long memorandum and backing it up with a variety of exhibits consisting of court dockets, police reports, witness statements, media accounts, and even a letter to the cops from Tonya.

The author seemed to be unaware of the distinction between the possessive *its* and the contraction *it's*, but some of the stuff blew my head off all the same. In my line of work, prostitutes rarely come into the story in a big way. Mistresses, yes. Prostitutes, no. But this was a prostitute-mistress, jumbling up the sex with secrets and money.

And murder.

Addressed to Gus Jr. and his sister, Patricia, the report made its point in the first line of the executive summary. "Our clients' concern for the safety and well-being of their father is well founded." It turned out that Tonya hadn't just been a prostitute. She'd taken on an impressive variety of professional personae for a woman of such limited educational background. She had the documents to show that she was an ordained Presbyterian minister, and she was also a member of the press under the name of Catherine Barrington, with a passport to match. (Curious about the name Barrington. I Googled it and discovered that the Barrington name can be traced back to AD 1236 in England. Its motto? "Virtute dignus avorum," or "Worthy to bear the dignity of our ancestors." I had to hand it to her; Tonya Pryce had balls.) As I studied the report, with an exhibit detailing her criminal activities that ran a good fifty pages, she seemed to me less a con than a con artist. She painted herself whatever color she needed to survive, from the snow white of a Presbyterian minister to the mottled gray of a check kiter or the jet black of a murderess.

Or potential murderess. The cops once arrested Tonya for conspiring with a thug to kill a man who had emerged as the key witness against her in a case involving a stolen check she'd tried to cash. Got that? Here's the important part: the man she conspired to kill—his name was Ed Power—was friends with Tonya's husband, Mark J. Steele Sr., and Ed had been sending Mark some tidbits about Tonya's new career as a prostitute while Mark was in the army in Kuwait during the Gulf War. That pissed off Mark, as you can imagine. Well, the fact that Power would tell him this stuff really pissed off Tonya. "I hate your ex-husband so much I'm going to kill him," Tonya had raged at Power's ex-wife, Diane. All this according to the police.

Diane thought that Tonya had to be kidding. If she was going to do such a thing, why tell his ex-wife first? Wouldn't that blow up any alibi? An even better question: since they were headed for divorce, why did Tonya care so much about what her husband knew about her new line of work? But she did. She absolutely did. She repeated over and over: *"I am serious, I am going to hire someone to kill him."* She had it all planned out: they were going to burn Ed's house down, with him in it. And she wanted to draw Diane into the plot. Tonya's thinking was that if Diane knew, she could make sure her daughter, Melissa, was nowhere near. It was perfect. With her ex dead, Diane would gain sole custody of Melissa. And Tonya would be done with the blabbering Ed Power. A couple of days later, Tonya discussed the job with a guy named James Campbell, in his pickup truck.

But by then Diane had squealed. She'd gone to the police—who came for Tonya and arrested her for conspiring to commit murder. She wallowed in jail for a few days until she was somehow able to scrounge up the $2,600 needed for bail. But Tonya always did some of her best work in jail, and she'd cooked up a counterstrategy by the time she was sprung.

The short of it was that if Diane was going to produce stories about her, well, two could play at that game. Tonya did a little reconnaissance work and then arranged to bump into Diane at a doctor's office, where they had a conversation that, under the circumstances, must have been pretty strained. Right afterward, she ran to the police to swear out a lengthy statement claiming that Diane had said she was filled with regret for making up all that stupid shit about Tonya's plotting to burn up Diane's ex, which was too ridiculous for words. That story was all that stupid Power's idea, just a way of sticking it to Tonya. He'd "forced Diane to say those things about me," Tonya wrote in a statement for the police. And she sent copies to the district attorney, the governor, both state senators, all twelve Massachusetts congressmen, and the local newspapers. Tonya claimed that Power threatened to have DSS take the couple's other child, Paul, away from Diane if she didn't cooperate. So Diane had had no choice! In closing, Tonya struck a ladylike note: "I would like to suggest that you give as much weight to these words as you gave to Diane's previous words." *She* was the victim here. She recited the particulars:

> [Diane's groundless assertions] got me arrested, thrown in jail bail of $2600, my children were almost kidnapped by my mother in law, I lost my job while I was in jail for not showing up. We were evicted from our home because I couldn't pay the rent after losing my job, we had to move into a homeless

motel. I had to go on welfare, food stamps, and I had to sell
my furniture in order to come up with money for a home in
September.

True or not, and not is the better guess, the letter did its work,
clouding the whole issue in she said/she said claims and counterclaims.
Tonya was never charged with any crime. Her threats to commit murder and arson were stripped from the record.

The Power matter was a sideshow anyway. The main event was
Tonya's endlessly unfolding divorce from Mark Steele Sr., a burly
sometime construction worker, which started about 1990, continued
through his deployment to Kuwait, and went on for ten years more.
"An unusual messy, and volatile, on again, off again divorce," the report called it. No question about that. Mark or Tonya had been issued
six restraining orders in eight years, starting in 1985, when Tonya first
sought protection from Mark a month after she first filed for divorce.
The pattern was always the same—an assault and battery charge, then
a filing for divorce, then remorse, then reconciliation. Then repeat. It
happened in October 1985; January 1986; May 1987; June 1989 (when
Mark charged Tonya with assault and battery); October 1991; and on
April 22, 1992. It wasn't until Tonya filed for divorce on October 27,
1992, that it stuck, and the marriage was officially dead on January 29,
1993. But there were still a lot of legal details to go through, like child
support, alimony, division of property, and health insurance, and from
that point on, the court records are filled with matters pertaining to the
fallout from *Steele v. Steele*—complaints for contempt, for modification,
and yet more motions for temporary restraining orders against one side
or the other out of fear of physical violence.

Tonya was no angel, but then Mark was no prince. He was wildly
manic-depressive, veering from zany, mile-high, dot-pupil mania into
blithering zombiehood. When he was up, though, he could be wicked
scary. In the fall of 1992, in the move that precipitated the divorce, he

tried to strangle Tonya with a nylon stocking, and only failed because she managed to kick him in the balls and then slam him against a doorframe. In a manic spree a year later, he burst into a church, and while a dumbfounded priest watched, Mark placed pills on the altar, expressing his gratitude for God's curing his jock itch.

In 1995 Mark was arrested for again trying to strangle Tonya, this time with rope. He had nearly succeeded. She passed out, and he left her for dead. He was pretty drunk at the time, and he went outside to puke, and then drove off. He was sent to the county prison while he awaited trial.

Tonya took up the cause of battered women and took to the airwaves to talk about how she'd been strangled and beaten by Mark, and on one TV show taped at her house, she pointed out signs that someone had been prowling about in the dark, trying to break in. Tonya told the interviewer she was planning to leave town and to change her identity so her husband would not be able to find her. Obviously, this was not the smartest way to split—by telling everybody first. But this may explain the phony passport.

While she was getting divorced, Tonya got into the sex business big-time. The previous foray, the one that Ed Power squealed to her Mark about—that was just for pin money. She'd started out turning tricks on the tony North Shore—in Hamilton, Wenham, and Beverly. But she had a feeling the local cops were onto her, so she moved to Rowley, a few towns over, and started running a call-girl operation out of a rented house. It was going pretty well. She brought in as much as twelve grand a week. Tonya also ran a karaoke bar on Eastern Point in nearby Gloucester as cover for all the call-girl money. It also helped to build her customer base.

That's where she met our man Gus Sr. After retiring from business management, he'd moved to Wingaersheek Beach to live year-round in what had been his summerhouse. A rich, lonely widower, he'd turned up at the karaoke bar for a few laughs. Tonya must have seen the dollar signs, because she took him upstairs for one of the extras she gave her better customers, and he was soon a regular.

But for Tonya, the call-girl operation was the main thing money-wise. She had a half dozen girls working for her, most of them teen-agers. She advertised their services in a Boston tabloid, the *Phoenix*, under innocent-sounding names like Virgin Bride, Dancing Girl, and Cheerleader. Tonya gave herself more of a roar. She went under Shasta, the "Lion Tamer." She changed the name of the service regularly to make it hard for the cops to track, and she shifted operations from town to town too. In the end, her little company was delivering the goods in a deserted office in nearby Lanesville, with only a mattress for furniture.

Tonya was never much good at secrecy, and by now her activities had attracted the attention of cops from four neighboring Cape Ann towns, plus the state police. And they all swarmed in when Tonya, re-sponding to a request for Shasta, met for a quickie at the Lanesville office with a skinny, middle-aged greaser who turned out to be an un-dercover cop. The room was searched, and investigators found a raft of sex toys, peekaboo costumes, lubricants, and condoms. When the cops went to Tonya's house with a search warrant, they found computer discs detailing who, when, and how much; cell phones with stored numbers of favored clients; and a fax machine for sex business communications. Plus thousands of dollars in cash and traveler's checks. Tonya was ar-rested for soliciting and for "deriving support" from the prostitution of others.

When she appeared for her arraignment in the local district court, the newspapers dubbed her the North Shore Madam, but Tonya played the Presbyterian minister's wife, appearing in a virginal sweater with a lace collar, pleated skirt, and flat shoes.

It was great news for Mark, still rotting in jail as he awaited trial. The assistant DA who was bringing the attempted murder charge against him didn't relish the prospect of relying on a front-page hooker as his star witness. He decided to drop the charges, so long as Steele paid up on the fifty thousand dollars in back child support and alimony payments and stayed a hundred feet away from Tonya. He agreed and was once again a free man.

Tonya, however, was facing serious jail time for prostitution and solicitation. "[My ex-husband has been allowed] to get away with as close to murder as you can imagine," Tonya railed to the papers. Then she added: "They said I'd be crucified on the stand. [But] I'm willing to take my chances." Several months later, when Tonya showed up in court to offer a plea on the prostitution-related charges, she was defiant. She wore a lusty crimson dress that dripped off her and a Southern belle's wide-brimmed chapeau that angled off her head. The outfit said I'm a whore and I'm proud of it. She pleaded guilty to all charges and got five years in the Framingham State Prison for deriving support from prostitution and another year for soliciting. Somehow Tonya's personal plea struck a sympathetic chord in the judge. He declared himself willing to suspend the sentences if she stayed away from the "adult entertainment industry." Tonya gratefully agreed.

She moved to Beverly and avoided any further arrests for two years—until June of 1997, when the Gloucester police picked her up for prostitution and courteously tipped off the Essex County DA that the North Shore Madam was back in business in a new venue. The DA summoned Tonya to a hearing forthwith, to determine if this lapse of hers warranted jail time.

Tonya was headed to court when she evidently had a change of heart. Her Chevy Lumina was found abandoned in the parking lot of a Beverly country club, several miles from the Salem courthouse. Inside was a copy of *Hustler* magazine, a box of clothes, several sets of keys, and a note from Tonya requesting that her car and clothes be given to friends.

She was gone.

☙❧

THE SALEM PROBATE COURTHOUSE IS NOT FAR FROM THE SALEM Witch Museum in the old part of town, and it's maybe three-quarters of an hour from my office. It's a tired old structure, and inside it seems like any other cluttered, municipal building. I drove there straight from my house, first thing in the morning, the filing papers tucked away in my briefcase. It was a bright, warm summer day, and I found it a little odd to be in a suit, hurrying into the courthouse, when most of the tourists around were dressed for the beach. Still, there was no time to waste. I went right in to First Assistant Registrar Julie Bianco and filed my papers. She told me I'd be seeing Judge Martin—Phillipa Martin—who usually sits in the Cambridge courthouse. She's very sharp, no-nonsense. She and I always got along pretty well.

"Mr. Nissenbaum." Judge Martin greeted me from the bench with a smile. "What are you doing here, so far from Cambridge?"

"Stalking you," I joked.

She smiled but said nothing, and pulled up her copy of the papers I had just filed with the registrar. She'd read them, so there was no need to explain how Tonya had failed to pay the nursing home bill and how the children suspected that she was draining her husband's brokerage account. I didn't go into Tonya's history either. There would be time for that later. Besides, you never know which way something like that will cut. Lots of women have a checkered past. That doesn't mean they can't be loving wives, or that their husbands wouldn't want the best for them. Besides, Tonya had done her time, so the court had to assume that she had emerged from her prison term rehabilitated. This was, after all, a system of *corrections*.

I kept it simple. I explained that the children were asking that Gus Jr. be appointed a temporary guardian for their father, Gus Sr. That would allow him to take legal control of his father's finances.

"But he has a wife," the judge interjected. She knew the papers cold. "And we can assume that her interests are not, shall we say, perfectly aligned with her stepchildren."

I resisted the impulse to smile, but I always admired judges who quickly come to sensible conclusions, even if they don't serve my clients' interests. "I understand, Your Honor," I conceded. I was not going to waste any breath arguing that one. "But my clients wanted me to ask."

"And now you have my answer." She smiled. "But under the circumstances, I'll appoint someone else as a temporary guardian for Mr. Pryce, so long as he or she is not related. Do you have anyone in mind I should consider?"

I'd prepared for this by calling a couple of lawyers in Boston, and another in Andover, which was much closer, to ask if they'd serve. Ricky Haddad, a hardworking young lawyer who I thought would be the best choice, was located in Andover. As I expected, she picked Ricky. She said she would issue a formal notice of order to get him started. It would only last ten days, to allow Tonya to respond.

"Anything else?"

"Quite a few things, actually." I requested an array of restraining orders that would put Gus's assets off-limits to Tonya. "Also, I would like you to revoke any power of attorney or health care proxy that Mr. Pryce Sr. may have signed in favor of his wife."

"That is a long list, Mr. Nissenbaum."

"Yes, it is," I replied. "But this is an unusual situation."

Judge Martin looked at me. "Yes, it is." She thought for a long moment. "The requests are granted."

"Thank you, Your Honor."

"Now, who is going to represent Mr. Haddad?" Ricky could be his own lawyer, but then, as the saying goes, he'd have a fool for a client.

"I am, Your Honor." I explained how his interests in looking after Gus Sr. would be identical to the children's, so there would be no conflict.

"Agreed," she said, nodding once vigorously. With that, court was recessed.

⚭

I CALLED RICKY BY CELL FROM THE COURTHOUSE AND TOLD HIM HE'D been appointed. We talked over strategy, and when I had his okay, I went into the registry office where Julie Bianco had already prepared some legal documents pertaining to Ricky's appointment and the restraining order against Tonya. Then I performed one of those legal maneuvers that lawyers don't even think about and that are probably head-scratchers to everybody else. Representing Ricky, who was representing Gus Sr., I filed a "complaint for divorce" by Ricky, on behalf of Gus, to end his marriage to Tonya. Talk about playing God. Who were we to do that? Well, we had our reasons, chiefly that Ricky was convinced that if Gus only knew, he'd divorce Tonya for what she'd done. Besides, Tonya's treatment of her last husband didn't bode so well for this one. A divorce action was the quickest way to freeze all her assets. She couldn't sell the house or anything else. And once we served the papers on Gus's banks and stockbroker, she could not drain his accounts. Otherwise, all of Gus's assets might soon be gone. Poof!

Once I had the papers, I took them to the deputy sheriff's office and asked his staff to serve Tonya right away. Once those papers were in her hand, she was iced. Then, feeling celebratory, I went for a grilled cheese and an extra-thick coffee frappe at a nearby sandwich shop.

While I ate, I checked in with Ricky again. He'd known all about the North Shore Madam, and he couldn't wait to take her on.

"So where do I start?" he asked me.

"With the construction at the house." I passed along what Gusty had told me on the phone. "We need to figure out what's going on and stop it."

"Any idea how?"

"Just tell the contractors they might not be paid, and they'll put their tools away. Believe me."

I gave him the address, and he said he'd get right on it.

"And let's keep each other posted."

"Sure thing."

Meanwhile, I'd work the money angle from the other end—at the stockbroker's.

Back at the courthouse, Julie Bianco had all the orders ready to shut down Gus's account at the brokerage house. "I figured you'd want that," Julie said.

I could have kissed her. I faxed the order to the stockbroker, drummed my fingers for a few minutes, and then called the firm to get Gus Sr.'s broker. I wanted to make sure the fax had gone through.

"Just got it," he told me when he came on the line. "Secretary just put it on my desk. You've got some good timing there. You should be in the business."

"Oh? Why's that?"

"We were just about to process two checks on the account. One of them's pretty big. I've got it right here in my hand. For four hundred thousand dollars. There's another one for ten thousand."

"Signed by?"

"Just a second. Got to put my glasses on. It's hard to make out." He paused for a moment while, I imagined, he examined the signature. "Looks like Augustus Pryce Sr. He's the signatory on the account."

"Did you check the signatures against what's on file?"

"Once we got your instructions, I pulled up his card. Got it right here."

"And."

He paused again. I pictured him comparing the two signatures under a magnifying glass. Finally, his voice came back on the line. "Well, to my eye, it's not much of a match. To tell you the truth, it's not even close."

"Makes sense," I told him. "Pryce has been in a nursing home for the last month with end-stage liver disease. I don't think he was able to hold a pen, let alone have any idea what he was signing. They say what the checks were for?"

"Looks like one is made out to Tonya Pryce. The memo line says 'home repair.' That's for four hundred thousand. The other is payable to a lawyer, and it says 'lawyer—home repair.'"

"Four hundred grand for home repair?" I repeated. "Sounds like a lot to me."

"All depends."

"So you're not going to put those through, right?" I asked, just to be sure.

"Not with this court order. No, sir."

I asked him to send me copies of the checks for my records and then snapped my cell phone shut.

I wondered about the timing. Why such a big check now? Did she sense the deadline was coming—the day when her sugar daddy would be no more—so she decided to grab for everything as soon as she could? Hard to figure it any other way, which made me think that Tonya really was true to her profession: taking cash for services rendered.

I was on Route 1, heading back to my office in Boston, when Ricky rang me back.

"So how'd it look out there?" I asked.

"My God, Jerry. There was all this stuff going on. It was like they were redoing the whole place from the inside out. Electricians. Carpenters. The gas guy. People putting down hardwood floors, measuring kitchen counters. At least, that's what I think they were doing. It was this big construction site. Must have been a dozen people there sawing, hammering, milling around."

"Was Tonya there?"

"No, but I found Tonya's new general contractor. Joe Basile, I think he said. He was there in his truck, looking at some plans. I knocked on his window, told him who I was, and then I showed him my papers and explained how I was acting on behalf of Mr. Pryce. And I was sorry but all this work here had to stop."

"How'd he take that?"

"He just cussed out Tonya, called her a little bitch and a few more things, and said he knew this whole thing was screwed up. He just knew it. Apparently, Tonya had wanted everything done in a huge rush, so everything would be set when her husband got home from the hospital. Paid him extra for a rush job. He asked for thirty-two hundred, but she offered to pay thirty-six. Joe figured, how weird is that? You also don't get back from the hospital and jump right into a hot tub. Then he got out of his pickup and blew a wolf whistle and told everybody, 'That's it, you gotta stop now. Pick up your tools and clear out. I'll let you know when you can start in again.' That didn't go down so well, but there wasn't much they could do."

Then it hit me, why she'd go wild on the house. The house was going to be hers, free and clear, after Gus died. The more money she put into it, the more valuable it would be. It made sense for her to draw down the brokerage account, since she'd never get it, and put the money here.

To nail that down, I called Towers—Gus's Texas lawyer—and brought him up to speed, promising to fax him notice of Ricky's appointment as temporary guardian and my notice of appearance as his attorney.

"Big day for you," he told me genially when he came on the line.

"It's all about the real estate, isn't it?" I asked him.

"You could say that." He chuckled. "When you see the will, you'll see."

"Why's that?"

"Because of what you just said. I couldn't tell you before, but you probably figured it: she'll get the house, all hers. Won't get much else. Just a hundred fifty grand or so. Oh, and an education trust for her to get a master's at Tufts."

"A what?"

"She was working on some bullshit degree, I can't remember."

"How much for that?"

"One hundred twenty big ones."

"Nice."

"Yes, he was. But the numbers are fixed. There's nothing there she can increase, which she's not gonna like. That's why she went nuts over the premarital agreement. It would have left her just how she was before the marriage. No way she was going back to *that*. You kidding?"

✆

I CALLED GUSTY ON MY CELL TO LET HIM IN ON EVERYTHING WE'D gotten done. I started talking about Ricky's appointment, but before I could get to the brokerage account, the renovations or anything else, he interrupted me. "I guess you haven't heard the latest," he said.

"What?"

"My father's gone."

"*What?* What do you mean, gone? You mean he's—he's dead?"

"No. Tonya went to the nursing home and took him. Just whisked him away. He's disappeared."

"But she can't do that!" I shouted. "She was served with a restraining order and notice of Ricky's appointment. She can't just take him."

"Well, she did. Just a few minutes ago. Came in to the nursing home and just . . . took him. He's gone."

"Do you have any idea where?"

"Nope." He sounded really tired. "I don't have any idea. That's what my sister and I are trying to figure out. He's not home. I had a neighbor check. Beyond that, no, I have no idea where he is. None. He could be anywhere. What a fucking bitch."

For a moment, I was speechless. Then I said it too: "What a fucking bitch."

CHAPTER

FIVE

TONYA HAD JUST PULLED OFF ANOTHER VANISHING ACT. FIRST she disappeared on her way to her court appearance, and now this. What was with that woman? It seemed like she didn't just ignore the law, she ignored the laws of physics. Things that are in plain sight are supposed to remain in plain sight. Right? Well, not so far as Tonya Pryce was concerned. She could be there and then—blink!—she could not be there. Then again, the disappeared rarely stay disappeared. And Tonya had turned up last time after all, but it had taken a while. After she dumped her car in that Beverly country club lot, she got to the other coast, which was pretty impressive, and managed to lie low in California until the other big impetus in her life got the better of her. Her need for publicity. She was asked to appear at a hookers' convention in Las Vegas, and she simply could not resist. While she was there, she couldn't resist taking the podium to tell the tale of her life as the North Shore Madam. And when she was telling it, she couldn't resist noting with some pride that, in fact, a warrant was currently out for her arrest for having jumped bail back in Massachusetts.

She probably shouldn't have mentioned that. Because somebody in the audience thought it might interest the police. And sure enough, before the week was out she was bound for Massachusetts in one of those flying cattle cars they reserve for criminal transport. A couple more days and she was in Salem Superior Court on her way to the Framingham pen to serve six years.

This time, I called Ricky back and said this was probably a stupid question, but did he happen to see Gus Pryce at the house by any chance? Ricky thought I was joking, which I probably should have been.

"Gus?" he asked. "The old guy?"

"Yeah—you check the basement?" It really wouldn't have surprised me if Tonya had hidden him down there.

"There is no basement. No, come on, Jerry. You really think she'd do that?"

"I'm not going to rule anything in or rule anything out."

So I put my investigator, Ted McCallum, on it. I didn't hear back for over an hour, but when he reached me on his cell, he confirmed what Ricky had said: there was no sign of him, or of anyone, at the house. No one answered the bell when he rang, and he didn't see any sign of life in the house.

But McCallum did discover one thing when he asked around. Just a week or two before, Tonya had appeared at the nursing home with a rotund local lawyer named Jason Englehardt. Tonya had brought Englehardt along to help persuade her dying husband to give her power of attorney. So they'd come to Pryce's bedside, and she held Gus's hand and told him how much she loved him, and said that there was just this one thing she needed him to do. Somewhere in there Englehardt remembered he'd need a notary public to take Pryce's oath. But he hadn't thought to bring one along. So the two of them went tearing around the nursing home, trying to find somebody who was commissioned as a notary public. There actually was one, but she didn't want any part of these shenanigans, so they came up empty.

Was Tonya trying to get Gus to give *her* power of attorney now? Is that why she abducted him? If so, where would she take him, and for how long? A hotel? I had my staff check around, but we came up empty. A motel? Ditto. Did Tonya have any friends in the area? Not that we could determine. I even thought of camping sites before I realized that was ridiculous, even for her. I would have called the police, but what was I going to tell them? That an elderly man had been abducted by his wife? Not much difference between that and going for a drive. Yes, she wasn't supposed to take Gus from the nursing home. But that didn't make it kidnapping.

Days went by. Gusty kept calling to see what I knew. And I kept calling to see what he knew. Neither of us knew anything.

༒

WE'D SECURED RICKY'S INITIAL APPOINTMENT AS TEMPORARY GUARD-ian without consulting Tonya. The court granted it on an emergency ba-sis, recognizing that if Tonya was allowed to contest it, she could delay the appointment indefinitely while she went right ahead and dropped Gus's brokerage account to zero. But that emergency appointment only lasted ten days. If we wanted ninety days more, we'd have to argue for it, going nose to nose with Tonya and her lawyer.

Considering that Tonya had just abducted Gus, I didn't know what to expect. Would she really show up? For that matter, would *Gus* appear?

The court was to convene at ten. I arrived early, as always, to get settled in and found myself in some suspense as the appointed hour drew near. Where was Tonya? Would Gus materialize? Finally, the doors burst open, and there was Jason Englehardt, loudly proclaiming that he was Tonya Pryce's lawyer and he was bringing evidence that Gus required no temporary guardian. Then came Tonya, with Gus shuffling along behind her, clinging to the arm of a heavyset woman I took to be a nurse (whom I dubbed Nurse Ratched).

I'm not sure which Pryce, Mr. or Mrs., startled me more. Tonya looked pretty good, but cheesy good, like she belonged in a small-market TV newscast. You didn't want to get too close. She had ultra-shiny golden hair that was gray at the roots and a stagy, *Sunset Boulevard* way of moving that commanded space and attention. She always told the newspapers she was forty-three, but it's the skin I go by, and I could make out enough tractor marks under the pancake makeup around her eyes to put her on the other side of fifty. Still, her chassis was in pretty good shape for all the miles on it.

Gus Sr., on the other hand, was like the walking dead. His hair had turned a wispy gray, his skin was papery, his shoulders sagged, and his gut ballooned from his liver disease. He gazed toward Tonya with rheumy eyes, unspeaking, the breath making a whistling noise as he strained for air.

I introduced myself, and told Tonya that it was good of her to bring Mr. Pryce back. "We were all getting a little worried about him," I told her.

"There was no need for that," she replied airily. "He was under the care of his loving wife."

"But not at your home," I said.

She reared back. "No, not after what you've done to it. He wouldn't have been comfortable there."

❧

The whole point of this little exercise was to determine Gus Pryce Sr.'s competence. Did he need a temporary guardian or not? To determine the matter, the two sides assembled around a large conference table in a back room. All except for Tonya, who was obliged to remain in the hallway, much to her distress. She didn't like it if she wasn't the center of attention or in control. Ricky sat across from Gus at the conference room table; I sat next to Ricky.

He started out by asking how Gus was doing.

"Fine," Gus replied.

"Where have you been staying?"

"With her." He nodded toward Nurse Ratched.

"Why not at your beach house?" Ricky asked, innocently.

Gus looked perplexed. "I—I don't know."

"Weren't you supposed to be in the nursing home?"

He glanced nervously over at Nurse Ratched again. "I—," he began, but said nothing more.

He was pretty out of it. He'd obviously been coached to deliver prepared answers, but he flubbed most of them. Unexpected questions left him at a total loss. I'm not sure he knew where he was. When Englehardt asked about the household expenses, he did it in such a way that Gus could answer with a simple yes each time. When Ricky asked more open-ended questions, Gus had to do more, and he kept getting bewildered. After just a few minutes, Gus's head dropped down toward his chest. He seemed pretty worn out. When he spoke, I could hardly hear his answers.

"So tell us, Mr. Pryce, how is your health?" Ricky finally asked, trying to sum it all up.

"Not too good," he admitted.

☙◗

BY NOW, JUDGE MARTIN HAD HANDED THE CASE OVER TO THE RUDDY-faced Judge Burl Dorfman, who normally presided on the bench in this jurisdiction but had been on vacation when the case got started. I provided an objective summary of what had gone on, up to Tonya's taking Gus from the nursing home. Ricky described his evaluation of Gus, concluding that he was not competent.

"Just look at him, Judge," I concluded, turning back to the long wooden bench where Gus was slumped, almost comatose. "If you were to put him in the witness box and spend just a few minutes asking him questions, you'd see that he needs a temporary guardian to protect his interests. And Mr. Haddad is willing to continue to do that."

Speaking for Tonya, Englehardt did his best to harrumph his way through the counter-case, claiming Gus was just "a little ill," that was all. And who had Mr. Pryce's interests more at heart—his loving wife, or a total stranger like Mr. Haddad?

I quickly replied, "Your Honor, I'd like to believe that most wives care enough about their husbands not to drain their accounts the moment they are incapacitated. But no one can argue that is the case here."

Englehardt started to speak, but the judge gestured for him to be silent. He had heard enough, and decided that Haddad was to continue in his duties for another ninety days. Gus was to be returned immediately to the nursing home.

∽

THERE WAS A STORY IN THE *BOSTON HERALD* THE NEXT DAY ABOUT THE return of the North Shore Madam, and it mentioned my role in the case. That afternoon I got a call in my office that Mindy said I should take.

I picked up the receiver. "Jerry Nissenbaum here. How can I help you?"

"I don't think you can," a woman said. She was worn sounding. "But I bet I can help you."

"Who am I speaking to," I asked, trying not to sound impatient.

"Marcia," she said.

"And your last name?"

"I'd rather not say." She let that sit there. "It's about the Pryce case. The paper said you were involved."

"That's right."

"I know the woman. Tonya Pryce. We—worked together."

"Where was that?"

"In the house."

Then I remembered. There had been a Marcia Stowe in the detec-

89

tive report. She and Tonya had been going at each other, and each had sworn out 209A orders—restraining orders—on the other. There must have been five or six between the two of them. Just like with Tonya's ex. That was her way of showing affection.

"I've got some information for you." She paused.

"I'm listening."

"I can't tell you over the phone." Huffy now.

"Well, I'm not going to meet with you until you tell me what this is about."

"Shit. Well, okay, then. It's—" Marcia stammered for a bit. "Fuck! How to say this? All right." She took a breath. "Okay. I'll just tell you. We were going to murder him."

"Who?"

"The guy. Gus Pryce."

"No, *who* was going to murder him?"

"Me and Tonya."

"You two were going to murder her husband? Now, how were you going to do that?"

Silence.

"Marcia?"

"All right. All right! I'll tell you. We were going to push him down the stairs."

I almost laughed. "Down the stairs. That's how you were going to do it?" I had to pause a moment to collect myself. "That's how you can kill somebody?"

"If he's drunk, yes. The guy was always fucking drunk. Always."

"Doesn't seem too likely to me."

"We had a backup plan."

"And what was that?"

"We were going to pump him so full of Viagra his eyes were going to bug out, and he was going to have a heart attack." She gave out a snort of laughter. "Serves him right, the little fucker."

I decided Marcia was out of her mind.

"You think I'm making this up," Marcia said.

"Well, I'll admit I don't exactly know how to take this."

"I've got it all on tape."

"You have Tonya Pryce talking about murdering her husband, Gus Pryce, on tape?"

"You bet your ass."

"Really, Tonya?"

"Yeah, the cunt. We were driving, and I got her to talk all about this shit. Swear to God. I got the tape right here in my pocket. That's why I called you. I want to nail her ass."

The tape. Of course—Russell Towers had mentioned it. He said he'd told Gus about it, and he'd just laughed it off.

"Why are you doing this?" I asked now.

"I've got my reasons." Airy now.

"The A and B?" Assault and battery, as Marcia well knew.

"Maybe. The bitch took my Harley."

The conversation went on, with a lot of dubious explanations and genuine venom. I kind of liked her, actually. All charged up, determined to nail Tonya. I knew the feeling. They'd known each other from prison. They were cellmates, then bunkmates, and then intimates, whispering stuff to each other. Marcia was a straight-out lesbian. Seriously butch. I met her later, and she looked like a fireplug with hair. Tonya was whatever the situation required. A lot of their prison talk was about Gus, who was visiting Tonya every few weeks. When Marcia got wind of the fact that he was hot to marry Tonya, she got all excited. Tonya should marry the geezer! Yes! He'd be their meal ticket! Tonya would fix the will so everything came to her when Gus croaked. To keep an eye on everything, and on Tonya, Marcia would live with them as the maid. That was an Addams-family touch I found even more hilarious when I actually met the woman. She was about as maidly as a front-end loader. Still, I couldn't ignore the plot. The idea of terminating Gus by pitching him down the stairs or stuffing him full of Viagra wouldn't be so funny if it worked.

Whether or not success was likely, and regardless of whose idea it was, this was evidence of a conspiracy to commit murder, and that was enough for me. If I could prove that Tonya married Gus to kill him, that should be plenty to get the marriage annulled. If a murder plot wasn't enough, what was?

But it would help to have Tonya on tape. All excited, Marcia offered to come right in and play it for me. But before I could let that happen, I had to press her for more details. Massachusetts has strict laws against taping someone without their permission. Even listening to such a tape could be a five-year felony, and there are other places I'd rather spend five years besides a state can.

"But it wasn't in Massachusetts," Marcia assured me.

"Well, where was it?"

"I—I don't know. We were in the car. Driving up from Florida."

"So you're saying you could have been in any state between Florida and here?" Not too helpful.

"I'm pretty sure it was Connecticut."

"Pretty sure?"

"Okay. It might have been New York."

New York would have been okay. You can tape people unawares in New York. But you can't in Connecticut. And I wasn't going to take that chance. I'd have to put the tape on hold.

☙❧

I WAS STILL MULLING IT OVER A FEW DAYS LATER WHEN I GOT ANOTHER call out of the blue, this one from a man named Alan Brinker, who said he'd once been Marcia's husband, a concept I found hard to imagine. He told me that Tonya had called the house once looking for Marcia. Marcia had let Alan in on their plans to kill Gus, and he'd told her to stuff it. He didn't want to hear about anything like that. So when Tonya called, he told her the same thing. "That's all Marcia's idea," she told him. "I had absolutely nothing to do with planning it. I was just going along for the ride." He wanted me to know what kinds of people he was dealing with. I thanked him for the information. It corroborated the murder plot—without requiring me to listen to the tape. It would allow me to try to get the marriage annulled. An annulment would cut Tonya out of Gus's will, saving his estate some serious money.

൞

THE SAME DAY, RICKY CALLED ME, ALL BREATHLESS. "GUESS WHAT," he said.

I couldn't guess, but as it turned out, I could imagine the answer all too well.

"She tried to sneak Gus out of the nursing home again."

She'd tried just the night before, after visiting hours. She'd come with that Nurse Ratched, and the two of them hauled Gus out of bed and, holding him up on both sides, started shuffling him down the hall. They didn't know that Ricky had outfitted him with an alarm bracelet that would go off if he left the building with anyone but the staff. They'd gotten him through the first double doors, but when they hit the second, the alarm sounded, and both sets of doors automatically locked, imprisoning them all in the anteroom in between. Finally, a nurse and two beefy security guards broke in on the threesome. Tonya was furious. "Can't I even take my husband out for a fucking ice cream cone?" she yelled. "Jesus fucking Christ!"

"Absolutely not," said the nurse coolly. "Not for a patient in Mr. Pryce's condition."

"Fuck you! I can too." When the security guards tried to intervene, she screamed at them. "Get the fuck away from me!" The security guard held his ground. "Fuck off! This is my fucking husband!"

The nurse ran to call the police. There was a wall phone just outside the double doors, and she called 911 and loudly explained the situation to a dispatcher.

"Screw this," Tonya said, and she tried to push her husband past security. "I'm fucking out of here. I am so sick of you."

Haggard and bewildered as he stood there, Gus might have toppled to the floor if the security guards hadn't grabbed him and held on. With that, Tonya quietly surrendered control of her husband. The nurse buzzed Tonya and Ratched through the far doors and watched them exit the building. Then the nurse and the security guards helped Gus limp back to his bed.

Ꙍ

AT THAT POINT, TONYA'S MAJOR ACTIVITIES WERE AVOIDING HER depositions, providing bullshit documentation of her expenses, and running up illegal charges on Gus's credit cards. She had a particular fondness for the sorts of appliances that are advertised on late-night TV. We needed to get a full account from her of the various financial stunts she had tried to pull, plus any documents that would show her actual spending habits. She'd asked the court for five thousand dollars a week from Gus for beach house rent, a daily massage, vacations, entertainment, nail care, and the like. We were trying to put a stop to all that. But to do so we'd need to review her claims that all these were reasonable expenses.

The woman was wily; I'll give her that. For each deposition, you have to plan everything well ahead of time. We'd set up a time, clear it with everyone involved, reserve a conference room, arrange for a stenographer, get all the lawyers on board. Then I'd drive to Andover, getting there early so we'd be all set up, and then . . . we'd wait. And then we'd wait some more. No Tonya. Her lawyer had no clue where she was. I should say, her *new* lawyer—a stuffy woman named Laura Hopkins— since the old lawyer, Englehardt, had to withdraw because he'd been a

94

witness to the attempt to secure power of attorney from Gus. That made him the subject of a deposition and probably a witness in any trial.

There was no sign of Tonya, no explanation for her absence, and no indication of her whereabouts. She'd vanished again! Nobody knew where she was. So we'd pack it in after wasting about five thousand dollars of billable time between my preparation time, everyone's travel, and the hours spent sitting there doing nothing.

But I can be persistent, and I got a court order requiring her to attend a third attempt at a deposition at Ricky's law office in North Andover. By now, Hopkins had also bailed on Tonya, and she was represented by the courtly, befuddled Randall "Happy" Douglas. The court ordered Tonya to appear with her documents at ten o'clock. We were all in our places around the conference table when we heard a heavy, drumlike sound, accompanied by a grunting sort of breathing, coming up the back stairs near the office. It was Tonya, wearing a medical collar, no less. And she was lugging a copy box full of papers, presumably the ones I'd requested, which she set down on the table with one last groan.

I had requested that a sheriff be there to serve her with a summons on a complaint for contempt I had filed against her for violating the orders of the court. Serving is a bit like tag. You don't have to get the papers into the person's hand; you just slap them on her any way you can. Now, seeing him reach toward her with the papers, Tonya danced away, her arms up. "My mommy told me never to take anything from a stranger," she said teasingly. The sheriff had been around, and he tucked the papers inside her handbag. Officially, that was "good service." Tonya fished out the paper and tossed it on the floor, but it was too late. She'd been served, and she was legally obliged to act on its requirements. Knowing this, Happy Douglas picked the paper up and tucked them in his jacket pocket for her.

Depositions are interviews, basically, but interviews with an edge to them. Question—answer—question—answer, and so on, all morning and afternoon. Nobody likes to be deposed, and tempers can flare. But people usually stay seated and keep their voices down. Not Tonya. No, not Tonya. She went nuts.

It started when I offered to get another box of papers she'd left at the foot of the stairs. Before I left, though, I shut off my cell phone and set it down on the window sill across from her. From the way she acted, it might have been an AK-47. "That's a camera phone!" she screamed. "You're taking pictures of me! That's illegal! I'm getting out of here! You can't do that!"

"Tonya, it's just a cell phone," I told her, holding it up for her. "See? It's off. And it's not taking any pictures." I stuffed the phone in my pants pocket.

"But that's illegal!" Tonya screamed. "That's illegal! It is! You can't do that! Stop!"

Tonya started to bolt from the conference room, hoping to take refuge in the hall, just as Ricky's secretary, an imposing woman named Marnie Tams, came in to see what the yelling was all about. They collided, and Tonya tried to shove Marnie aside, screaming, "You assaulted me! You assaulted me! I'm going to sue!"

"For God's sake, nobody tried to assault you," I told Tonya. "Don't be ridiculous."

Now, Marnie had been a victim of hideous abuse from her ex-husband, and the combination of getting shoved by Tonya, hearing the word *assault*, and seeing all the craziness gave her flashbacks. She slumped down into a chair and started to cry these big heaving sobs. Ricky helped her up and ushered her into the next room.

"She bodily assaulted me!" Tonya insisted.

Once Marnie was safely outside, Ricky turned back to the room and closed the door behind him.

"Oh, you want to kidnap me now?" Tonya demanded, her green eyes flaring. "This will be reported to the police."

"Go right ahead," Ricky told her, disgusted.

Tonya's eyes swept around the room. "You people are in big trouble now. I am ending this meeting. I'm not staying. I was assaulted by a secretary."

"Cut it out. You were not," I told her.

She started to pull the box of papers toward her.

"Leave that here," I told her. "Remember, the judge ordered you to produce these documents and to be deposed today."

"Fuck you. I won't stay."

That's when I lost it. I shouted at her that she was a "freakin' idiot." Not the worst language, but not the sort of thing a lawyer wants to see on a deposition transcript either. Tonya had gotten to me. This is what she does.

"You're under arrest!" she yelled.

"Rosalie—" I tried to get her attention by using the nickname she'd acquired in prison. But it didn't faze her.

"You are in big trouble," she snapped. "You'll be disbarred, mister."

"I'll be disbarred? You will be behind bars, madam."

With that, she scooped up the box as if it was empty and clattered down the stairs. She grabbed the other box at the foot of the stairwell and, kicking one box across the pavement and carrying the other, she somehow made her way across the parking lot. I didn't know whether I should race out there and try to drag her back to the deposition, call the police, or just scream bloody murder. But in the end I just watched her go, kicking and carrying, until she made it to the street, where she flagged down the driver of a pickup truck and climbed in with her boxes, taking off once again for parts unknown.

ⅮⅯ

WHEN TONYA FAILED TO COOPERATE FOR THIS THIRD ATTEMPT AT A deposition, I amended her contempt complaint, requiring her to explain to Judge Dorfman in the Essex Probate Court why she'd flouted the will of the court. The appearance was set for ten o'clock on Tuesday,

October 4, and by nine thirty, the courtroom was jammed with press, all there to catch a glimpse of the illustrious, almost legendary North Shore Madam and record her latest legal high jinks. She had made it onto the front page of a number of the local papers, and even the *Globe* had given the story heavy coverage inside. But, of course, ten o'clock came and went, and our diva had not showed. For anyone else, I would have waited. For Tonya, I called McCallum, my investigator, and asked him to find her. No problem. He drove down to the Pryce house and spotted her Toyota in the driveway. He pulled in, parked, knocked on the door. No one answered, but when he went around the side to look in the windows, he could see that the front door had been barricaded with a huge chair. When he peered in, he saw Tonya sprawled out, either asleep or unconscious, on a mattress on the living room floor in front of a blaring flat-screen TV.

After McCallum sent word, I told Judge Dorfman that we had located her.

"Well, what do you want me to do?"

For a moment, I just looked at him. I debated whether to say, "You're the judge." Instead I replied, "Issue a warrant for her arrest." I did not say: they call it the law for a reason.

He looked past me at all the press. "Okay. I'll do that."

Did I mention that Judge Dorfman is the worst judge in the state? Dumb as a post, lazy, arbitrary, imperious, and vengeful. Let's just say: I was not a fan.

The cops were gathered and duly authorized to arrest Tonya. When they arrived, McCallum was waiting for them. They pounded on the front door and flashed their badges through the window. Tonya's son Shawn loomed inside. Turned out he'd been there all along with his girlfriend. He shoved the big chair aside and opened up and said okay when McCallum asked if he could come in with the cops. The place was like a construction site, which is what it had been when the workmen scrammed. There were wires everywhere and scraps of wood and bits of plumbing pipe and sawdust. The inside water had been turned off, so someone had run a hose in through the window from an outside tap, and it went all across the living room, and left a stain on the expensive new wooden floors where the water had dribbled out.

The kitchen counters had been removed, and with the pipes stopped up and the electricity off, nothing worked. The place reeked of garbage, and there were pizza boxes, food wrappers, and empty beer cans strewn everywhere.

Tonya was a mess. She'd obviously just been woken up by the cops, and she looked sick: pasty faced, disheveled. She was wearing only a filmy T-shirt and no panties. When she talked to the cops, she'd tug suggestively on the neck of her T-shirt, like it was an offer.

No soap. "Get dressed," they told her. "You have an appointment before Judge Dorfman this morning, and you're late."

"Fuck off," Tonya said.

"Get dressed and come with us," the cops repeated. "And if you won't get dressed, we'll take you like this." One of them reached for the handcuffs on his belt. "All the same to us."

She got dressed, although not quickly.

Somehow she made herself decent. And when the squad car delivered her to the courthouse, and the print reporters and the photographers and the TV cameras all descended, she was ready. She knew how to act with the press, how to give them only what she wanted. She moved slowly, gracefully, as if she were the Queen of England.

The assembled media throng went wild as she made a grand procession through the hall, up the wide stairs, and onto the second floor. TV lights gleamed off the marble walls, photographers' flashes fired, and the halls echoed with shouted questions from all the reporters. She moved ahead of them all, then turned out of the long hall and slipped into the ladies' room with a female deputy right behind her.

When she finally emerged, Tonya had her medical collar on again. If she was a diva for the media, she'd be a victim for the judge.

Once she arrived in the courtroom, Dorfman asked her to explain why she had failed to show up for the deposition.

"I'm so sorry. I overslept, Your Honor," she told him wearily. It looked like her head was being propped up by the collar. Her whole body seemed limp. "I've been on some very heavy pain medication." All of it for her neck and back. "It's from all the stress of my husband's illness and all these lawsuits." The pain pills had kept her up until three. So she took sleeping pills to see her through the night. "But I couldn't wake up."

Dorfman listened to all this with a blank expression. "You still need to show up for court, and for your depositions, Mrs. Pryce."

"I understand, Your Honor. But they want me to bring all these boxes of documents, and with my back, I—"

"Do your best," Dorfman interrupted. "Now, I'll give you thirty days to reschedule this one. Deputy, you can release Mrs. Pryce. Next case."

Thirty more days! After all this! On a matter that was literally life and death? I couldn't believe it. Tonya could simply ignore the rules that everybody else had to live by. Dorfman wouldn't listen to my objections. Tonya still wasn't deposed, and I was getting steamed.

There was a tenderness in Dorfman's voice when he spoke to Tonya, a sympathy, I'd never seen before—and one that had certainly never been directed at me. I watched how he looked at her, and how she looked back at him. And then it hit me like an anvil to the head. He'd done her. He'd been one of her clients. It explained why Dorfman put up with all her other shenanigans, which no judge, not even the most lackadaisical, uncaring ones would accept. Although he had been married for twenty-three years and had five children shortly after he became a judge, he took up with a little sexpot on the courthouse administrative staff, which is a little like doing it at high noon on Salem Common. A secret like that doesn't hold much past the first orgasm. To keep his job, he got a divorce and married his princess. And now this. He had to have banged Tonya Pryce. And now he had to be nice to her, to keep her mouth shut.

❧

WE WERE PLENTY BUSY IN THOSE THIRTY DAYS, DEPOSING THE CON-
tractor about the cost of all the additions, which he placed somewhere
north of three hundred thousand dollars; keeping the Pryce children
apprised of the developments; hiring a neuropsychologist to evaluate
Gus Sr.'s cognitive state (which was not good, and getting worse by the
hour); studying up on the likely prognosis of a poisoned liver; filing motions to allow Ricky to take charge of the finances; and conducting a
thorough inventory of Pryce's holdings, from his real estate down to his
automobiles, of which he had several.

One of them was a dark blue BMW, which was nowhere around.
Tonya said she knew nothing about it, so Rickey reported it stolen.
Well, guess what? A few days later, a local patrolman named Ferrara was
tooling along Route 128 in Gloucester in an unmarked cruiser when a
car went roaring by him at almost a hundred miles an hour. A dark blue
BMW. Ferrara gave chase and pulled it over. And yes, this was indeed
Pryce's dark blue BMW. Tonya's son Shawn was out joyriding with a
drunken friend named Pete. In the back were heaps of antique quilts
they'd stolen from Pete's grandmother to sell for drug money. All of this
was in violation of Shawn's parole restrictions, which were put in place
after he got caught knocking over some local gas stations. Nice family.

❧

ALL THE WHILE, GUS HAD BEEN DECLINING. INITIALLY, THE DOCTORS
said that he had a few months to a few years to live. Now they said it
would be weeks. Toward the end of October, three months into the
case, it had gotten down to days. He had been moved from the nursing
home to Addison Gilbert Hospital in hopes that the doctors there could
better manage his care. No one was expecting a cure. But we were hoping at least to save him from too much pain. End-stage liver disease is
relentless, and it was doing a job on Gus. Finally, when October gave

way to November, it was clear that it was finishing up its work. With the support of Gus's two children, Ricky had asked the court to permit him to give the doctors a Do Not Resuscitate, Do Not Intubate order. Tonya fought that furiously, since every day Gus lived offered her another day to exploit his fortune. It was all money to her. She told Gus's children that she would agree to the DNR/DNI order for a million dollars. The children were aghast. Lacking her permission, I had to ask the court to appoint yet another lawyer to act as the court's investigator to determine if the DNR/DNI order was what Gus would have wanted. At a hearing the next morning, the lawyer reported that yes, he would have. This time, Tonya didn't contest it; she didn't even show up.

You don't enter into an end-of-life order like this lightly. Ricky and I needed to talk the whole thing over with Gus's doctors. Very early the next morning, on November 2, I drove up to Addison Gilbert Hospital. Gus's condition had deteriorated severely, and the doctors were ready to implement the court's DNR/DNI order immediately, saying it would be cruel not to. As it was, they were giving him IV fluids and some medication to keep his blood pressure up, plus a little morphine to ease his pain. They also had him on oxygen.

Gus's room was on the top floor of the hospital, with blazing sunlight stopped by pulled curtains. Stretched out, his skin a shiny yellow, Gus lay utterly still in the bed except for the slow rising and falling of his chest with each breath. His face was limp, his eyes closed, and his arms lay flat and lifeless on either side of him. If you didn't know better, you'd think he was dead already. He was seventy-six, but he looked a hundred. I leaned over him, and I said a Hebrew prayer asking God to preserve and protect Gus and to grant him peace.

We told the doctors to hold off on the DNR/DNI until Gus's children could get there. Gusty arrived a little later that afternoon. Patricia was stuck in New York. Gusty hovered worriedly over his father, sat at his bedside, and stayed through the afternoon.

Tonya never did show up.

I made sure that the hospital staff kept hold of Gus's possessions—his wedding band, Rolex watch, and some other things—to keep them out of Tonya's clutches. When the end came, they were to be given only to Ricky. An administrator nodded in agreement.

At five o'clock, we asked the doctors to follow the DNR/DNI order that we had filed with the hospital, and they agreed. They increased the morphine and stopped the blood pressure medication, and about a half hour later, with Ricky, me, and his son, Gusty, by his bed, Augustus Pryce Sr. died.

ॐ

As the widow, Tonya got control of Gus's body. So the question was, what would she do with it? Would she take it to a funeral home? Have a proper funeral? Or would she simply make off with it, as she had tried to do so many times when Gus was alive? Fortunately, she took the funeral home option. Tonya wanted the estate to kick in for a twenty-thousand-dollar casket with all the extras, but settled for the forty-five-hundred-dollar variety. Since Gus was Catholic, a fact unknown to Tonya, the kids wanted a wake. Tonya said that would be fine—for two million dollars. Appalled, the children organized a lovely service, at a private home, without their father's body. Gus had always been just a gaunt, sickly figure to me. But I learned now that he'd been decorated for bravery in World War II, and that he was a sports nut—a golfer and sailor. He had season tickets to all four Boston pro teams. And he'd been a hockey dad, taking young Gusty to the rink at all hours of the day or night.

Tonya had the proper wake at the funeral home. The first night, only her two kids came. The second night, no one showed up at all, not even Tonya. It was just Gus in his casket, all by himself.

Meanwhile, Tonya was frantically trying to get a church service together. Since she herself was Lutheran, she tried for a Lutheran church, but the minister would have nothing to do with her. Finally, the Unitarians came through. With her diploma-mill divinity degree, she would be the minister.

The service was beyond depressing. It was a huge church, but there couldn't have been more than a half-dozen people there, along with a tired pianist to bang out some hymns on a twangy piano. Tonya's two kids, Gus's longtime estate planner, and a few others were way up at the front. Ricky and I were way in the back, with a vast ocean of empty pews in between. Gusty and Patricia skipped it, and I can't blame them. The casket was up by the altar. Tonya whisked in from a side door, decked out in a flamboyant black dress and a cute little black hat, with a gothic cross dangling off a slender chain around her neck. "I've never led a service before," she breathed from the lectern. No joke. She didn't know the Lord's Prayer, and couldn't find it in the Bible. She said how "marvelous" it was to see so many people here to honor Gus. But, of course, almost nobody was.

∽

GUS'S DEATH ENDED THE DIVORCE CASE. NOW WE HAD TO FIGHT OVER the estate. By the nature of the deed, Tonya now owned the house outright. And the will also gave her $150,000 and another $120,000 in trust to pay for a master's degree she falsely told Gus she was getting at Tufts. It took a year to figure that out—because this was Tonya. Gusty wanted me to keep fighting the annulment case and to go to civil court to win some of the money back. This is when Tonya's antics started to catch up with her, for the civil case was heard in the superior court, where Judge Brennan took a dim view of her various attempts to subvert the legal process and nailed her. The only question was, how much? What were the damages?

By now, she'd hired yet another lawyer, a pleasant young man named Matt Doyle, whose office was just a few blocks from mine. So one day I called him up and asked if we could have lunch to talk the thing over. He said sure, and I went over there with some tuna sandwiches and milk. In his office, I noticed all the pictures of his kids on his desk and on the bookcase. He was divorced but obviously a devoted father. There were other pictures of him in the Peace Corps in Thailand. I told him a few things about growing up in Somerville. We got to know each other a little, and that's important. It established a basis for trust.

Then we got down to it. We agreed that Tonya would keep the house, which was worth at least a million.

"What about alimony?" Doyle asked.

"From a dead man?"

"She wanted me to ask."

"I think you know my answer to that. No."

The will promised $120,000 in trust—but it could only be used to pay expenses toward a master's degree at Tufts. But by then I'd discovered that she wasn't enrolled in any such program. "She'll never get that money," I told Doyle. "But the children want this over, so I'm authorized to say that if she forgets about that college money, they would not object to her getting that other money, the $150,000 outright."

"I'll see what I can do."

And we were done. Doyle got Tonya on the phone later that afternoon. By five o'clock, I had the answer: agreed.

It wasn't until we were in court to certify all this with the judge that I asked Tonya the question that had been troubling me. This was very close to the offer we had made at the very beginning of the process, almost two years before. Why didn't she accept it then and spare everyone all the trouble?

She batted her eyes at me and cooed, "Oh, Mr. Nissenbaum. That was then. This is now."

෨෬

It was an exhausting case, one that depended on the energy of our madam to frustrate and deceive us at every turn. It showed how far people can go to take the law, even divorce law, into their own hands.

And I have to say, our madam came out well ahead of where she'd have reached if she'd abided by the rules. To me, divorce work is an effort to impose law on lawlessness. But our madam inverted that. More exactly, she didn't even acknowledge the law's existence, or imagine that it might possibly apply to her. Me, I take only those deductions I am entitled to, and make no claims I can't substantiate. That is the world of reason and order. And usually, I succeed in pulling these antagonists inside that bright circle where right is right and fair is fair. That is what I live for, seeing justice done. I never did reel Tonya Pryce in, though. She stayed outside, never facing the consequences of her actions. In fact, she profited from them.

When the case was finally over, I assumed we'd seen the last of her, but I bumped into Officer Ferrara in the Essex Probate Court a year or so later, and he pulled me into a quiet corner to tell me he had some news about that Tonya Pryce. She was back in business. She'd started up a new establishment, one with a male-to-female transsexual as the pimp/enforcer. "Tonya and the tranny got into a screaming fight over money. It got so loud that neighbors called the police." One of the cops to respond was Ferrara. Neither of the two combatants pressed charges, although both of them were scratched and bloodied. With the police on notice, Tonya closed down the operation, and she retreated once more to her beach house, as a widow by the sea.

"I haven't heard of anything from her since. Not a thing," said Ferrara, shaking his head. Then he smiled. "But I bet I will."

Part Three

◆◇◆

THE
MONEY

CHAPTER

SIX

NOBODY EVER CRIES ABOUT THE MONEY.

They'll cry about losing the kids, about seeing the marriage dissolve, about leaving the house. Those issues will get both sides heaving and sobbing.

But the money? No.

And I've seen cases where hundreds of millions of dollars changed hands. That's a lot of money to pass out of your life—or accept into it, if you are on the receiving end. You can bet that a client's hand tightens up on the pen when he signs that check. But you never see tears.

Anger, yes. It's a shameless and grotesque intrusion into people's lives! It's a tax on being male! It shows no understanding of women! It's feminazi socialism—taking from the man according to his abilities, giving to the woman according to her needs! It's macho sexism, encouraging an all-powerful patriarchy! And on and on.

But I don't buy any of it. Frankly, I think the law makes sense: the marriage is a partnership to which both sides contributed equally regardless of their salary. And as a partnership, the proceeds from the course of the marriage should be split right down the middle. That's the principle governing the law in most states. In Massachusetts, where I practice, it's called "equitable distribution," and it means half and half. Unlike in other states, even inheritances and gifts are up for grabs.

On some level, I think people get this, which is why they don't cry. Beyond a certain sum, the money is all status anyway. I'm thinking of a CEO with two hundred million dollars in assets, who got all bent out of shape when he had to cough up half of it to his ex-wife after he exited their thirty-year marriage. I asked him what difference the money really made to him. I mean, really, what could he do on two hundred million dollars that he couldn't do on one hundred million? "I can own a bigger plane." There it is. At one hundred you have to settle for a smaller one. How tough is that?

It doesn't mean that some people won't fight over every last nickel. For them, it's war, but it's war played on an Xbox. The idea isn't to kill; it's just to win. And the money is the score. You give up less than half—victory! You get more than half—victory!

Then again, there are plenty of people in divorce court who are out for blood—or at least for revenge. They aren't content until they drive their ex-spouses into the gutter and take everything they have, or ruin them by forcing them to spend everything they have. I try to keep my clients from doing that. But I've had cases where my clients have bankrupted themselves to fend off nuts bent on destroying them. There are plenty of psychopaths who don't use the legal system. They abuse it. Their victims are the clients who need me the most.

I'm thinking of Jessie Marks, a sweet, stay-at-home mom who'd been trapped for years in a hideous marriage to an abusive stockbroker named Randy Marks. Truth be told, Jessie may have been too sweet—and credulous—for her own good. Back when they were first considering marriage, Randy had gotten so riled up during an argument that he had started to choke her before he came to his senses and let her go. When she tried to leave him, he went into the classic batterer routine. Sobbing, he got down on his knees to beg her forgiveness and promised he would never, ever do that again. She softened, gave in, married him, and bore his son. Everything was okay for a while, but then the attacks resumed. It was horrendous. He'd call her ugly names, then claw her with his fingernails, choke her, throw her to the floor, and stomp on her. She called 911 and had Randy arrested, only to recant in hopes that her husband would reform. But he never did, and Jessie finally scooped up the kid late one night and snuck out to a friend's place—and called me.

Jessie didn't want revenge. She just wanted to get out alive and be rid of Randy. She was even willing to share joint custody since, brutal as he had been to her, Randy had been a decent father to their son. But that was not enough for Randy. He wanted sole custody, claiming that Jessie was an unfit mother. To show the judge that he was an exemplary human being, he wore a suit and was unfailingly respectful to everyone in court, including Jessie. Since Jessie had never gone to seek medical treatment, had taken no pictures of her bruises, had hidden her bruises from her friends, and had never spoken of his brutality, she had little evidence of any abuse to offer in court. To assert Randy's sterling character, his lawyer called any number of character witnesses, starting with his first wife, and all of them attested to his fine behavior. I objected, claiming their testimony was beside the point because as our expert testified, batterers don't batter everyone, only a select few, and often only one. And besides, the sole question was whether he battered Jessie. But I got nowhere.

The truth is, the whole trial was beside the point. It wasn't a legal case at all, but a war of fiscal attrition. As a stockbroker, Randy made $250,000 a year; as a stay-at-home mom, Jessie made nothing. All she had was a $500,000 inheritance from her parents. And all she wanted was joint custody, child support, and a divorce. Well, Randy's lawyer dragged the whole thing out, staging legal sideshow after legal sideshow to drain her money. There was nothing I could do to hurry things along. Randy would win by losing, leaving Jessie with no money for a lawyer to fight back when he brought the case again, as he surely would. We did win, but it took forever, and she ran up a bill for $600,000 to do it. No way I was going to bankrupt her, but I can't work for free. I just asked for half and waived the rest. Sure enough, some years later, when Randy came after her again for sole custody, Jessie appeared in court without counsel, lost primary custody of her kid, and could see him only two Sundays a month.

That's tragic. To try to keep such things from happening, before we undertake any case, we do a litigation risk analysis. It's a fairly scrupulous workout to see if the client is likely to come out ahead. We tally up likely assets, estimate their value, consider the issues, project our fees, evaluate relevant law, and then weigh it all to see if the scales tip in favor of proceeding or not. But, as with Jessie's insanely vengeful husband, there can be wild cards.

Until you actually get into a case and start mucking around, it's all guesswork, and you can be way off. Motivations, secret agendas, credibility—all these are hard to predict, not to mention the difficulty of doing a reliable accounting of the value of someone's assets. You might think that I'd be on more solid ground in dealing with financial records of the money that is at stake in a case. Actually, money—cash money, or its many equivalents—is a lot harder to find than you'd think, especially if the other side is determined to hide it. Sure, if it's in a checking account, with a current balance of $47,785.87, that's easy. And if it's in an equity account, with stocks valued at $6,456,231.45 at the close of trading this afternoon, that's also easy. *At that moment.* But balances shift, markets tank, holdings suddenly and perhaps mysteriously get liquidated. And maybe there are other banks, or other investment accounts, that the other party never said anything about. Maybe the money is stashed in an account under another name, with a phony social security number, and maybe it isn't here in the United States but in a country or region that is particularly secretive about such things. Like Kuwait, the Cayman Islands, or Monaco. Good luck there.

At least that's money stored as money, with a dollar value everyone can agree on. Lots of times money is hidden away as something else. It can be anything from a stamp collection to James McNeill Whistler paintings.

But let's start with real estate. It's popular because most people never plan to cheat their spouse out of a hunk of cash. What's more, if they did buy a house for that purpose, they aren't likely to be very good at it. Deceit takes practice.

Most of the time, the house in question—that handsome, three-story Victorian on a quiet street in suburban Weston, for example—is pretty easily appraised based on "comparables." Those would be similar houses nearby that have sold recently. It gets trickier when these houses are strewn across the globe, as often happens, or if they are really weird.

A contractor turned developer, Eddie Felzer owned nine extravagant houses around the working-class suburbs just south of Boston, each one more wacked-out than the next. The crown jewel was a place in Quincy I called Eddie's Erection. It was a knockoff of the massive Italianate Hearst Castle in San Simeon, California, if you can believe that—all done in brick. (A New Yorker, he also had a miniature Gracie Mansion.) It was just a ridiculous house, and it wasn't improved much by the mausoleum-like interior and the garish, copper-roofed pool house by the kidney-shaped pool in back. An arrogant little toad, Eddie drove a Hummer around town. Eddie's bosomy wife, Darlene, liked to throw swimsuit-optional, drunkenness-mandatory pool parties there, which accelerated the decay of the marriage, since Eddie wasn't invited.

Eddie had spent $5 million building his palace, and he insisted that $5 million was what it was worth. God knows why, but Darlene wanted that house. But she wanted it valued much lower so it would count for as little as possible in the settlement. That way she would get more of everything else. It all came down to comparables, and how many other Hearst Castles were there in Quincy? Right. The next most valuable single-family home in the whole city was $2.1 million. But our appraiser came up with enough comparables elsewhere to put the Erection at $3.2 million, and even that was generous. Eddie's lawyer was outraged. But at the trial I made my point by getting Eddie up on the stand, showing him a picture of a real dump, and asking him how much he thought it was worth.

He shrugged. "Probably not too much."

"Try twenty-two million," I told him.

"For *that*?" His face all scorn.

"Yes, because it's on Nantucket, and it's sitting on thirty-five acres. Yours is in Quincy, on almost no acres. You get the difference?"

He said nothing, just clenched his jaw.

The judge leaned down to ask him, "Isn't that what they mean in real estate when they say, 'Location, location, location?' "

I had no further questions.

The thing is, chiselers chisel, and liars lie. That's what they do. It's their job. Eddie didn't push it only on his Erection. With that Gracie Mansion knockoff, he put in a $150,000 atrium and a hundred other wildly expensive features in the run-up to the divorce just to screw Darlene over. If the cash was out of his bank account and put into a new house where its value would be appreciated only by him, Darlene wouldn't get it. Clever—but not clever enough, as it turned out because the judge awarded that house to Eddie, valued at what it cost to get it built. Eddie also downplayed the profits from the string of video stores that funded his real estate empire. It was a million a year, easy, but he declared just seven hundred grand to ease off the income taxes. Plus, since the value of a business is a function of the income, it also dropped the value of his total asssets, reducing the sum total for Darlene's half. He pulled the same stunt on some of his rental property, never reporting a good portion of the rent and thereby cutting its value too. When I got Eddie's accountant up on the witness stand, I pressed him so hard on these evasions that his lawyer freaked, asked for a recess, and huddled with the accountant in a panicky conference.

When the accountant went back on the stand, he pleaded the Fifth. Suffice it to say that Darlene came out of that marriage in pretty good shape, at least financially.

ഔ

You start to think this way, and you realize that everything is money—everything you see, and many of the things you do. It's almost like the world is one huge bank, and everything in it has a dollar value. But, again, for some things the value is obvious, and for others it's a head-scratcher. As with Eddie's Erection, a house can be a pretty good head-scratcher, and all the more so if it is hidden away on another continent.

Stephano Papadimitriou tried that strategy on his ex-wife, the willowy Corinna, and it nearly worked. Born in Athens, he had met her on a beach on Crete when she was island-hopping with her family one summer. He spoke flawless English, and was soon joining them for meals. When Corinna returned to Boston, Stephano followed, and they were married six months later. But Stephano also possessed a bullying manner that only came out after the marriage. With Corinna's dad's money, he'd started a T-shirt shop in Provincetown, and then another in Key West. The better he did, the meaner he got. With Corinna, he started with sharp words, then it was slaps and shoves, and then he was beating her with his fists, leaving nasty bruises and sending her once to the emergency room. One afternoon when she was taking a shower to clear her mind after a fight, he lurched into the shower stall, grabbed her by the arm, dragged her across the living room, and threw her stark naked and dripping wet out into the street. Then he locked the door behind her, and no matter how much she cried and pounded and pleaded with him to open up, he wouldn't let her back inside.

A neighbor took her in, but Corinna was done with the bastard. Unbeknownst to Stephano, she was pregnant, and she gave birth to a son seven months later. Terrified of what he might do, she didn't dare actually start divorce proceedings against Stephano for another ten years. In all that time, Stephano never laid eyes on his son or paid a nickel to support him. By then, she was working in her family's own clothing business, and she'd pulled her life back together. Ready to start divorce proceedings, she called me. When she came to my office, she was resolute. When she mentioned Stephano's name, her whole body stiffened.

Stephano was living in Key West by now, and had knocked up a new girlfriend, so he was eager to get divorced. The issue was money. Stephano claimed he earned a measly twenty-five thousand dollars on his federal tax return, but Corinna was sure he was just crying poor. She had snooped around a bit and discovered that he was living in one of the Keys in a gorgeous stucco-sided house with a view of the water and a nice pool. And he was driving a Lamborghini. Meanwhile she was raising their son in a basement studio.

To get a fix on the volume of business he was doing at the T shops, I had my private eye Ted McCallum skulk about for a few days, drifting in and out of the stores in both Provincetown and Key West, to see what he could pick up. He reported that both were beehives of activity with brisk sales and maybe a half-dozen employees each. He couldn't be sure, but it looked to him like money from the cash sales went into a different register than slips for the credit card purchases. In Key West, McCallum followed Stephano one afternoon as he left the T-shirt shop, strolled down the street, took a left, and, at the end of the block, stepped into a high-fashion women's clothing store called Shasta. A records check with the Florida Secretary of State revealed a business certificate for the store. It had only one listed officer, a man who turned out to be Stephano's personal lawyer. That was enough for me to link the enterprise to Stephano. When McCallum went inside to look around, he saw that an online apparel store was run out of a back office. That was Stephano's too. As was the high-end shoe business whose products he offered online.

But how much was he making? We knew it was way more than twenty-five thousand, but we couldn't put a number on it. Days, then weeks, went by, at considerable expense for Corinna, and nothing else popped out for McCallum, so we requested a formal deposition. Stephano's lawyer kept telling us that Stephano wasn't there, that he was sick, that he was nursing an ailing parent. A hundred excuses why he couldn't show up. It's a strategy we run into all the time. He figured the harder he could make the easy things, the more likely we'd give up on the hard ones. Well, we don't give up so easily.

Finally, I had Stephano at the table across from me. He was powerfully built, with thick black hair and heavy cologne. He coolly evaded most of my questions until I asked him to furnish me with financial documents that would establish his annual income. It was like I'd shoved his finger into a light socket. He suddenly lit up. "Why—you think I'm lying?" he shouted, and slammed his fist down on the table. "You think I'm a liar?"

I assured him that I wasn't drawing any conclusions. I simply wanted to see the underlying financial facts, as I was entitled to do under the laws that govern divorce cases. With that, he swept his hand across the table, knocking a glass of water onto the floor. "Okay, then. Okay! You'll have your goddamn papers."

"Thank you."

Then he wagged a finger at me. "But I'm not an accountant. I never look at papers. They are not going to be laid out all nice."

"Just get them," I said.

They were available a week later. He refused to send them, or to copy them, so I had an associate, Shelly, examine them there in the back of his T-shirt store in Key West. She was given a folding chair by a small, rickety table in a small room lit by a single 25-watt bulb that dangled from the ceiling. There, she went through what proved to be three huge boxes of material, each one the size of moving boxes for clothes, not for books. The documents might have all been thrown into the air and then scooped up and pitched into boxes in a big jumble, with all the dates mixed up, along with the types of records, and the topics. And there were extras in there too, like pizza box and burger wrappings.

Shelly stuck with it for three full days, making careful descriptions of the content of the material she uncovered, and got down about six inches into the first box. Finally, she called me up, practically in tears. "It's impossible!" she told me.

I appealed to a judge to require a more normal production of documents, but he decided that Stephano had no obligation to be neat.

There are other ways to get financial information. I asked Shelly to go into Stephano's T-shirt shop there in Key West, buy a couple of T-shirts, and pay by check. When the check came back, it was stamped with the name of the bank and the account number into which the check to Stephano had been deposited. We subpoenaed those bank records. It was just as McCallum had suspected: not a penny in cash was deposited.

So what was Stephano doing with the cash? We knew he had it. McCallum had seen cashiers taking in fistfuls of dollars. Was he hiding it in a vault someplace? Buying art? Putting it in gold? It could have been any of these, or lots more. There is no shortage of valuable objects in this world—and dubious characters who are happy to take cash for them, no questions asked. But where? If we didn't know, we could do nothing for Corinna except waste her money.

Then we got lucky. An anonymous tip came in to the answering machine at my Boston office late one night after everyone had gone home. Tips can resolve divorce cases just as they can solve murders. As it happened, it wasn't a tipster, but a tipstress, a spirited young Latina to judge by her voice. Without giving her name, she said she'd worked for Stephano at the Key West store, and she spoke bluntly about her employer. "He fucked me," she said, "until he fired me." On the phone she didn't come right out and say that she wanted to slice his balls off, stick them on a skewer, roast them over an open fire, and then feed them to the nearest bloodhound, but that was the impression I got. "You want to know about the money? Check out his employees. All the guys look just like him. No joke. Just like him. Dark, olive complexion, tall. Why? Because he flies them to Athens under his name and using his passport—and they take twenty thousand dollars in cash with them. In hundreds. Stick it in their pockets. No big deal, got it? He's building a house with it on one of the islands. I don't know which. Find the house, and you find the money. Fuck him. Bye."

This was long before caller ID, or ✱69. I never figured out who the caller was, but I did verify from banking sources in Athens that it would indeed make sense for Stephano to bring in dollars for drachmas. The government offered a special pink receipt for cash that came in to the country if—and only if—it was used in domestic real estate construction. The country was that desperate for hard currency. In exchange, the foreigner escaped taxes.

Through the International Academy of Matrimonial Lawyers, I found a divorce lawyer in Athens and worked with him to take the next steps. He hired a couple of Athens-based detectives who knew their way around the banking system. They tracked payments from Stephano's account and saw that some of the money went to materials purchased on the tourist island of Mykonos. The detectives discovered there was indeed a new house on the cliffs outside the town of Little Venice, ran a title search, and discovered it was owned by a Papadimitriou. It wasn't Stephano, though, but Ernesto, a man whose birth date would have made him eighty-four. A retired shoe salesman living off the Greek government's social security benefits in a tiny apartment in Athens, all of which perfectly matched Stephano's father. The Mykonos house was the only villa of any size going up in the town. All the locals knew of the crazy Greek American who would pay anything to get the very best.

When we brought Stephano back in for a second deposition and showed him pictures of the seaside villa, he denied everything. "That's not my house," he shouted. "It's my father's. It's his name on the title. Look and you'll see."

"We did look, and we did see," I told him, and I pulled out a copy of the deed. "Ernesto Papadimitriou," I read. "But he's a retired shoe salesman on social security. How can he afford a house like this?" I pushed the photographs at him.

"It's his house," he replied heatedly. "That's all I'm telling you. I have nothing to do with it."

I asked him to produce his father so we could depose him.

"No," he replied. "I can't do that. He is in Greece, and he's too sick to fly here." He offered no proof of that, however. No doctor's certificate or hospital record.

So again I appealed to the judge. This time he gave Stephano a choice: either pay to fly me to Athens with a stenographer to depose him there or fly his dad to Key West. Stephano chose the latter. Fine. I was happy to take a little vacation in Key West. So I flew down there, hired a translator and a stenographer, and we met Ernesto in the same dreary conference room where I had deposed his son. I was waiting for him when he arrived. He seemed worn, and his clothes hung off him, but he didn't seem seriously ill. Stephano's lawyer, a younger man who favored flowery ties, directed him to a chair. An assistant supplied some fragrant tea, which was not offered to me.

I explained the procedure, that he was under oath, and that this deposition was the equivalent of court testimony. Then I got to the point.

"Do you own a villa in Greece?"

The translator, a slim lady with heavy eyebrows, put the question to him in Greek.

He nodded. "Yes, sir," he replied, via the translator.

"Where is it?"

He looked down at the tiled floor. "I'm not sure. I'm a very old man. My son could tell you."

"Is it on Mykonos?"

"Yes, that's right." He smiled, relieved to have the answer. "Mykonos." He smiled again, as if he was thinking about the island and the sea.

"Tell me, where on Mykonos is it?"

"I—" He stopped, sighed. "I'm sorry. I do not know. My son knows."

"Well, can you tell me what town it's in?"

"I'm sorry. I . . . well, I—" He stopped again and looked at me.

"Take your time."

"I am sorry to tell you I do not know," he said finally. "My son knows," he added helpfully. Ernesto's lawyer's eyes drifted up to the ceiling. Ernesto looked apologetic, but said nothing.

Finally, I showed him pictures of four villas from the village of Little Venice. "Are any of these yours?"

"Yes." Certainty in his voice.

"Which one?"

He looked at them carefully, first one then the other, and then tapped the photograph on the right, which I had labeled Exhibit B. "This one."

"This one, did you say? The one marked Exhibit B?" I repeated, to get his response on the record. A little drama wouldn't hurt either.

"Yes. That's right."

"Actually, it's Exhibit D. This is the one your son says you own."

Ernesto looked crestfallen.

It was not a good moment for Stephano. The house turned out to be worth $2.5 million, which put Corinna's share of just this one asset at $1.25 million.

Since Stephano filed his divorce in Florida, I worked the case with another lawyer down there. Once we had all the information from the depositions and detective work, we went to trial. Stephano insisted Corinna had done nothing to create the value of these assets in the decade since he'd been gone. The judge set him straight, saying that she had been doing something potentially far more valuable: raising their son. Corinna did well. Once the current value of the house in the Keys and the other businesses were added in, her share of the total holdings came to nearly four million dollars. And it could have been more, but before we could get a reliable valuation on Stephano's retail assets, Corinna said to stop.

She'd had enough to free herself from Stephano and put a nice chunk of change in her pocket. That wasn't the case for the girlfriend. By now she'd had two kids by Stephano, but that didn't make any difference. After the Corinna result, the viper tossed her out of the house—clothed—along with the kids. And then she called me too!

☙

MONEY IS NOT ALWAYS HIDDEN IN HOUSES, NOT BY ANY MEANS. IT CAN be secreted in another currency that is really hard to track or tabulate. Supermarket coupons, for instance. You laugh, but they can be a big deal. Say a supermarket prints up one hundred thousand coupons, to be redeemed in the store for a dollar discount each on a bottle of Clorox. That's like handing out one hundred thousand dollars in one dollar bills, since people are saving a dollar on their Clorox. Customers get most of the coupons, but the store owner can use the rest himself. How? By skipping the Clorox, popping two thousand coupons into the till, and taking out two thousand dollars and sticking it in his pants pocket. Do that once a week, and it can add up. When you have ten stores, it can really add up.

But wait, you ask, isn't he just taking that money from himself? Well, yes—except he's taking it right off the top, and not reporting it, thus saving himself more than 60 percent in corporate and individual taxes combined. And in a divorce scenario, he gets the benefit of running down the store's value—which, again, is a function of its income—with every dollar he peels off, so it's worth that much less for the soon-to-be ex-wife.

I run into these sorts of shenanigans all the time. Another case involved a strip joint in the Combat Zone here in Boston, where the bar served watered-down drinks to clients too stupid, too distracted, or too drunk to notice. The bartender kept an account of which stripper sold which drinks—a ledger that was separate from the official one for the IRS. And there were separate places to put the payments. Any cash payments for the watered-down drinks went into shoeboxes on the floor. All other payments went into the cash register.

I got the short course on all this from Stephanie, whose husband, known universally as Billy C., ran one of the sleazier outfits down there in the Zone. She was a bartender for him. Knowing her husband, she had taken the precaution of spiriting away the true books, just in case. And she knew where the cash that those books recorded was being concealed: in several spacious deposit boxes around town, each one stuffed with a million dollars in twenties, fifties, and hundreds. Stephanie knew the box numbers, but did not have the keys.

When Billy C. started knocking her around, she called me to say she wanted out. She laid out the bar's cash situation. I called up Billy C.'s lawyer, a man I knew to be a little heavy on the jewelry, and I said that we had an "unusual situation" here.

"And why's that?" the other lawyer asked.

A pair of divorcing tax cheats can't exactly take each other to divorce court, I told him. Because the two cosigned the fraudulent tax returns, neither could testify against the other without bringing them both down.

"That's right, we have an unusual situation," the lawyer agreed.

"And the money was all earned during the marriage, right?" I asked him.

"That's right."

"And so they should divide it up equally?"

"Yes."

"I haven't actually seen what is in those safe-deposit boxes. Have you?"

"No."

"So our clients can go down into the vaults and pull out the safe-deposit boxes and divide up the whatever is in there, right? And she can get another box to put her portion in?"

"Right you are." The man was being very agreeable.

"We don't want them filing anything in court, now do we?"

A bit of nervous laughter. "No, we don't."

"And they can go to the Dominican Republic for a quickie divorce. No muss, no fuss."

"Exactly."

I felt like a champion.

Three weeks later, I got a call from the other lawyer. His first words were: "Guess what."

Well, in my line of work, there is only one answer. "They're reconciling," I said.

"How did you know?"

"Just a hunch."

I called Stephanie right away. "Are you sure?" I asked her. Billy C. was a bad guy, and I did not trust him as far as I could throw him, which was not very far. Stephanie had indeed re-upped, but this time she had taken a precaution. She had managed to spirit away half his vault holdings, a stash she called her "fuck you money." She laughed one of those wonderful, raspy, two-pack-a-day laughs. "If he screws around on me again, I'm rich and I'm gone."

That one turned out okay.

But a similar case involving a lady dispatcher, not so much. Taxis are like strip bars. It's a cash business, with a lot of possibilities for financial sleight of hand. Priscilla handled maybe fifty cabs a shift, and she was very good at keeping them all straight and occupied. Her husband, Fernando, owned the business. Shady is as shady does. And this guy had the usual second set of books—plus a second set of bedmates. Classy guy that he was, most of them were strippers and would-be strippers, and he was not shy about buying them bling. Finally, Priscilla told him to go blow. Fernando shoved her, then slapped her around pretty good.

Priscilla decided to split, and she called me. We were six months into the case when the other lawyer gave me the "Guess what" call.

I called Priscilla up and told her straight out, "Don't." Something about Fernando scared me, and I was afraid of what he might do. She said no, no. He'd never meant to hurt her, he was devoted to her, and he promised to give up his screwing around. He loved her! And besides, she had a copy of that second set of books, if it ever came to that.

"Not if you're dead, you don't," I told her.

"You worry too much, Jerry," she told me.

I found out about it when I came back from vacation. Madeline and I had been down in St. Croix for ten days, and I was glancing over the *Herald* when I got back. I saw an obituary for the wife of the owner of one of the city's biggest taxi fleets. She'd been found dead on the front seat of her car, an apparent suicide. She had died from a single bullet wound from the gun that was found in her hand. I called up the DA's office, the police, and the funeral home, and told them what I knew about Fernando, and what I was afraid had happened—that this was no suicide. The DA canceled the funeral, which angered Fernando to no end. But I told his lawyer I didn't give a shit. The police investigated, but nothing ever came of it. When Priscilla was finally buried in a municipal cemetery, her secret went into the ground with her.

ତ୍ରତ

WHEN YOU HAVE ALL YOUR VALUABLES IN A SECRET BANK VAULT SOMEwhere, your greatest possession may not be the riches themselves but a knowledge of their exact location and access to the key. And that is true of the great money hunt that I engage in. It's all about knowing where to look, and knowing what you have when you find it.

I figured out how this worked in a divorce very early on in my career, long before I was handling the high-end customers of today, when I represented a knife grinder. I knew something about knife grinders. Back when I was growing up in Somerville, I'd always hear these men outside, yelling up to the houses, "Knife grinder! Grind your knives! Knife grinder!" Like that, once a week. And the ladies would come out of their houses and down onto the sidewalk and hand over small canvas bags that contained the knives to be sharpened. Most times, the knives weren't bought but leased. The grinder would swap a sharp knife for each dull one, charging maybe ten cents for the sharpening on top of the fee for leasing, and then be on his way.

Well, in one of my first divorce cases, I represented a knife grinder, Giovanni, known to everyone as Jojo. He handled the chefs of all the fancy restaurants, not just in Boston, but a good ways up the North Shore. It was a long route, and driving around in his panel truck, it took him from Saturday night at eleven until Sunday noon to get it all done. At each stop, he'd trade a bag of sharp knives for the bag of dull ones that the chef left hanging off the back door of the restaurant. In each bag, the chef would leave up to ten dollars per knife to cover the weekly cost, maybe forty bucks in all. Jojo reported only twenty-five thousand dollars to the IRS, but he confided to me that he actually made far more.

And his wife knew it too. He'd learned the trade from her father. She knew that he didn't keep the true numbers in the books, which were only for the IRS. The real ones were in the route book, which detailed the number and types of knives at each address and matched up the sequence of hooks for the knife bags in the back of his truck.

Knowing all this helped Jojo's wife only up to a point. If she revealed his true earnings, she might bring the IRS down on him, true, but she'd also cause a heap of trouble for herself too, since she cosigned the return. They settled amicably, and fairly, I thought. She got the house, he the business, and he kicked in some child support and alimony. But I got dinged. I couldn't represent Jojo in court, because I'd have to sign off on his financial statement, saying that I didn't know of any unreported assets or income. That I will not do. I don't lie to judges.

But it established the principle: the real numbers aren't necessarily the ones that get written down.

ᏁᏇᏁ

The days of knife grinders and strip bars are behind me. At least I assume so. The businesses I'm looking at nowadays are usually housed in gleaming skyscrapers. Any snooping is done at my desk in my Federal Street office or after hours in my office at home in Boxford, when I'm doing what amounts to forensic accounting, digging out the details of some hotshot's income and net worth from a slew of tiny-type documents like SEC filings, annual reports, and employment agreements.

I've given seminars on the topic of "Determining Reasonable Compensation for Executives of Closely Held Businesses." My talk was meant for appraisers, accountants, and other professionals in the trade, but it's a gold mine for divorce lawyers. If you're trying to get a handle on the full compensation of a CEO, it is always a little out of reach. There's always something more you don't know. The best you can do is make your best guess based on the known sources of income and tokens of value that these potentates have coming to them in the agreements and records you can find. Tally them all up and good luck. Most likely, even the executive can't tell you everything she gets or how much she's worth. Sure, she knows all the digits that make up her six- or seven-figure salary, and sure, she's got the notice about the stock options somewhere. But what about the value of the other freebies that don't come with a price tag—all the stuff you read about in the papers these days, like country club memberships, private airplanes, company cars, free parking, limo service, personal trainers, luxury box seats at sports events, drivers, membership in airline "clubrooms," lifetime health club memberships, daily shoeshines, and adoption assistance plans, just to name a few of the perks of office for these sultans. And this is to say nothing of the usual stock appreciation rights, education benefits, IRAs, 401(k)s, profit-sharing plans, golden parachutes or golden handcuffs (depending), life insurance, et cetera. I could go on. The money is sprinkled about like fairy dust, some of it ending up in plain sight, and much more of it hidden in the grass. My job is to find it, wherever it lies.

 める

USUALLY, THE SPOUSE KNOWS. IF THE HUSBAND IS A WEALTHY EX-ecutive, for example, and his wife is home raising the children, he'd probably assume she doesn't. Well, she may not have an MBA, but she's still got ears. After Val Larkin's husband, Max, started spending a lot of time in Seattle "on business," she overheard him saying on the phone to someone that a college girlfriend lived out there. When she passed that bit of news on to us, we discovered that Max Larkin had recently purchased a three-million-dollar love nest out there, a condo overlooking the bay—something we probably would not have found otherwise. There were other slips. Over drinks one evening at a Copley Plaza bar downtown, Val heard him mention to a golfing buddy something about a Goldman Sachs account. That's where he'd parked his share of the proceeds from taking his company public. And she heard him brag to his mother that he'd set up a trust fund for each of their two infant kids. For ten million each, we found out.

Max thought it was plenty to cut in Val for just 25 percent of the assets he disclosed even though they had all been accumulated during the course of the marriage. He didn't realize that she had a critical piece of leverage: she knew that he was trying to strike a deal for a new round of venture capital money for a company he'd just founded. He was dealing with a Swiss investment company, an extremely cautious, conservative firm whose partners weren't likely to be especially excited about the idea of handing one hundred million dollars of their money over to a free-swinging CEO who might lavish a good piece of it on a mistress.

And he'd somehow missed the clause in the divorce's restraining order that required all marital assets to remain in place until a court could divide them. Since Max bought the Seattle condo well after the divorce complaint, we brought a complaint against him for criminal contempt of court, claiming that move violated the temporary restraining order against such financial transactions. Then we moved in for the kill. We served him with notice for a deposition in which we wanted him to detail the nature and length of his relationship with his girlfriend. Miraculously, Max's offer to Val jumped from the original 25 percent to meet my demand: 50 percent of all his assets. Done. As Lyndon Johnson used to say, "Grab 'em by the balls, and their hearts and minds will soon follow."

For this reason, I sometimes tell my clients to try to pull together a thorough record of their spouses' affairs—business affairs, I mean, but the other kind too—if they are thinking of a divorce. Everything's material. As with Val, these records can lead us to lines of investigation we might not have uncovered. And revelations of affairs can color a judge's impressions of a spouse's character in unfavorable ways. More to the point, the fuck-arounds worry that they will.

Aurelia knew she wanted to split from her Lebanese husband, Assad. He was short, just five foot two, but domineering. He was in the aluminum siding business, and he'd dallied with over a dozen of his women customers. Aurelia was furious and disgusted and embarrassed and everything else, but she was from a very traditional background and didn't believe in divorce. So she hung in there for fifteen years until she couldn't stand it anymore. Then she called me.

Her husband's business had done very well, and he'd banked maybe two million dollars. But he was represented by Monroe Inker, who'd argue anything for money. He claimed Aurelia wasn't entitled to a penny because she had withdrawn emotionally from the marriage ten years before. Monroe was either a fanatical legal advocate or a small-town bully, depending on the day. Except, that is, for days when you couldn't figure out just what he was. I remember one of them, and it was a day we had to do a deposition for the Assad case. My son Benjamin was a newborn around then, and we used to bring him into the office with us. That day Madeline was in court, so I brought Benjamin along when Monroe deposed Aurelia. Well, of course, Benjamin delivered this big, groaning poop right in the middle of it, and Monroe craned his neck around.

"What the hell was that?" he demanded.

I explained that Ben had just relieved himself, and Monroe acted like maybe we should evacuate the building.

"Well, should I stop?" he asked, referring to the deposition.

"No, no," I told him. "Keep going with your questions. I've got a bottle right here, and I'll just pick him up and nurse him a little."

Monroe wasn't sure about that, but he continued—until I finished with the bottle and set Ben down on a plastic pad to change him.

Monroe glanced down at me, horrified. "*What are you doing?*"

"I'm changing him. Don't worry. I'll be done in a second."

"You're what? *Good God!*" He leaped out of his chair and dashed out of the room.

I finished up with Ben, wrapped up the diaper, sealed it in a plastic bag, and dropped it into the wastebasket, then waited with Aurelia for Monroe to come back. And waited. Monroe didn't return for almost twenty minutes, as if it took that long to handle a diaper.

"Well, where is it?" he asked, when he finally returned to the conference room.

"Where's what?"

"The diaper."

"Sealed in a plastic bag in the wastebasket. Why?"

"*What?*"

God forbid that Monroe should touch a wastebasket containing a bag with a diaper in it. He dashed out of the room to get a secretary to remove the wastebasket and empty it and with that he finished Aurelia's deposition.

Monroe was just as rigid about any settlement. His position on the Assad case was simple: nothing for the wife. Not a red cent. Well, when the case came to trial, I got Aurelia up on the stand to testify about what a bastard Assad was—how he'd stay out till two in the morning with one of his floozies and then, when he got home, wake Aurelia up to demand that she serve him dinner in bed. To add to the humiliation, she slept on the couch, while he had a massive king-size mahogany bed, and he stretched out under the covers with his legs apart while he ate his dinner off a silver tray.

Assad insisted he was devoted to his son, but on cross-examination I got him to admit that from kindergarten through sixth grade of his son's parochial school, he had attended just one of the annual Christmas pageants and one parent-teacher conference. Worse yet, he didn't even know the name of the school. Strangely, he never referred to his beloved son by his name, Mohammed, always calling him "the boy." I could see the judge getting irritated at that.

Finally, I got Assad to admit that he'd had sexual affairs with eleven other women, whom I named. Aurelia had provided the list—names, dates, everything. And then I asked Assad, "How long did each affair last?"

Assad reared up on the witness stand. "These weren't one-night stands," he thundered. "These were serious relationships. I don't just have sex with someone and throw her away. What kind of man do you think I am?"

The judge, who had been taking notes, suddenly stood up, threw his pen down in a fury; shouted, "Recess!" and stormed out of the courtroom.

Up on the witness stand, Assad looked dazed by this sudden turn of events. Monroe rushed up to him, grabbed him by the arm, and escorted him out to the lobby. As he went by my table, I heard Assad ask, "What happened? Did I say something wrong?" And I heard Monroe snap, "Yeah, you fucking did. The judge hates you, and you're going to get screwed."

Monroe had always insisted that Assad would pay my client nothing, not a penny, and that we were wasting Aurelia's money and my time by pursuing a trial. Now Monroe changed his tune and sheepishly agreed to the judge's recommendation that my client get half the assets, child support for Mohammed through college, a college trust fund, and five thousand dollars a month in alimony for Aurelia for life. Monroe, of course, blamed his client. Monroe Inker never failed; only his clients did.

ᘓᘔ

In theory, sex has nothing to do with the financial outcome. In most no-fault states, the court can't get into who did what. Here in Massachusetts, what's termed the "conduct of the parties" is a factor the judge will keep in mind in awarding alimony and dividing up the marital property, with good conduct winning a better deal than bad. And multiple adulteries can certainly color things, as they did for Assad, and cause a judge to come down harder on an adulterer than he would somebody else.

Such hanky-panky can get pretty expensive. Like sixty million dollars worth of expensive. My client, the silver-haired Bessie Hunter, was nearing sixty when her husband, Rick Pearlman, decided to trade her in for a younger model. This happens, but in this case Rick made the mistake of choosing a younger model by the name of Tiffany, who was head of human resources at the large privately held company Rick ran. Even this might not have been so bad except that, in her position, Tiffany was the one to hire the outside consultant who decided on Rick's bonus. This companies do not like.

To keep Bessie quiet, Rick's offer to her became significantly more generous, jumping from a third of his holdings to 50 percent. And the holdings were extensive, consisting not only of the $120-million interest in the company but of a vast array of perks like vacation homes, aircraft for flying to Florida State and Virginia Tech football games, a daily car wash and polish, tickets to NASCAR races, several golf club memberships, helicopters, and frequent-flyer miles that we would normally overlook (but that ran into the millions). The alimony went from little more than nothing to half his salary from now until his retirement. Since he'd met my demands, we said sure.

I told Bessie to clam up on the subject of Tiffany, since it was to her benefit to keep Rick in his job. This she did, for a year, but then she slipped the news to some board members, who went to town with the information and got Rick fired—for cause, in the lingo, which meant that Rick was out on the sidewalk and all sixty million dollars of his compensation package went to zip, which meant Bessie would be receiving half of zip.

Rick didn't just let it go. He appealed to arbitrators and got the decision reversed when he persuaded them that, in fact, he hadn't had an affair with Tiffany at all, only with three secretaries. And that was fine because they had no say in his salary, perks, or position. Unfortunately, it wasn't so fine for Bessie. Her ex still didn't get his job back. He was merely able to recover many of his benefits, and Bessie only got half of those, and none of his multimillion-dollar annual salary and bonuses. Had she followed my advice and kept her mouth shut, she'd be a lot better off financially speaking.

CHAPTER
SEVEN

Big earners sometimes don't understand that, over a long marriage, even if the other spouse has never worked outside the home, that person, usually the wife, has made a financial contribution to the marriage by taking care of the house and the kids. Sometimes lawyers argue otherwise, that the big earner is somehow entitled to a larger share because of what is sometimes called the "genius factor." The theory goes that Mrs. Ted Williams didn't make Ted Williams a great hitter. But as it happens, the Massachusetts Supreme Judicial Court has addressed that exact issue in deciding genius is not a relevant factor in the section of the divorce code that determines the amount of alimony and division of property. Contribution is a factor; genius is not. But sometimes it takes a little nudge to get the other side to see that.

That was the issue at the heart of the Worthington case. But there was lots more to it. More than other types of cases, money wars range all over the place, wherever the wealth is located, and the fighting is fiercest where the financial stakes are highest. And lots of times, it isn't just husband versus wife, but a much larger family affair, as the in-laws sometimes get involved too. They may have a financial stake in the outcome, and there can be some family pride involved as well. One side or the other can close ranks like the Sopranos, determined to drum the ingrate out of their family and leave him starving in the gutter, his life in tatters. The in-laws in such a scenario can be parents who act vengefully against a son-in-law or daughter-in-law they feel was never good enough for their child. Or the in-laws can be siblings, whose own internal alliances can bring a united front of indignation against a spouse who's dared to cross one of their own—even as they double-cross each other.

In the Worthington case, the in-laws were three brothers. Obviously, only one was a party to the divorce, but all three might have been, to judge by how they acted. Bound together in the family firm they owned and ran, they'd been sucking the cash out of it for years to fund their many extravagances, like their ninety-eight-foot motor yacht, *Victory III*, custom-made in Istanbul, with a four-man crew plus a gourmet chef who doubled as a masseuse.

But with the three brothers in cahoots like that, which of them had the money? And where? All the many mysteries of money came into play in this case. And even more mysteries of meaning. Why, for instance, would anyone go so nuts over a matter like this that he would pursue the case for more than eighteen years, ruining not just his own life but those of his two brothers and the several cronies he'd enlisted to advance his scheme? All three brothers had the money at one time or another, and they played a kind of three-card monte among themselves as they slid assets from one to the other depending on who needed the cash, who needed the debt, and who they wanted to cheat. Their job was to hide, and mine was to seek.

The wife was the former Emily Stovell. She was my client. The brothers were the Worthingtons, and they owned Monadnock Press, a printing firm in New Hampshire that was one of the country's largest, producing magazines, catalogs, brochures, advertising supplements, and newspaper inserts for publishers across the United States. It had four hundred employees, massive German-made rotary presses that cost ten million apiece, and railroad tracks that ran right up to the back door, for moving the colossal rolls of paper in and the printed matter out. Monadnock had been started by their spry, enterprising father, Jeffrey C. Worthington, back in the forties. He'd been one of those Yankees whose reputation for probity exists only because nobody ever thinks—or dares—to look at the facts too closely. When old man Worthington died in the late seventies, the company was passed to his three sons: Jeffrey Jr., Richard, and Thomas. Emily married the first of them, Jeffrey Jr. The father had deliberately left his two daughters out of the company, and they'd both moved to the West Coast and gotten married out there, rarely returning east.

The Worthington men had all gone to Bowdoin, as their father had, and Emily told me that just about everything in their houses had a *B* on it. Jeff was short but tough, with a marine's jutting jaw, and he had made a name for himself at Bowdoin as a 140-pound wrestler, winning something like twenty straight bouts and snapping one guy's arm. Emily had met him at a mixer the summer before her senior year; the night ended in the back of his Buick. It was her first time. "It wasn't that great," she told me later. "It was never that great with him." After Bowdoin, he'd gone straight for a business degree at Harvard, another family tradition; joined the family company; and then taken over as CEO when his father died. He'd done well, tripling revenues in fifteen years, but the profits hadn't kept up. It took Emily eighteen years to fully figure out why.

Proper New Englanders, the three brothers had all sent their kids to boarding schools, and they all owned huge houses in nice Waspy towns. Tall, imposing Richard settled up in Kennebunkport, with a big shingled place by the sea. He and his wife, Anne, were very social and, through the boating circuit, had made the acquaintance of Walter Cronkite, after which he mentioned a party of theirs in a memoir, which sent them straight to heaven. "They'll never let you forget it," Emily told me once, wearily. The slight, wispy-haired Thomas had an old sea captain's house in Duxbury. Jeff's house was by far the biggest, a vast place, all glass, on the water in Marblehead on the North Shore—complete with a deepwater dock for what the locals called "the monster," that ninety-eight-foot *Victory III*.

Jeff and Emily had married after business school. There were worrisome aspects to Jeff, no question. He had an angry streak, and he sometimes belittled her because she didn't have a business degree. But Emily loved the enthusiasm he brought to the relationship, the wild intensity. He was always whisking her off to a luxury hotel in the Swiss Alps for a long weekend of skiing, or to some five-star resort in the Caribbean for a week in the sun. But the romance started to taper off once the babies came, and the two moved into separate orbits. They had three daughters. He got into boating, which took him away for hours, days, or even weeks at a time, and his business involved a lot of travel too. She stayed home with the kids.

As the fun went out of the marriage, some bitterness set in, and it turned seriously bad when the last of the three kids went off to boarding school just as the big five-o loomed for Jeff. Of course, it loomed for Emily too, but that was the least of her problems. Now that it was mostly just the two of them in their big glass house, Jeff wasn't home nearly so much, and when he was, he always seemed to have a bottle of Maker's Mark handy. Often distant, he could be moody, and it didn't take much for him to turn furious about some stupid little thing, which made her a target if she walked into his gun sights when he was loaded. He'd get on her about her weight, her hair, or some little thing like her interest in the *Times* crossword or the color of her cell phone. Anything. He never hit her, although it wouldn't have surprised her if he had, but his words cut pretty deep.

Jeff was starting to screw around too. She could sense it. He was losing interest in sex with her. It had been years since he'd peeled off her clothes at night like he used to. Some of the neighborhood wives on the North Shore were known to be on the make. Emily never knew which ones had captured her husband, but she knew that one and then another of them had. She didn't want to know the details. The women were mostly Botoxed dimwits, and she figured that, after a few of these encounters, Jeff would get the urge out of his system, and that would be it. Instead, it seemed to get worse. Phone conversations would stop when she came in the room. He was out at odd times.

And then one Sunday morning, it was in her face. She'd planned to attend the service at the Congregational church in town. But after she settled into her pew, she suddenly felt ill and had to hurry home. She came up the long drive and pulled up by the kitchen door. As she made her way up the back stairs, she heard the side door slam, and she could see, out the big atrium window, a young woman racing barefoot across the lawn, hurrying away from the house. She was barely dressed and clutched her shoes to her chest. It was Sasha, the daughter of her best friend, Suzie Driscoll, who lived three houses down. Sasha, running nearly naked from her house. Sasha, who'd just turned twenty-four. Perhaps it was just her illness, but she rushed to the downstairs bathroom and threw up. When she went upstairs, she found her husband still in bed.

"You sick bastard," she said.

He got up and, without pulling on a robe, headed to the bathroom. "I gotta take a shower," he told her.

☙

Emily slept in the guest room after that. She scarcely spoke to Jeff. They rarely ate together, and when they did, they passed the meal mostly in silence. Still, it took a week before she could summon the courage to file for divorce. That was June of 1988.

She'd started with my competitor, Monroe Inker, and, true to form, he'd thrown around a lot of indignation, demanded a lot of documents, made grand plans, and then, when Jeff's lawyer proved resistant and the matter became complicated, lost interest in the case. That was after five years of litigation. So she'd tried another lawyer who was even less successful. Emily called him SFB, short for "shit for brains." He hung in for six years, but screwed up so badly, Emily was thinking of suing him for malpractice.

That's actually why she came to me one snowy day in December 1999. Not to take her case, but to decide if she should go ahead with the suit against SFB. As we talked, she asked me, just hypothetically, how I would proceed with her case now that the two previous lawyers had made such a hash of it. I'm not sure I would have seen her otherwise if she had asked, straight-out, if I would take her on as a client. I make it a rule—I call it Nissenbaum's Third Law—never to be the third lawyer on a case, no matter how tempting, because if a case has already gone through two lawyers, it is so thoroughly screwed up that it is nearly impossible to get it unscrewed up. And I have more enjoyable ways to waste my time.

At that point, Emily was more than eleven years into it and, incredibly, she had only just gotten divorced. Monroe hadn't even gotten the case to trial, although he agreed to have an arbitrator try the case, which might have been an okay idea. Arbitrators can be good for highly complex cases like this one, which can require the exclusive attention of one well-trained and experienced individual over a long period of time. Unfortunately, the case ended up in the hands of Clarence Dibley, who, while knowledgeable, was known to be unbearably slow and thought by some lawyers—and not just the ones on the losing side—to have a drinking problem.

If Emily's lawyers were bad, Jeff's were worse. The first one, Sam Sharpe, bled Monadnock ink. In his midforties by the time I got on the case, he'd worked for Monadnock his entire career, where he'd risen to become chief counsel. Then he became Jeff's divorce lawyer too, which created all sorts of complications since, as chief counsel, he was a witness and participant to one of the key incidents in the case. So Sharpe had to pull out and hand the divorce job over to the eminent Walter Burns—until his license to practice law was suspended for billing his clients for construction fees on his new house in the Adirondacks. But for Burns's claim that he had a brain tumor, which was surgically removed, that impaired his judgment, the Board of Bar Overseers would have probably disbarred him. By then, Sharpe had left Monadnock, so the case went to his successor, the frail, spindly Martin Bacon, who likewise did double duty, representing Monadnock and Jeff Worthington, despite the conflict of interest. Bacon remained a figure of some mystery since he hadn't yet appeared in a courtroom on the case.

Right away, I liked Emily. There was almost a foot of fresh snow on the ground the morning she arrived, and it seemed like she might have come in on skis. She had ruddy cheeks, piercing green eyes, and a crackling laugh, as if she was overjoyed by everything except the antics of her ex-husband. And she was such a bundle of energy that I figured that if only we could plug her into the power grid, she'd light up the whole East Coast. She was from a military family on her mother's side. All the men had fought for their country practically since the Revolutionary War, and a cousin was currently deployed in Iraq. Emily had gone to Smith, but never held a regular job outside of volunteer work and gardening. Now, after eleven years of her divorce case, she had developed such a feel for divorce law that it struck me that she could have prosecuted her case far better than the clowns who had preceded me.

And she had an encyclopedic recall for the documents in the case. By 2003 she was more than fifteen years into it, and the documents, if stacked up, would have reached halfway toward the moon. If anything had been printed on paper, she had it. Spreadsheets, memoranda, annual reports—God knows what. She had arranged them all in her basement, lining them up chronologically and then cross-indexing by topic. It was like a mini Library of Congress down there. The basement had a cluster of rooms, and every wall was lined with documents. At one point, I needed a certain figure that was in one of the documents, but I couldn't for the life of me remember which. Emily was visiting one of her kids in Colorado, so I didn't think she could help, but I was desperate and called her on her cell and explained what I was looking for. She said, quick as anything, "Yeah, we got that."

"Where?"

"It's in the basement. I'll have Gina get it for you." Gina was her house sitter. Gina was not much smarter than a dachshund.

"Gina?"

"Jerry, I know where it is. I'll tell her. Don't worry."

About an hour later, an e-mail came back with an attachment: just the information I was looking for. Somehow Emily had remembered which room in her basement stored the document, the shelf, the form's location on the shelf, the title of the document, and the page.

And I thought *I* was good.

As Emily laid the case out to me, the issue was one of simple theft— that and a cover-up to hide it. She contended that the three Worthington brothers had been skimming off all the company cash they could get their hands on—depleting the company income, reducing the money available for capital investment, and thereby cutting the book value of the company, since that value, as we have seen, was a function of income. All of these financial maneuvers had greatly lessened her share of her largest marital asset. "And we're not talking nickels and dimes, Mr. Nissenbaum."

"Jerry," I corrected her.

"Jerry." She smiled. "We're talking millions of dollars. Literally millions. Maybe ten."

"What makes you think so?" I asked. "We're going to need hard evidence. You have any?"

"Jerry, I know they are doing this."

"But, Emily, we need proof."

"Well, they live a lot better than they should be able to. We certainly know that. Not on their incomes."

"What do they declare on their tax returns?" I hadn't had a chance to go through the documents.

"Try $230,000."

"That's all?"

"And Jeff has his boat, a huge house, a country house, the use of private planes, three private school tuitions between prep school and college, and I could go on. None of that's cheap."

"But that doesn't mean that he's been stealing from the company to get it."

"Well, I think it does."

And that was it in a nutshell. To Emily, finding the money was like finding the girlfriend. She knew the girlfriend was there. To her, nothing could be more obvious. But the trick was proving it to others. And the thing was, girlfriends are a lot easier to find than money, especially if all the top executives of the company are bent on concealing it, particularly if they can get their underlings—the independent accountants, the independent in-house counsel, the senior staff—go along. Before she came to me, she had lost the first trial; Arbitrator Dibley awarded her almost nothing of what she thought she was due. What's more, since Monadnock was privately held, it had no obligation to the SEC to file any public financial statements about its income, expenses, cash flow, executive compensation, or any of the other things that you can get instantly from a company like IBM. Yes, divorce court requires a respondent to cough up the relevant financial information, but it is easy to cheat, since there are so many ways to hide the truth, or to fake it entirely. And as I soon learned, Monadnock Press was not exactly transparent. It was like one of those huge, granite mountains up there in New Hampshire, with no handholds for climbing, and no holes where you can see inside.

And then there was Jeffrey Worthington Jr. That guy put the stone in stonewall. He was a liar pure and simple. Yes meant no; and no, yes. Or at least, that's what I thought at first. Until I realized his answers bore no relationship to the truth whatsoever. Yes could mean anything, and no likewise. Which meant that, too much of the time, we had absolutely nothing to go on. Nothing hard and fast that everybody could point to and say, "That, ladies and gentlemen, is a fact." We were grabbing smoke.

ᘓᘔ

WHEN EMILY ARRIVED IN MY OFFICE THAT FIRST MORNING, SHE'D brought with her a full carton of documents. It had stayed at her feet as we talked. But eventually she said that she'd love it if I would take a look at "some stuff." Before I could help her, she hoisted the box up, and then set it down on the conference table with a thud.

"I got all this from Jeff's place," she said, setting her hand down on the box.

"He gave it to you?" I asked, incredulous. That didn't sound like Jeff.

"Not exactly."

I just looked at her.

She told me the story, although it might have been better if I didn't hear it. Annoyed at being stonewalled, she'd driven up to Meredith, New Hampshire. The company printing plant was up there, as well as a place she and Jeff had rented in the woods. He moved up there full-time when the divorce started. She figured that if he was up there, so close to the business, he'd probably have a lot of the company documents in the house too—balance sheets, financial memoranda, transaction records. All the things that her dim-witted lawyers had not been able to obtain. So one morning when he was in Boston—

"Don't tell me you broke in," I interrupted.

"I didn't!" She paused a moment. "I didn't have to. The back door was unlocked."

This was off in the woods, so no one was around. She'd pushed the door open, stepped inside—and then an alarm had gone off! A terrible, high-pitched screech. If I'd been in that situation, which I wouldn't have been, I'd have bailed. But Emily is fearless, and she kept right on and stepped into the living room, with the alarm screaming in her ears.

Then the phone rang.

She figured it had to be—hoped it was—the alarm company, and picked up. Even though she cupped a hand over her other ear, she couldn't hear anything over the din. So she just shouted, "This is Mrs. Worthington. Sorry, I accidentally set the alarm off here on Franklin Road. And I can't remember the code."

It was indeed the alarm company, lucky for her. To verify that it was Mrs. Worthington, the attendant needed to ask her a security question.

"What's Mr. Worthington's mother's first name?"

That was easy. "Virginia." She was the only Worthington Emily liked.

"Thank you," said the attendant. He shut the alarm off.

She was in, and since her name was on the lease, she was entitled to be there. Otherwise we were looking at a B and E.

Jeff is not the neat and organized person that Emily is. Rather than tuck documents away where it would have been a crime for Emily to look at them, he spread them out over virtually every surface for all to see. She plucked out a carton's worth of the most interesting documents, hauled them to a copy shop in Meredith, and then returned the originals to the desktops where she'd found them.

Before she left, she took a moment to poke around the house. She noticed some dresses in the bedroom closet, jewelry on the bureau, and racy underclothes in the dresser drawer. Clearly, the girlfriend Jeff claimed he didn't have had moved in. Other women might have ripped the clothes to shreds and tossed the jewelry in the toilet. But Emily simply left by the door she'd come in. She had other ways to take her revenge.

We spent a couple of hours going through the box. I'm painstaking, since I never know what piece of information might blow the case wide open. Emily was going through them with me, and she suddenly sprang up, holding a document in her hand.

"The lying little bastard!" she exclaimed.

She set the document on the table and flipped it open to a page for me to look over. She stabbed it with her index finger. "Look at this."

I read the page. "The Victory III Trust, and a lease from it to Emily and Jeff for the rental."

"The lying little bastard. That's his goddamn trust—and his goddamn house! And look at the name of the trustee."

"Martin Bacon."

"He's Monadnock's house lawyer! That's conflict of interest, isn't it? Gotta be."

"Could be."

"Is, Jerry. Is. That's the thing. Nothing is straight. Jeff rents from himself through this secret trust, so he can hide the income *and* the asset from me. And he has Monadnock pay the rent as a business expense. And he has his lawyer, who is also Monadnock's lawyer, cover for him. And this is just to hide, what, a property worth two hundred thousand? That's nothing! But that's what we're dealing with here. Nothing is what it looks like, and everybody at Monadnock is covering for everybody else. If you don't understand that, you don't understand anything."

It had been a long time since I'd been lectured by a client. And other times, when it happened, the client was usually 180 degrees off. Not this time. Not with Emily. She was right on. I could tell that even then.

"Got it," I said.

"Do you?"

"Yes, Emily, I do."

"Good." She smiled, looked at me, her green eyes gleaming. "You're hired."

 co

IN DIVORCE CASES, THE MONEY ISSUES ALWAYS COME IN TWO PARTS. There are the assets, and there is the income. Most of the time, aside from your ability to use your income to buy those assets, these are separate and independent matters. You own a house in the south of France

and another in Nassau—that doesn't affect your $425,000-a-year in-
come as a senior VP at Bose Corp. If you get a raise, those houses aren't
worth any more, or any less. But that's not true when you own the company you're drawing the income from. A company is valued as a multiple of earnings, after expenses like salaries and bonuses are taken out.
If the net earnings are $2 million, and the multiple is five, the company
is worth $10 million. Easy. That multiple is debatable, but the relation-
ship between value and bottom-line profits isn't. So the more income
that Mr. Owner sucks out of Owner Enterprises, Inc., the lower the
profits—and the lower the value of the company. This, of course, sticks
it to Mrs. Owner, who, in a divorce case, is due half that value. But at
least she has a shot at making it up on the income side, for she may well
be entitled to a good chunk of Mr. Owner's inflated income as well. For
her, the doomsday scenario is when Mr. Owner is secretly drawing off
money to boost his income, without acknowledging it in financial statements to the IRS or to her. Then Mrs. Owner gets whacked on both
sides—receiving a smaller award of child support and alimony, because
they are pegged to the artificially lowered income of her ex-husband,
and a lower payout for the devalued assets too.

This was the situation that Emily thought she faced. She was convinced that somehow her husband and his brother Richard were surrep-
titiously tapping into the income stream at Monadnock, only she didn't
know where. For her, the financial implications were extreme, and they
explained why she'd already held out for more than a decade, and would
hang in for seven years more. Jeff claimed that Monadnock Press's revenues were such that the company was worth about $10 million (split
between Jeff and Richard, since by then Thomas had resigned from the
company). Since she expected half of Jeff's half, that meant she should
receive $2.5 million. Not chump change, but just eyeballing the scope
and scale of the operations, Emily was convinced that the true value of
the company was at least five times greater, or $50 million. That would
push her share up to $12.5 million.

After Emily laid out for me the Worthington matter, and I started to dig into the documents, I began to see a dark haze of obfuscation over all areas of the case. But as I learned more, I came to realize that the darkness gathered to a nearly jet black over two areas of conflict. And in time it became clear that the case would turn on how much light we could shed on each of them.

The first one was a specific incident, one that occurred on a single afternoon. It was on Sunday, June 19, 1988, about a week after Emily discovered her husband's affair with Sasha and exactly ten days before she formally served Jeff with divorce papers on June 29. It was definitely that Sunday, according to Monadnock records, and buttressed by testimony by Jeff and Richard, their outside accountant, and their chief house counsel, Sam Sharpe, who would soon be doubling as Jeff's divorce lawyer. And it was a pivotal meeting of the brothers, in which they discussed a restructuring of the printing company. The gathering was at Sharpe's place. Indeed, it was the event that caught him in a conflict between being counsel for Monadnock and for Jeff simultaneously, eventually forcing him out of the divorce case. Otherwise, he'd have to question himself on the witness stand.

In their testimony, the Worthingtons, Sharpe, the Monadnock independent accountant all described the event as a bit of fun for the boys, with a little business thrown in. Sam's wife, a flight attendant, was off in the Far East for the long weekend. So he'd invited the Worthingtons and that accountant over for a cookout during an afternoon Sox game, before they did some paperwork designed to shore up the company's precarious finances.

The timing here is key. Once Jeff was served on June 29, 1988, with divorce papers, he would be subject to a TRO, a temporary restraining order that forbade him to conduct any transactions that might affect the value of the marital estate. Given the fact that Emily was sleeping in the guest room and could barely speak to him without hissing, Jeff had reason to think that she was headed to divorce court. And he would also have reason to make moves to lessen the financial impact. That Sunday was Father's Day. Because of the effect of those transactions on Emily, I call it the Father's Day Massacre.

The brothers insisted that they had to make a move because Monadnock had hit a credit crisis. Strained by rising expenses and pressured by increasingly anxious bankers, Monadnock needed to raise heavy capital quickly, or it risked going under. Jeff said he'd taken the extreme step of exploring the bankruptcy option the previous summer, although he had obviously never pursued it. The First National Bank of Boston had extended the company a $10 million line of credit but was threatening to pull the plug if the Worthingtons didn't put in more cash to shore up the company's debt-to-equity ratio—a key indicator of financial health. The bank wanted the two brothers to put up $750,000, which they could take back in Monadnock stock. To cut the company's costs, the brothers also imposed a 10 percent pay cut on all Monadnock employees, including their own elderly mother, Virginia, who drew a salary in the marketing department.

To come up with his share of the $750,000, Jeff said he had to scramble. He was already overextended. His first thought was to take out a second mortgage on the big glass house he owned with Emily. It already carried a $400,000 mortgage, but that was nothing compared to the equity. Even though he didn't show much income on his tax return, he thought he had enough assets to get another $250,000 out of the house. But he'd need Emily's signature. During that spring of 1988, when he and Emily were having a rare relaxed moment on the deck of the ninety-eight-footer that was docked at the house, Jeff made Emily a gin and tonic, a stiff one, and then poured her another. Then, in a soft voice, Jeff brought up the question of the second mortgage, and tried to sweet-talk her into cosigning the relevant documents. He had the papers right there, and a pen.

No matter how much gin was in her, she wasn't going to agree to that. No way. She didn't want to be on the hook for a $650,000 mortgage on the house, not while he dumped all the cash into the floating money pit they were sitting on.

"Go mortgage your boat," she told him angrily.

Now he started shouting at her. "You don't know what it's like to run a company! You don't know anything about business!" He leaped up, and the way he leaned in on her, she was afraid he might hit her. She tossed her drink overboard and ran back inside the house. That night, she slept in the guest room with the door locked. It wasn't long afterward that she spotted Sasha dashing across the lawn.

ဖ၀

THE THIRD WORTHINGTON BROTHER, A SCRAWNY LITTLE WEASEL named Thomas, had also been involved in the company, and his tale was instructive. In sagas of this kind, the part stands for the whole. If something is rotten here, something is likely to be rotten most everywhere else. Thomas had been Monadnock's treasurer, third in command after his older brothers, until, in 1987, a year before the divorce, the other two found that his chiseling had exceeded even their own. Somehow he'd used Monadnock assets to buy himself a private plane, a helicopter, a restaurant, and a farm in Kentucky. How he did all that on the sly I can't imagine. *A helicopter?*

Thomas was gay, so he moved in very different circles from the other two brothers, and it is remotely possible that they didn't know too much about his activities. When pressed by the creditors, Thomas insisted that he'd just "borrowed" the money for these purchases from Monadnock and that he was planning to pay the company back. Someday. By now, his first loans, however, were overdue by over a decade, and he'd never paid a penny in interest.

In other families, blood may be thicker than water, but here money was thicker than blood, and his brothers were seriously pissed. They threatened to file criminal charges against Thomas unless he walked the plank, giving them his share of the company and resigning from his seat on the board. That was it for Thomas at Monadnock.

Then Jeff and Richard went after their mother, the elderly, infirm Virginia Worthington, who passed her days painting landscapes and serving on cultural boards. The matriarch of the family, she was still connected to the firm her husband had started, just enough to draw that salary, and benefits, through the marketing department. She also drew extra money from some property she owned beside Monadnock's printing presses, where she rented out some storage space. Virginia's building had been heavily damaged by a fire that had started on Monadnock property. Playing the devoted sons, Jeff and Richard offered to handle the reconstruction. But, true to form, they wildly inflated the damages for insurance purposes, understated the insurance money they did collect, fixed up the building on the cheap, and pocketed the extra. They were also seriously behind on the rent they owed her.

When it came to money, Virginia was like Emily. She may have been untutored, but she wasn't dumb. When she figured out what her sons had done, she confronted them and demanded full payment. As with Emily, they claimed not to know what she was talking about. So she took them to court, won all the money she claimed, and then received treble damages when the judge found her sons had defrauded her. I'm sure that made for some interesting conversations around the Worthington family dinner table at Christmas.

With Thomas gone, Jeff and Richard were left in sole charge of Monadnock Press just when they found out from the banks they needed to come up with that $750,000 to sweeten their balance sheet. In depositions and at trial, Richard insisted that he had gone ahead and taken out a half-million mortgage on his house. (Unlike Emily, Richard's wife, Anne, was apparently okay with taking on such a debt.) That left $250,000 for Jeff to secure. Jeff had turned to a small bank that he had frequently done business with, the New Hampshire Bank and Trust Company of Meredith, better known as Meredith Bank. It was the bank for an unlikely nautical corporation that the two brothers had created, N.H. Bay Sailing. Meredith Bank offered Jeff an unsecured bank loan for the $250,000. Perfect. For some reason, though, Meredith Bank reconsidered and insisted on collateral after all. Jeff offered up the ninety-eight-footer, which he'd built for more than $3 million, but Meredith Bank wouldn't take it. With Jeff tapped out, Richard agreed to cover his brother's quarter million by mortgaging a condo he owned in Miami. That's where the deal stood: Richard would come in for the full $750,000 and take back equity in return—exactly 2,117 shares of treasury stock in Monadnock Press.

Whatever the explanation for such a maneuver, it caused Emily's stake in the company to drop from half of Richard's half share to half of a lot less, some 19 percent of the company. If the company was worth—as Emily had always assumed—a healthy $50 million, her share had dropped from $12.5 million to $4.75 million. If the company was actually worth the pittance Jeff claimed, half his 19 percent would be worth peanuts, less than $1 million. That's why I call this the Father's Day Massacre. Because Emily got creamed.

ℰℐ

THEN THERE WAS THE SKIMMING, WHICH EMILY ALWAYS CONTENDED was a regular feature of Jeff's and Richard's lives. With a company like Monadnock Press, you probably think of its value in terms of all the publications that rolled off those four huge $10 million presses to be hauled off from the loading dock by freight train. But a printing plant doesn't just produce product. It also produces waste, surprisingly valuable waste, that, when collected and sold, can seriously fatten its bottom line. "Scrap" they call it. Mostly it's the trim left behind when the paper is cut down to size, and it can all be reused, making it worth good money. There are also recovered inks, the reusable cores that the paper is spooled on, and plenty of other things. You don't just put all this stuff out in recycling bins. Monadnock had a deal to sell the Maine Paper

Company all this extra stuff. Jeff acknowledged it during discovery in the run-up to the first trial, claiming Maine Paper had paid $79,000 in 1989 for everything that Monadnock sent down.

This didn't sit right with Emily. She knew the total had to be higher, and probably much higher given the volume involved. This was when Monroe was still on the case, and he sent down a stiff letter demanding a full accounting, but the accountants at Maine Paper just said sorry, this was all they had. When SFB made the same request of Monadnock, he asked to see all the corporate checking accounts so he could track any other money coming in from Maine Paper.

Two were of particular interest, and both of them were held at Meredith Bank, the bank that Jeff had turned to in his effort to get a $250,000 loan. Neither account was in Jeff's name; both were in his brother Richard's. One of them was listed as "Richard Worthington, Monadnock Press Incorporated, New Hampshire." Another had it slightly different: "Monadnock Press Incorporated, Richard Worthington." Even though Richard was not a party to the divorce action, he had retained a lawyer, and the lawyer immediately jumped in and got a protective order on the first account. That was our man Sam Sharpe, who had been Jeff's divorce lawyer until professional ethics forced him to withdraw. But he stayed on as Monadnock's corporate counsel. Now he jumped back into the fray as the personal lawyer of another Worthington, Richard.

Sharpe acknowledged that the first account was active, but he asserted it was personal and of no concern to the court. In his reading, it was Richard Worthington *in care of* Monadnock. The second one, he said, was to Monadnock, *to the attention of* Richard Worthington. SFB was free to look into that one, but it proved to be little used and of no interest.

Arbitrator Dibley agreed that the first one was indeed a personal account, and therefore had no bearing on the matter of Jeff's finances. But Emily did not give up. That account—which became known as the "dash-nine" account because it ended in -9—remained a focus of her attention. What she didn't learn until I got into the case was that she, SFB, and Dibley were all looking at the wrong end of the account number in trying to determine its relevance. At Meredith Bank, the two numbers at the *beginning* of an account number indicated whether they were personal or corporate. In this case they were 01, digits that to anyone at Meredith Bank might as well have been lit up in neon—for any account number that began 01 was not personal. It was corporate. It meant the Worthingtons were lying.

∞

I don't know if I'm good, but I am occasionally lucky. Because a week after I signed on to the case, Emily called up all excited to tell me that she had just received by UPS a box of documents from the FDIC regarding the dash-nine account at Meredith Bank. By now, a former VP from Meredith Bank had tipped us off to the fact that this was a corporate account, not a personal one, and that had enormous implications for her divorce settlement, since it was the company she was shooting to get a percentage of.

"Were you expecting it?" I asked.

"Not for a while." She gave me one of those great laughs of hers. "I mean, Jerry, I put in a Freedom of Information Act request for this back in—when the hell was it?—1994! That was five years ago! Can you believe that?"

It turned out that Meredith Bank had gone bankrupt, so its records were seized by the FDIC, which froze them because the president of the bank, Ernest Pierce, was being prosecuted for fraud. The first trial ended in a hung jury, but the feds bagged him on the second, which Pierce could have appealed, dragging the case out all the longer, but he let the clock on any appeal expire and went to prison. That was the year before I came on the case. When the Pierce trial was finally over, the FDIC started tidying up its Meredith Bank files, and somebody remembered that there was a woman from Marblehead who wanted stuff pertaining to a Monadnock Press account that started 01 and ended -9.

"You busy?" Emily asked.

"Not too busy to look over that stuff."

Emily was at my office within the hour. She sliced open the box, dumped the material out on the conference table, and started laughing with glee to have so much information under her control. Information that might at last reveal the nature of the money that flowed through the dash-nine account. It wasn't five minutes before we were hollering. Hollering! For damned if the bulk of the checks weren't from . . . the Maine Paper Company. Yes, Maine Paper. It was sending Richard Worthington payments for Monadnock scrap that he deposited into a corporate account that he insisted was personal. It was going to be pretty hard for them to explain why. It was not as if the scrap was ever Richard's personal property. What's more, once we dug through it all, and stacked up every last Maine Paper check, we could see there was a ton of money here, way more than the $79,000 a year that Jeff had claimed in sworn testimony.

I pulled out my trusty little calculator, went through all the checks, tallied up the weeks they represented, worked it out to an annual basis, and discovered the year's total came out to more than a million dollars—$1,129,480 to be exact. That's when we started hollering all over again, and not just because it caught Emily's ex-husband and former brother-in-law in a bald-faced lie. It was because it was a very big number, and if it was at all typical for the last five years, it was going to make the former Mrs. Jeffrey Worthington a stunningly wealthy woman. Right then, I couldn't think of any client that I would rather make wealthy.

Under the law governing domestic relations, there is a provision called rule 60(b), which allows a party to a divorce case to file for a new trial if there has been fraud or newly discovered evidence. In this case, we had both, and I told Emily that I was going to ask for a new trial. She grabbed me and kissed me on the cheek.

❧

I WAS IN COURT BEFORE JUDGE MARGERY O'DONNELL WITHIN A FEW weeks, and Walter Burns—his license restored—was there to argue the other side. Most judges spend hours in the chambers reading up on the relevant documents before they emerge onto the bench to preside over the trial. Judge O'Donnell does everything on the fly. She's always hurrying along, with various clerks fluttering after her, her robes swirling around behind her. If it weren't for the rapid click of her heels on the marble floor, you might think she'd left the ground altogether, swooping down the hallway like some massive black crow. As she goes, her head is always buried in some documents she's keen to peruse before she bursts into her courtroom.

Once she was settled on the bench, she asked Burns and me to step forward.

"Mr. Burns," Judge O'Donnell said, peering at him over her spectacles, "have you read Mr. Nissenbaum's pleading?"

"Yes I have, Your Honor."

"Have you looked at the checks attached to the motion?" I'd included copies of the checks from Maine Paper that had been deposited to the dash-nine account.

"Yes, I have, Your Honor," Burns repeated

"Well then, can you give me any reason why I shouldn't vacate the divorce judgment? Can you think of any argument that this is not newly discovered evidence? Why I should not send this matter back to the arbitrator?"

Burns could usually come up with something in such a circumstance. But he could do nothing but agree.

"Fine," said O'Donnell. "So entered."

So, eleven years into the case, armed with the new information about the dash-nine account, we'd start all over, bulldozing away virtually everything that my predecessors had done on the case. It was as if they had never existed, all their work for naught. It was my case now.

∽◦∽

WHEN YOU UNDERTAKE A NEW TRIAL LIKE THIS, THE FIRST THING YOU do is go through discovery again, as if you have never gone through it before. The other side is legally obliged to give you the documents you ask for even when doing so is like handing over a .357 Magnum and pinning a bull's-eye on their heart. When they have suicidal documents like that, ones that will kill them on the spot, they have several options, and I have seen all of them. They can delay, claiming they can't find them because they've lost them, or they have been destroyed, or they already gave you the originals, and if you can't find them that's your tough luck. They can give a smidgen of the "good stuff," enough that you'll think you have all of it, but not enough that it will kill them, and you won't press them for the rest. Or they can completely overwhelm you with material, delivered by front-end loader and dropped on your head, with the good bits sprinkled in like one-carat diamonds in sand. Or they can choose that last course without including any good bits whatsoever.

Jeff considered his various options and took that last one: the whole-lot-of-nothing approach. This provoked two full years of increasingly furious demands from me to fork over what we were asking for and had a right to see, extensive appeals to the arbitrator listing everything we wanted and comparing it to what we'd received, and pleading with Dibley to enforce the law and force Jeff to comply. We'd asked him for documents pertaining to the dash-nine account and to the Father's Day Massacre. We were very precise, asking for invoices and memoranda and much more, pertaining to a few key periods, along with a variety of supporting documents. Finally, they relented. We would have our documents.

Well, what came back was delivered by moving van. Literally. A huge truck roared up the driveway in Marblehead, then backed in toward a rear door of Emily's big glass house. The house has one huge open space on the first floor above ground level, with a warren of smaller rooms above and below, and Emily had cleared one of the biggest ones downstairs to receive all the documents. The War Room, she called it. She had set it up like a factory in reverse, a place to take in all the documents, sort them, process them, scan them, and then store them. Well, the movers delivered box after box after box, so many that, when they were done, the room was practically all boxes. But Emily merely rolled up her sleeves, with this eager look in her eye. She, along with my then-paralegal, Wendy, and a forensic bookkeeper, Margie, spent weeks and weeks unboxing everything, picking through the documents, cataloging each one. arranging them chronologically by category, and storing them in the basement, where she had installed a dehumidifier of archival quality. Each one of them went through every page as it was scanned in.

And they found not one thing of value. Not one! Not a single figure, date, or incident that would in any way call into question the line of argument the other side was proposing, one that we had determined had to be 100 percent, pure grade, stinking bullshit.

I fired off another motion to Arbitrator Dibley, laying out in detail how Jeff had been so absurdly unresponsive. Dibley ordered him to produce what we were after. So a few more weeks went by, and another moving van pulled up to the house and made a delivery that was suspiciously similar in size to the previous one. Once again, Emily, Wendy, and Margie went through it all. Once again, it took months. And . . . it was exactly the same stuff, just organized differently. I could probably have filed a complaint for contempt against Jeff for rope-a-doping us.

But there is always another way, and now I realized what it was—to try to get this information from Monadnock's independent accountant, the high-strung Burt Childreth. Surely he'd been given copies of at least some of these documents by the Worthingtons, but accountants aren't like lawyers or targets of a divorce action. They don't shred. They retain. I bet he had kept the good stuff.

Well, when I made my request at the next hearing, it was as if I had jabbed a fork into Burns's eye. In return, he did everything but bite me to keep me from persuading Dibley that this was a necessary and legitimate approach.

Dibley sided with me. "I can't see why this isn't a good resolution. Can you, Mr. Burns? This way, we won't have to trouble you or your client any further."

Burns's Adam's apple was working overtime again. "But, Your Honor—"

"I don't think we need to discuss this matter any further, Mr. Burns."

"No, Arbitrator Dibley."

"So ordered."

Every bit as retentive as I had expected, Childreth refused to let any documents leave his office. So we hired a scanning company to pay a house call. Once again, I dispatched our little detective squad: Emily, Wendy, and Margie. And they set up their little disassembly line there, with each person taking apart each document and giving each sheet a once-over before it was finally passed to the scanner.

There were at least 250,000 pages altogether, many of them black with text, and all of them requiring clear-minded, close attention. With something like this, just a few words or numbers—a name, an amount, a date—can make all the difference.

Sure enough, out of those 250,000 pages, Emily spotted one that contained information that applied nitroglycerin to the elaborately con-cocted fabrication that Worthington had created. She told me afterward that it was all she could do to keep from shrieking there at Childreth's conference table, where all the documents were arrayed, when the key evidence appeared in her hands. Once everything was scanned, and she could hone in, she found four documents more, but the first one was enough for her to rush outside and call me on her cell phone.

"I've found it, Jerry!" Emily told me, breathlessly.

"Found what?" I asked.

"A letter. From the bankruptcy lawyer, Reginald Wilkins, to Childreth."

I remembered the connection. Jeff, Richard, Sharpe, Monadnock's CFO, and Childreth all testified they'd gone to see Wilkins in Nashua, New Hampshire, more than a year before the Father's Day meeting. Of course, SFB didn't think to ask for any records to establish that date and just took Jeff at his word, which nobody should ever do in a case, especially when it suddenly comes out during the other side's direct testimony on the witness stand.

Emily continued, "But remember how that visit was supposed to be back in 1987?"

"Yes."

"It wasn't. It was in 1988. July 16, 1988. That's when Wilkins sent a cover-his-ass memo to Childreth, Jeff, and the others who were there, to confirm what he said at the meeting. And that meeting had occurred just a few days before the memo, on July 12, 1988. July 12, Jerry. That's like a month after the Massacre."

"And well after the temporary restraining order," I chimed in.

"So he's screwed, right?"

"If it is the way you say it is, my legal opinion is that he is screwed, yes."

To get everything straight, I had Emily read the full document to me over the phone, and I was staggered by how incriminating it was. It was the proverbial little birdie, the one that speaks nothing but the truth. After all the lies in the case, the sound was refreshing. As Emily read, I could tell that the memo was even more damaging than she'd said. She was all excited about the July 12 date, which was plenty incriminating. But as she was reading along, she hit a reference to a "Form

UCC-1 Financing Statement" to protect Richard. Since it meant nothing to her, she hurried right by it. But I asked her to hold on a second, to read that part again even slower.

"Sure, why?" she asked.

"Just do, please."

When she was done, I said, "Well, holy shit. There it is."

"What?" she demanded.

"That just blows them out of the water. They are dead. All of them, the whole conniving Monadnock team—both Worthingtons, Childreth, Sharpe, the whole lot. Dead. And you are going to be a very rich lady."

CHAPTER
EIGHT

THERE WASN'T TIME TO DISCUSS IT RIGHT THEN, AND I WASN'T comfortable speaking of legal strategy on a phone that might be monitored. So Emily came in that evening, after a long day of scrutinizing and scanning documents. She had every reason to be exhausted, but I had scarcely seen her so energized, as if she'd just had her third cup of espresso. All the documents had been scanned for delivery to her office computer, but she'd sent the critical one on for me to look over. I'd printed it out and had it on my desk when she arrived.

"So what's the deal?" she asked.

"Whatever they say happened on Father's Day, it didn't."

She picked up my copy of the letter. "How do you get that from this?"

"It's all about that form, the UCC-1. The UCC stands for the Uniform Commerce Code, which oversees business lending. It proves that there was never any loan. Period. Never."

Emily looked at me blankly. "What form?"

"The UCC-1. It's like a mortgage the bank records when you use real estate to secure a loan, except that a UCC-1 is used to secure business assets. So if Monadnock was taking out a $750,000 loan from Richard, it would issue a UCC-1 that specifies $750,000 worth of collateral—the printing presses, the inventory, the desks. All of it is pledged to secure the loan. Once Monadnock paid off the loan, Richard would cancel out the Form 1, mark it paid, and return it to Monadnock. Bang. Right then."

"Okay," Emily said slowly, not quite following.

"Emily, listen. If Monadnock truly had paid Richard $750,000 on June 19, 1988, by trading that debt for those shares of stock, the company can't still owe him the money on July 12, 1988, now, can it? That debt is all done. Over. Finished. There is no need to pay it off again. Right? So no UCC-1 could properly be issued."

Emily just watched me, obviously unsure of what to say.

I kept on. "Think about it. In the first trial, Jeff and Richard claimed, and have claimed ever since, that that $750,000 had *already* been paid off when it was converted from a loan into equity—those 2,117 shares worth of Monadnock stock—during that Father's Day meeting on June 19, almost exactly a month before. So why, on July 16, would the bankruptcy lawyer be writing anything about a UCC-1?"

"Because that Father's Day meeting never happened?" she said hesitantly.

"Exactly! Because it never happened. That's the only possible explanation. It never happened. If Wilkins had slipped up on the dates, and somehow wrote July 12 when he meant to say June 19 for that Father's Day meeting, Childreth would surely have corrected him. Look for that in the files, but I'd be astonished if it were there. Wilkins wouldn't mess up something like that. The point is, if all this had gone down, as the Worthingtons claimed, on June 19, there would be no UCC-1 on July 16 or any other day, for there would have been no loan. You with me?"

"I think so."

"But if it *hadn't* gone down as Jeff and Richard claimed, there *was* still an outstanding $750,000 loan, which on July 16 could be secured by a UCC-1. That means Jeff and Richard were indeed the lying, thieving bastards that I always took them to be, and this letter"—I reached for Wilkins's letter and shook it—"is proof of it."

"Lying, thieving bastards." Emily broke into a big smile. "Exactly."

Wilkins' ass-covering letter was proof that the supposed meeting on Father's Day was a total fabrication, a fiction concocted out of backdated documents and then sworn to in court, and a figment of Jeff's and Richard's desperate desire to do anything they possibly could to keep Emily from her rightful share of the assets that had been built up during her long and miserable marriage. Jeff had the idea that the money was his and only his, and that the woman who had supported him through thirty years and three children was a stick figure to be abused at every turn. The financial transaction that so conveniently drove down Jeff's share in the company from 50 percent to 19 percent—which he claimed occurred before Emily's divorce action prohibited such moves—never took place that Father's Day, or at any other time before she sued for divorce. No, Father's Day was just a family holiday, nothing more.

I continued. "And if Jeff's share did not go down to 19 pecent, then your share didn't either. If it stayed up with his brother's, at 50 percent, your share is 25. And that's what will make you ten million dollars richer than you ever thought you'd be."

"And him ten million poorer," Emily added happily.

"That too."

In the next few days, Emily uncovered four other letters that made it crystal clear that we had it dead right: Jeff, Richard, Sharpe, and Childreth had phonied up the whole deal and backdated transactions to cover their tracks. We referred to these documents as the five smoking guns, and the four conspirators as the four donkeys. The first gun was Wilkins's deadly letter from July 16, 1988. Then there was Monadnock's general counsel Sam Sharpe's letter dated July 17, 1988, to the company's bookkeeper, a Ms. Walker, sending along a copy of Monadnock's $250,000 note to Jeff and asking her to keep it in a safe place until Jeff paid it off. Well, fine. Except that, under the Father's Day scenario, that note supposedly was *already* paid off the previous month right after it was assigned to Richard. Then, two days later, on July 19, the third smoking gun detailed Sharpe's sending Richard the original of Jeff's $250,000 note and telling him to return it when Monadnock paid it off, even though this, likewise, had supposedly already happened on that Father's Day.

Then, on August 1, 1988, Sharpe wrote both brothers and Childreth announcing the news that *now* he'd finally prepared the UCC-1 to secure the debt to Richard. And then Sharpe wrote a memo two days later, on August 3, proposing a scheme in which the brothers would pretend that back on June 19 Jeff signed his $250,000 promissory note over to Richard, and Richard traded the full $750,000 loan for 2,117 shares of equity in Monadnock pushing Jeff's share down to 19 percent.

August 3, long after such a move would have violated the TRO. Yet Jeff and all the Monadnock heavies had taken the witness stand in the first trial to solemnly swear to tell the whole truth, and then lied through their teeth in claiming that this transaction occurred at a time, in a place, and in a manner that it manifestly had not.

The kicker? It later turned out that Jeff never got a $250,000 loan from Meredith Bank in the first place. That money actually came from the dash-nine account. He'd simply taken the money from one pocket and put it in another. Whichever pocket it was in, the money was not his.

ⱺ

I HAD GONE INTO THIS THINKING THAT THE BEST I COULD DO WAS nail Jeff on the dash-nine account, since we already had developed some good information from the papers produced by FDIC that the brothers were skimming off those Maine Paper payments. Anything more than that I figured was too much to hope for; just cleaning up the dash-nine fraud would be a major coup that would win Emily some serious money. And I might have stopped there if Jeff had simply given up the relevant documents about that as we had asked, rather than drop moving vans full of trash on us. If he'd been more obliging, we would never have turned to Childreth, and we might never have found out the truth about the Father's Day Massacre. But that wasn't the way Jeff wanted to play it.

But that did leave the dash-nine account to handle, and eventually we managed to get hold of the key documents from a trove that had been stored off-site by the Concord Bank and Trust of New Hampshire, which had taken over that account after Meredith Bank went belly up. There's a daisy chain to records of this sort, especially if you have the total recall that Emily had for the full Library of Congress of this case. Some records linked to other records, which linked to still others. With each revelation, we opened the window into the Worthingtons' world of wickedness a little wider. First a crack, then a few inches, until finally there it was. The real world has its laws of gravity and photosynthesis and who knows what. The Worthington world had three laws only: (1) don't buy it if you can steal it; (2) don't steal it if you charge it to the company; and (3) always, always, always stick it to Emily.

Once we had the documents, we could do some damage. They were like sticks of dynamite, ready to blow the Worthingtons' lies sky-high. The fact is, whenever you conduct such a financial transaction so close to a divorce action, flags shoot up and sirens go off. The timing is just too suspicious. It is like when a spouse is murdered. The suspicion immediately falls on the other spouse. Well, this was a financial murder, and it should have triggered the exact same thought: he did it. I don't know why Monroe and SFB weren't able to make more of this in the first trial, but I had operated on this assumption from the moment I came to the case.

As soon as I had the five smoking-gun documents pertaining to the Father's Day Massacre, I knew I could go to town. I told Emily that I wanted to start by deposing Sam Sharpe, who had been both corporate counsel and Jeff's divorce lawyer. It was at Sharpe's house, after all, that the Massacre supposedly occurred.

This sent Emily into a panic. "Jerry, don't," she said, angrily. "Don't do that. *Please*."

"Why not?"

"You'll just waste our ammo. Sharpe will give one answer in the deposition, and then a whole different one at the trial once they've had a chance to prepare some line of bullshit. Jerry, you don't know how these people are. They just lie. They lie and lie and lie. That's what they do."

For the first time, she was nearly in tears. She tipped her head down and ran a sleeve across her eyes. It was the exhaustion. The whole ordeal was taking its toll. At that point, the case had consumed her for sixteen years, closing out much of a social life, constraining relations with her children, and draining her bank account so dry she had to take loans from her parents, to be paid back out of any award, if one eventually came.

"I've dealt with plenty of liars," I told her. "Divorce cases are all about lies." There is so little incentive for anyone on the losing side to tell the truth. Nobody ever gets nailed for perjury afterward, even when they have made up their testimony. "But once a deposition is on the record, you can't lie your way out of it," I assured her. "The words say what the words say."

She looked really dubious, her arms crossed, her chin down in her chest. These five letters were her trump cards, cards that she had spent all those years trying to accumulate, going up against some pretty nasty people, starting with her ex, and she couldn't bear the idea of my throwing them away.

"Listen, I get it," I told her. "Your ex-husband has been a total bastard to you, and you think he'll screw you to the wall if he has half a chance. I understand. But I've been in this game a lot longer than he has. You've got to believe me."

Besides, I went on, with Sharpe's deposition we had three advantages. "One, we know the truth; two, we can prove it; and three, he doesn't know what's coming."

Emily seemed unconvinced.

"All right," she said finally. "Just don't screw it up." She wasn't smiling.

Neither was I. "I never do."

The deposition was in my conference room. Although he was entitled to have a lawyer present, Sharpe came alone, which said something about his confidence level. Even though he was almost fifty, Sharpe was freckle faced, with thick reddish hair, and he looked like he'd still get carded at a bar. And unlike Jeff, Sharpe was extremely tall, nearly six foot five. He towered over me and everyone else in the room.

The deposition room was the usual scene—lawyers in dark suits all around a big table, each one fronted with a hefty stack of documents, like castle fortifications, all exchanging a lot of false pleasantries like "good to meet you" and "nice day" to fill the air until we got going. I wore a lively bow tie, brightly striped shirt, and snazzy braces; I looked like a peacock amid all the gray, even if I wasn't exactly sure what colors I was wearing. After all the work they had put in, I brought along Wendy and Margie and, of course, Emily. I didn't want her, or any of them, to miss this.

As part of the cover-up, I assumed that Sharpe had gone through Monadnock's records along with his own, pulling out any land mines that might otherwise have blown up in his face. But coconspirators can never be sure if they can trust each other. Although Sharpe probably asked Childreth and the others to destroy any potentially troublesome files too, he couldn't know if they had secretly retained copies for their own protection. Such caution only exposed Sharpe's vulnerabilities. If the files were retained, they were now flagged as worrisome. If he succeeded in removing the incriminating documents, he wouldn't know we had information he had to fear—or how to respond to it.

In a deposition of this type, surprise is your best weapon. But in this case, I wanted to sneak up on Sharpe, rather than hit him with a massive dose of the unexpected right away. Once we were sitting down in our chairs, we chatted a bit about the Red Sox, I got the paralegal to top off his coffee, and did everything but plump up his pillows. When he was all comfy, I began by reviewing his testimony from the first trial pertaining to that key Sunday, June 19, 1988, when he had asserted that he and the Worthingtons and Childreth had met at his house. He reaffirmed it all, including who was there and what they did. With each answer, I could sense him loosening up a little more as he became more confident that we were just going to go over the same ground. No problem. He smiled at me, as if to say, "See? Piece of cake."

Then, I asked him about the bankruptcy lawyer, Wilkins, and he confirmed that Jeff and several others from Monadnock, including himself, had gone to Nashua to see him about putting Monadnock into Chapter 11.

"When exactly did that occur?" I asked.

He glanced up at me, startled. "I—" A pause. "I'm not sure."

"But you testified at the first trial that it was before that meeting on Father's Day."

For the first time, his eyes betrayed a hint of anxiety.

"That's right."

"So, in fact, it was before that meeting?" I repeated.

"Yes."

"Was it a year before, would you say?" He'd testified to this previously.

"To the best of my recollection. Yes."

"Now, Mr. Sharpe, you were the chief counsel for Monadnock during this period?"

"Yes."

"Weren't you concerned that your CEO was contemplating putting your company into bankruptcy?"

"It was all hypothetical," he quickly replied.

"Meaning he wasn't really planning to do this?"

"Meaning he might." More forceful now.

"But, again, your testimony is that the meeting with Mr. Wilkins occurred well before the meeting on June 19, 1988."

"Yes."

"Would you like to reconsider that testimony now?"

I could see a bead of sweat on Sharpe's forehead. He sat there for a long moment, looking anxiously around the room.

"No," he replied.

"No," I repeated. "Now, Mr. Sharpe, didn't you testify that Mr. Wilkins pointed out that Richard and Jeffrey Worthington could improve the company's balance sheet by exchanging their $750,000 in debt for equity?"

Sharpe was proceeding very slowly now.

"I have the transcript," I nudged him.

"That is my recollection."

"And you have testified that you acted on Mr. Wilkins's recommendation at the subsequent meeting on June 19, exchanging Richard's debt for equity, those 2,117 shares of Monadnock. Is that correct?"

Sharpe must have sensed that he was being led into a trap, but he had no way of avoiding it.

I had the transcript in my hand, but he waved it away. "Yes, I have testified to that."

That's when I sprung it on him. "Then how do you explain this?" I pulled out the letter from Wilkins from July 16, 1988, almost a month *after* the Massacre, and placed it on the table in front of him.

It was the letter confirming that Wilkins had advised Monadnock to secure Richard's loan by issuing its $750,000 UCC-1. Sharpe's face paled as he glanced over it. I asked him to read it out loud into the record, which he did, his voice significantly weaker than before.

"Now, Mr. Sharpe, can we agree that Monadnock could only issue its UCC-1 to secure its debt to Richard?"

He glanced about the room, as if looking for a way out. "Yes."

"Can we also agree that you testified at trial that on June 19 Richard gave up his debt for Monadnock stock?"

Another pause. "Yes, that's right."

"Then how do you explain Wilkins writing that on July 12, 1988, almost a full month after that June 19 Father's Day—that Monadnock still owed Richard the $750,000?"

He looked at the document again and shrugged. "I can't."

"You can't explain it," I repeated. I paused to let that settle in. "Then how about this?" I handed him a copy of Monadnock's auditors' notes from June 30, well after the supposed big meeting on Father's Day. I directed him to one line of figures. "You see there that Monadnock's auditors confirm that the $750,000 debt was still outstanding, and not converted to equity?"

"Yes, I see that," he said weakly.

"If your trial testimony was accurate, how could it be that the debt had not been converted to equity on the company's books, Mr. Sharpe? Especially given that First National Bank of Boston was calling for it?"

He looked at the records, paused, looked again, and shook his head. "I don't know."

"You don't know. Did the company auditors—all of them extremely scrupulous, experienced professional people whom you knew—did they fail to make the proper accounting entries?"

Sharpe looked stricken. "I just don't know."

I pulled out another document. "Now, what about this letter you wrote on July 19, a month after the June 19 meeting, to Richard, sending him Monadnock's original $250,000 promissory note to Jeff and instructing him to hold on to it until it had been paid by Monadnock. Why would you ask him to do that—*when that note supposedly had already been paid?*"

"I—I don't remember," he said. His forehead was wet with sweat.

I went through two more of the five documents that Emily and I called the smoking guns. To every one of my questions, he replied the same way. "I don't remember."

At the end of it all, I gave him one last chance to come clean. "Do you have any explanation for these discrepancies at all?"

He shook his head one last time. "No."

"Now, Mr. Sharpe, isn't it possible that there is a reason? And only one reason? That there was, in fact, no meeting on June 19 and that, well after the fact, you backdated everything to a date before Jeff was served with the temporary restraining order?"

Sharpe turned combative, eager to defend the last shred of his dignity. "I never did that. No. Never."

Then I pulled out that last memo Emily had found. The fifth and final smoking gun. It had been intermixed with a long report on Monadnock's financial prospects and slipped past Emily when she was looking over the documents in Childreth's office before they went through the scanner. But Emily never left such important matters to just one pass, and she caught it a few weeks later when, after a strange premonition late one evening, she reviewed that financial material on her computer again. Sharpe had written the memo for his own files, with copies to Childreth and the Worthingtons. It could not have been more damning, as it laid out in stark detail everything that I had just asserted and Sharpe had denied. At my request, he read out the document; then, almost incredulous at the words it contained, he looked at it a long time, his shaking hands causing the paper to flutter a little. I glanced back at Emily, who was watching Sharpe intently, her jaw tight. Her eyes did not shift to mine.

"I see it. I know I must have written it. But I don't remember this at all," he said finally. "Not one word of it."

☙❧

WELL, AFTER THAT, THERE WAS SCARCELY ANY POINT IN HAVING A TRIAL. If Sharpe went down, they all went down. That is the flip side of any conspiracy. It's one thing to stand as one when the lies are working. When they aren't, everyone falls as one. And the lies had finally started to run out, exposing everything and everyone for what they were. Those boats, for example. Jeff and Richard each owned huge oceangoing vessels. Jeff's was that ninety-eight-foot motor yacht, *Victory III*. Richard, the younger brother, had a mere seventy-five-footer, *The Hope*. The titles to the ships were both held by N.H. Bay Sailing, which they owned. But all that corporation's operating expenses were paid for by Monadnock, which wrote them off as bogus sales expenses or chartering fees. We found the logs, and that showed the boats were sailed exclusively by the Worthingtons. It wasn't cheap to run them either. Between fuel, salaries, and maintenance, the cost ran over a quarter million. Just to gas them up could cost thirty thousand. But the boats ensnared the other henchmen in the plot, as Jeff and Richard took Childreth, Sharpe, Bacon, and some of the others out on lavish trips with their families to the Caribbean, around to Mexico, or over to Monaco. All completely for free, except that the others incurred a powerful sense of obligation that Jeff and Richard could convert into membership in a conspiracy that could cost the lawyers their licenses. That's how Jeff and Richard operated. They weren't attractive people, but they had jobs to offer and perks to give, and for such blunt men, they could be subtle, drawing in these coconspirators first with just a little favor, then a bigger one, and then one bigger still. By then their lackeys were in too deep to pull themselves out—in so deep they didn't even see it as in.

Such thievery was bred in the bone. It didn't start with Jeff and Richard and Thomas but with their dad. Jeffrey Worthington Sr., the company founder. An oil portrait of him hangs in the Monadnock hallway, and it adorns every annual report. Craggy-faced, with sky blue eyes, he could be a Calvinist preacher, the picture of Yankee probity. But no. He started his sons down the path when, from the earliest days of the company, he had his own personal bagman truck the Monadnock scrap to Maine Paper, where he dealt with a Worthington crony who was in on the deal. Old man Worthington made sure his delivery guy was paid in grocery bags full of cash, a portion of which the crony presumably skimmed off the top for his pains. Old Mr. Worthington would then slide the cash right into his pocket when the bagman returned.

By 1987, the old man had died and Maine Paper's new owners changed its policy, and it starting paying Monadnock in the normal way—by check. That's when Jeff and Richard opened the dash-nine account at Meredith Bank. It was just a place to hide those checks. It was the new version of the old man's grocery bag.

All the brothers knew how the game was played, and they all took to plundering the company in their own way. Thomas was the most flamboyant, and he had to be banished because he stole too much. There was a limit, even for the Worthingtons. To replace him, they had to find somebody quasi-brotherly to do the accounting while Jeff and Richard divvied up the dash-nine account.

Jeff hired Burt Childreth, a former Babson accounting professor who had started his own firm. He was frail and sickly, and the Worthingtons figured he wasn't likely to risk his income over some moral scruples. They tried him out as a consultant, then hired his accounting firm. It wasn't clear if Childreth ever noticed the dash-nine account, or if he chose to let it go. I'm guessing the latter. But it was fine with the Worthingtons either way. They got their money, hundreds of thousands of dollars every year for each of them, tax free.

Sometime in 1993, well after the divorce case began, Richard finally started getting anxious. The free money was piling up, Emily was digging around, and he was afraid the feds might notice. He decided to clue Childreth in on the true nature of the dash-nine account. In doing this, of course, Richard was taking a risk. Childreth could run to the IRS, restate all his financial statements—or resign in outrage. But Richard knew his man, and knew his company. He and Jeff had designed it as a place of wall-to-wall mendacity; it had to be for Richard and Jeff to continue their illegal practices. By now, Childreth and his family had gone out on the Worthingtons' boats for any number of long, extravagant cruises to the Caribbean, French Riviera, and elsewhere, all of it seemingly for free, although Childreth noticed that the expenses later popped up on Monadnock's books. Whether Childreth wanted to be or not, he was in. And Childreth came through for Richard and Jeff now. Childreth looked over the dash-nine account. For the first time, he betrayed a hint of uncertainty and brought in a retired IRS agent, who had specialized in fraud, for an examination. The agent came to the only conclusion possible—that it was monstrous, willful fraud. Still, Childreth carried on like it was just a bunch of numbers without any legal implications whatsoever. He told Richard that everything was fine, and he would simply amend their personal tax returns along with Monadnock's corporate returns for the last three years to reflect the dash-nine income.

Richard gave him a hearty slap on the back for that—and a few days later offered another trip on his boat, to Bermuda this time. Childreth prepared the various amended returns and asked Richard to make sure they were properly filed. They never were. Neither Childreth nor anyone else at Monadnock breathed a word about the company's amended returns to Emily, although Jeff was legally obligated to. And Richard asked Childreth to say nothing to anyone else. "Who needs to know, right?" he asked with a chuckle.

But the dash-nine numbers kept getting bigger. In 1996 more than a million dollars came into that account from Maine Paper. On the financial disclosure forms filed that year, Jeff listed his annual income at $233,000, and that was the figure on which child support and alimony were based. The true income, as Childreth well knew, was more than $750,000, and the discrepancy was making him very nervous. The IRS would be very interested to learn about it, and so would Emily. How could an auditor have missed it?

෨ඥ

CHILDRETH'S LIES PUT THE SQUEEZE ON JEFF'S LAWYER, MARTIN Bacon, just when Emily was turning up the heat on the whole dash-nine matter. On this score SFB was hopeless, but Emily was after Bacon. She knew in her bones the dash-nine account was corporate, not personal, as Richard and Jeff had claimed in the first trial. If so, she was entitled to an accounting. And if so, where was it? Bacon was already in a tight spot, since he served as Monadnock's corporate counsel *and,* by then, as Jeff's personal counsel in the divorce matter, even though those duties were no less in conflict for him than they were for Sam Sharpe. Like Sharpe, Bacon couldn't make a move except at cross-purposes, his right hand at war with his left. What helped Jeff hurt Monadnock, and vice versa.

Like a good soldier, Bacon cast his lot with Jeff and did whatever he could to protect him, not caring that it might hurt Monadnock. So he did not look at the dash-nine numbers. He never asked for copies of the account's checkbook, deposits, or canceled checks. Instead, he tried to stonewall, refusing to give us a speck of information about the account. But eventually he realized he had to cough up something. So he promised to provide formal affidavits regarding the question of ownership of the dash-nine accounts by five o'clock one Tuesday afternoon in April 2002. As part of Jeff's official response, that morning Bacon faxed affidavits to Jeff, Richard, and Childreth to sign, acknowledging that the dash-nine account was personally "owned, maintained, and controlled" by Richard. It was personal, personal, personal. If they said it enough times, maybe that would make it true.

Then he called Childreth to see how the affidavit went down with him. Not very well! Bacon might be protected by attorney-client privilege, but Childreth wasn't. He didn't feel like being thrown to the sharks. If Bacon was hoping for a tidy conversation between like-minded colleagues, he was in for a surprise. As Bacon's time sheets reveal, that call to Childreth lasted *four entire hours.* And it's plenty clear why: Childreth was not eager to sign a bullshit affidavit that could cost him his license and maybe send him to prison. However much the two brothers wanted to pretend otherwise, they both knew full well that the dash-nine account was not Jeff's or Richard's money, but Monadnock's money, which the two of them were plundering for their own pleasure, at the expense of the company *and* of Emily's interests in the divorce case that was just about the only thing anyone thought about anymore. Despite the endless conversation, Bacon made just one change. He removed the word *owned* from the phrase "owned, maintained, and controlled" in the affidavit regarding Richard and the dash-nine account. Richard didn't own it, which meant it wasn't his, which meant it was a corporate account after all, and therefore was now fair game for Emily. Now Childreth would acknowledge only that Richard "maintained and controlled" the account. Clever. It was factually correct, and substantively identical to the previous version, but escaped the most obvious liabilities. The only problem was that it marked a change that Emily's later lawyers—Wendy and myself—would likely pounce on if they were paying attention, which we damn well were. What, it's *not* a personal account anymore? After Emily had contested this very point for more than a decade? All the same, Bacon faxed that to Childreth, who immediately signed it and faxed it back to Bacon at his office at the Monadnock plant in Meredith.

Richard, however, wouldn't sign. When Bacon called him after finishing up with Childreth around three o'clock that Tuesday afternoon, Richard insisted that the dash-nine account was a personal account, and to hell with anyone who thought otherwise. It had always been a personal account, regardless of any stupid 01 in the account number. Of course, to say anything else would just get him into worse trouble. But to Richard, it was just plain wrong! He was entitled to that money, just as his father had been, and his brother Jeff was. It was his company, and it was his money, and if Childreth thought otherwise, he could go work for somebody else.

Richard left in the word owned.

So did Jeff.

When Childreth saw what Bacon said were the final affidavits come through the fax machine at his office, he quickly glanced through to make sure the changes had been made. But no: Richard's and Jeff's affidavits still claimed the dash-nine account was "owned" by Richard. Childreth's, however, did not. Panicked, he called Bacon up at the Monadnock office. They couldn't have the brothers' affidavits say one thing and his say another. That had red flags all over it. And sirens. And klieg lights. It was almost four o'clock now, just an hour away from the deadline. Bacon was not at Monadnock but in his car headed into Boston to drop off the documents at my office. The Monadnock operator put Childreth's call through to Bacon's cell. Childreth was merely the outside company accountant, not the lawyer, but he told Bacon that, as the affidavits now stood, two of them were lies and could land all of them in a world of trouble. At the very least, they needed to line up their stories. They couldn't have two saying this and one saying that, and there was no way that Childreth was going to lie about something like this.

He may have made some threat too, because Bacon, then out in the Boston suburbs, knew it was too late to get back to his office. It was just past four now, and time was getting pretty tight. If he was late in getting the affidavits to my office, that would send warning signals right there. As it happened, he wasn't far from the office of a former associate who'd put up a shingle in the suburbs. He rushed right in, and with scarcely a moment for pleasantries, asked if he could use his computer. There, Bacon went online to retrieve the file, frantically deleted the word *owned* from the first page of Richard's and Jeff's affidavits, printed out a new first page for each and attached to it the original seconds, which Jeff and Richard had signed, and had a messenger deliver them to my office a few minutes before five.

Bacon never told Jeff and Richard what he had done.

Bacon, however, had also prepared his own memorandum that would go to me and also be sent, with the three affidavits, to the arbitrator and to the court. In it he followed the line of the original affidavits,

asserting that Richard had indeed "owned" the dash-nine account—
even though Bacon had just changed the affidavits themselves to say the
opposite. He could have inserted the single word *not* before the word
owned in his account and made it conform to the truth. But lies breed
lies.

෧෨

SO IT ALL STARTED WITH THE OLD MAN AND HIS CHISELING, WHICH
his sons continued as if it was natural and right, and it led to the dash-
nine account and the efforts to hide it, which drew in others, until too
many people knew and there were too many stories to control and keep
straight. Those fabrications led to the lies about the Father's Day Massacre too. There would never have been a need for such a meeting if the
Worthingtons hadn't been bilking the company out of millions for a
decade before I came onto the case, to say nothing of the decades before
that. Nor would they have had to concoct this elaborate debt-for-equity
scheme, because there wouldn't have been nearly so much debt, if any.
And if Jeff had simply come clean about the dash-nine account, and furnished the documents we were seeking, we would never have stumbled
onto the truth about the Massacre.

But we did, and what it added up to was a massive case of fraud,
far larger and more audacious than anything we could have imagined
coming in. For this wasn't just a matter of a simple oversight. No, this
was a matter of a deliberate manipulation of facts that was widespread
enough to create an alternative reality. And once the deceptions become
that sweeping, you lose any feeling of solidity. It's more unstable than
a house built on sand. It's built on air. There is nothing to support it
except the perpetrators' determination to make you believe their lies
regardless of the facts.

The edifice was certainly shaking by the time I got through with
Sharpe. But it all came crashing down when we deposed Childreth.
By that point, he had gotten wind of how the Sharpe deposition went

down. Sharpe had emerged from that session like a prizefighter who had been hit with too many jabs to the head. Childreth didn't want to fight. Frail and sallow, he kept putting off the deposition, claiming illness. We had to file several motions to get him into his seat.

For the deposition, at least thirty people crammed into a windowless conference room downtown, not far from my office, all of them expecting a prizefight. Most of them were lawyers. And most of the lawyers were there for one good reason. Their clients could be next. Now that I'd found so much evidence of the conspiracy to commit fraud against my client, I decided to up the ante by going after the two Worthingtons and their various Monadnock foot soldiers, under the RICO statute that was initially designed to allow the federal government to bring charges against the mafia. Which was good, since what we had here was a kind of mafia. A Wasp mafia.

As soon as I saw Childreth, I recognized the guilt on his face, a hangdog, I-did-it look. He was perspiring heavily, he would not look me in the eye, he had no voice, and when we shook hands, it was as if I was greeting a dead mackerel. Once he was in his chair, he sat there limply, as if he might topple any second. With Sharpe, I'd tiptoed into the central issue because I needed to set up the big questions with a long line of small ones. Here I wanted to start pummeling Childreth before he had a chance to think. Shock and awe. Maybe it's cruel, but I have a job to do for my client, and nothing I would do to him could ever compare to what he had done to Emily.

Finally, we were ready to start. I waited for the room to quiet, and then I waited a little longer. I wanted the air to have that snap in it, the feeling of worried expectation. I had everybody's eyes on me when I finally spoke, and then, after the briefest of preliminaries, I hit him so hard with the first question that I nearly knocked him off his chair.

After he confirmed his position as certified public accountant for Monadnock Press, I asked, "Was there ever a time when you looked at or came across anything concerning Monadnock Press, or Jeffrey or Richard Worthington, that made you think that fraud had taken place?"

Well, you might think that was tame, but in a corporate context, with so many suits around and a nervous witness in the box, if you say the word fraud you might as well bring out a .44 Magnum, cock it, and press the barrel to his forehead. The breath went out of him, and his skin turned a corpselike gray. Childreth just looked at me with a pair of very sad eyes, or more likely, he looked through me, to some place where he could not be seen, not be judged. It was a fairly small room for thirty people. I could hear the air conditioner blowing. Not a squeak or whisper. It seemed like no one was breathing, or maybe all the oxygen in the room was just gone. Childreth turned to his lawyer, a stout character named DeMarco, who remained absolutely still, lest his client think he was suggesting a particular answer. DeMarco knew his client's obligation. He had to tell the truth, or DeMarco would quit as his attorney.

I waited for Childreth's answer. We all did. Waited and waited. I didn't move a muscle, and no one else did either. I wanted Childreth to feel the weight on him, the ache. Another minute went by—an eternity in this silent, motionless room crammed with so many people. I could almost see the wheels spinning behind Childreth's eyes, cranking and cranking in an attempt to find the perfect defense to a brutal question. He went through every piece of information he had ever known. But none of it had prepared him for this moment, when he had to choose between adding one more whopper to his pile of lies or seeing what the truth was like.

I could see the choice before him, and so could Childreth, and everybody else in the room. Nobody in the room had moved a fraction of an inch.

Finally, Childreth cleared his throat and coughed quietly into his hand. And then he looked at me.

"Yes."

DeMarco and all of the other lawyers in the room sprang forward in their seats, picked up their pens and started writing furiously on sheets of paper. But DeMarco made no move to restrain his client.

"On more than one occasion?" I asked.

"Yes."

"Tell me about each concern."

Just five words, but they provoked an outpouring of confession. I scarcely had to say anything more. Childreth laid out all the ways in which the three Worthingtons had siphoned off money from the dash-nine account to fund countless other scams, and how it had led to problems in producing an honest accounting for the IRS, and for the annual certified audit. He explained that he had hired the former IRS agent, who concluded that fraud had been committed, but he had been unable to persuade Jeff and Richard to come clean by acknowledging the true nature of the dash-nine account.

"And did they ever acknowledge it?"

"No, sir. They did not."

"Even though they knew the money wasn't theirs?"

DeMarco jumped in to object that his client wasn't a mind reader—

But Childreth answered anyway. "They knew," he said. "Of course they knew. They'd known from the beginning."

We moved on to other things—Monadnock's payments to maintain the yachts, to cover legal fees for Jeff's divorce, to acquire some land for Jeff, to buy first-class plane tickets and occupy vast hotel suites. The damage was done. Jeff Worthington had been outed, by his own accountant, as a fraud and a cheat who would do anything to deprive his ex-wife of her fair share in a divorce settlement.

The deposition ran on for four hours. By one thirty, Childreth looked so wasted that I started to worry about him. When DeMarco asked to suspend the deposition for the day, I didn't object. Two days later, Childreth went into the hospital, complaining of heart problems.

It took a quadruple bypass to cure them. He wasn't out of the hospital for weeks, and wasn't available to give further testimony for months.

There were other depositions, of course. But none as devastating to the other side as those of Sharpe and Childreth. We had breached their defenses, and there was no keeping us out after that.

You'd think Jeff Worthington would have settled after all the revelations. But no. He insisted on a second trial, conducted, like the first, by Arbitrator Dibley. It followed the same rules of evidence as a conventional trial, and all the usual procedures involving cross-examination and the like. It simply had an arbitrator in place of a judge. And it did take forever. Two weeks for the trial, and then three months for Dibley to offer his final ruling.

At any kind of trial, a lawyer always has to expect the unexpected, but I was pretty confident going in that we had what we needed to nail Jeff Worthington. We had everything, and he had nothing. A demon for preparation, I had been preparing my questioning of Jeff for weeks. I wanted to blow the guy sky-high. We had so much proof, so much inside testimony.

It was early on a Thursday morning when Jeff finally took the stand. Bald, chunky, and short, Jeff was not exactly the most prepossessing individual. But he was fairly well turned out in a polo shirt and sports jacket, and he radiated confidence as certain politicians do, often looking about the hall to see how marvelously well his lines were playing. Once he was seated and sworn in, I paced before him, sometimes turning to confront him, sometimes turning away, all the while slowly and methodically building up my line of argument brick by brick, and stacking all the bricks up just so, until they walled him in.

It took at least two hours before I was ready to get him to face the truth of the matter that had made his ex-wife's life a misery for so long. I'd gone through the dash-nine, the Father's Day Massacre, and many other smaller deceptions that had cost the company so dearly and robbed Emily of millions. Then I approached the witness box, wanting to see his reaction up close when I asked the next question. It was the key question of the trial, and the key question of the eighteen years that preceded it, and, indeed, the key question in the life of Jeff Worthington, and of all the Worthingtons. Yet it didn't matter which way he answered it. If he said no, he simply would not be believed; yes, and he was a monster.

"Would you then agree that, throughout these matters that we have just discussed, you have perpetrated a sweeping case of fraud on your ex-wife, Emily Worthington?" I asked.

I expected at least a moment's thought, but the answer came right back.

"Yes, I have."

Just like that. "Yes, I have." In the kind of casual tone you'd use if you were ordering a side of fries with your cheeseburger. Utterly matter-of-fact, and quite inconsequential. Yes, I have. Next question? Or are we all done?

What a monster.

And so, in a stroke, he admitted to what he had spent eighteen years trying to deny, and had enlisted others to deny, at tremendous cost in time and effort and money and stress to virtually everyone, it would appear, except himself.

Yes, I have.

There was more, of course. But it was pretty much over right there.

"That prick," Emily said. "He doesn't even care! Can you believe that? Ruined my life for eighteen years, and he doesn't even care!"

❧

THAT PART OF THE TRIAL WAS TO DETERMINE FRAUD. YES. DEFINITELY Dibley found there was fraud. Then came the money. How much was the company worth? And how much should Emily get? We were a couple of days into that when Jeff's side asked for a recess. Why? Because Blaine, Howard and Co., one of the largest printing companies in the world, had made an offer to purchase Monadnock.

That changed everything. Blaine Howard's offer would put a fair market price on Monadnock, making any other appraisal immaterial. And we finally had leverage. Jeff and Richard were desperate to cash out. But there was no way Blaine Howard was going to buy Monadnock with a nasty divorce case hanging over its CEO.

"It would be a legal circus," Bacon admitted to me.

"Well, then," I said, unfazed. "Let the circus proceed."

"Jerry—c'mon, *no*."

I looked at him, sensing his frustration. "You know, every time you say that, Emily's price goes up."

Blaine Howard was offering $42.25 million. Jeff owned half of Monadnock. So if Emily was due half of his share, she would receive $10.56 million in the sale. Not bad—and a whole lot more than when she started. I could goose that up some, but not too much. If Blaine Howard said no sale, Emily would have to return to arbitration and take her chances there. In the end, we offered to decouple the two parts. For $500,000, we told Jeff we'd end the divorce fight so he could conduct the Blaine Howard deal free and clear.

Jeff immediately agreed. With that, the long ordeal was over. Almost.

Free to negotiate without restraint, he succeeded in pushing Blaine Howard to just shy of $50 million—$49.3 million to be exact. When you included the real estate, Emily came away with over $16 million. Emily was stunned. For a second, I thought she might start sobbing. But instead she broke out laughing. The legal fees that Jeff was responsible for came to $1.32 million, and we had Blaine Howard wire Emily's share to us out of the money they were paying to buy Monadnock. Emily was in my office when the money arrived, and my bookkeeper cut her a check for her share. I held that check in my hands. I have rarely felt as happy as I did then. Along with Wendy and Mindy and a few other people from the office who had worked so hard on the case for eight years, I led Emily and the little group in the chicken dance, all of us flapping our arms and squawking as we marched about my office.

❧

EMILY'S OPPONENTS AT MONADNOCK DIDN'T FARE SO WELL. JEFF'S LAST attorney, Martin Bacon, faced disciplinary charges arising from his conduct in the case and was publicly reprimanded. The first attorney, Sam Sharpe, was charged with illegally backdating documents, making false entries in a corporate stock record book, and conflict of interest. The Massachusetts Board of Bar Overseers has held hearings into the question of whether to permanently disbar him from the practice of law.

Once he sold the company, Jeff took off on the *Victory III*. With the girlfriend whom Emily discovered at his Meredith hideaway, he set out down the Atlantic, through the Caribbean, farther down the South American coast, around the Cape, and out into the broad expanse of the Pacific. That was in 2007. He kept in touch with his children for a few months, and Emily heard about him from them. But then—radio silence. God knows where he went.

I'd always imagined Jeff had more money stored offshore around the world. We'd found a mysterious check for one million dollars, which was drawn on a bank in Andorra to cover the building of his boat, left uncashed. About a year after the silence set in, Emily got a call from her oldest daughter. Her father had called and told her that he was almost bankrupt. He'd sounded very tired. He was calling from a harbor somewhere in Central America, although he had carefully not revealed where. And the girlfriend had left him. Apparently, he had fallen for a Ponzi scheme that involved a high-level con artist who operated through one of the exclusive yacht clubs Jeff belonged to. Not Madoff, but another viper who hadn't surfaced in the papers yet. Bored with money, Jeff had let the man manage everything. And now he'd lost it all. Millions. He'd had to put the *Victory III* up for sale, but feared he'd get only a fraction of its value in a dying economy.

Emily had never trusted stocks, and she'd put every cent of her settlement money in U.S. Treasuries. She didn't need to make her money grow, just to hang on to what she already had. She was overjoyed that her ex-husband had gotten badly bitten by another SOB. "Serves him right, the creep!" she told me, when she called to pass along the news about Jeff. She'd stayed on in the big house in Marblehead, remembering how much it meant to her three kids and the grandkids who seemed to be coming along almost monthly. Seven and counting, last I heard. She'd removed the Library of Congress—her divorce records—and put in a studio space for herself and some bedrooms for the grandchildren. I get Christmas cards from her, birth announcements of grandchildren, and an occasional e-mail. Whenever I think of Emily, I do a little chicken dance in my mind, because I'm so happy that things came out right for her.

Part Four

·∞·

THE
KIDS

CHAPTER

NINE

THE KIDS ALWAYS COME FROM SOMEWHERE, AND HARRY'S three —twin two-year-old girls and a four-year-old boy—had their origin in the bar at his golf club in Naples, Florida. That's where, a few stools down, he spotted Loretta, a nicely shaped and heavily accented Russian blonde, glittering with gold jewelry, and just twenty-five. Harry was pushing forty, and he was a little heavy. But to Loretta, he must have seemed a lot younger and slimmer now that he'd sold his Internet company for twenty million dollars. And that made her look all the better to him too. He'd have jumped her right there, except she was with another club member, a balding cardiologist in his early sixties. The doctor was old enough to be her grandfather, but Harry didn't question it. He figured the guy was just lucky.

Not exactly. Loretta, it turned out, was a professional escort whom others might call a hooker. But Harry didn't learn that until several years later, after he'd lured her back to Winchester, Massachusetts, with him, married her, had the kids, and installed everybody in a big house with a tennis court, heated pool, live-in French nanny, and two Polynesian houseboys.

"I was happy," he told me afterward. Of course, if he'd been truly happy, he would not have been sitting beside a box of Kleenex in my conference room telling me the story. "I was! But Loretta—" He sighed and shook his head. "Loretta was a total pain in the ass." She quickly tired of being a full-time mom, so Harry got her into an MBA program at Boston University. Soon she was hardly ever home, which made him wonder a little. And when she was home, she seemed different. "She wasn't fun anymore, wasn't sexy at all," Harry said. "She seemed bored, distracted. Like she never had anything to do."

She started getting sloshed on the California pinots he'd introduced her to—at dinner, and before and after too. There were fights, nippy little ones at first, then some beauties. Finally, one night Loretta got bombed, stuffed the twins and the boy into the Lexus, threw some clothes for everybody into the trunk, and tried to drive off with them to his house in Florida. Harry was upstairs, but he'd seen all the commotion down on the driveway and heard the car start up. He flew down the stairs, dashed outside, and pressed the override on the master remote to keep the swinging gate at the foot of the drive from opening. Loretta jumped out, charged at him, clawed the shit out of his face, and ripped his shirt to shreds while the kids screamed in terror. Somehow he managed to hold her off long enough to fumble for his cell phone and call 911. When the cop cars roared up, blue lights everywhere, they looked at this man who had been all ripped up, and saw Loretta slurring her words and stumbling around, and they arrested her for public drunkenness. They took her down to the Winchester police station and put her in a holding tank to sober up. She used her one call to get a lawyer. Her first words to the guy when he got down there were, "I want a divorce."

That's when Harry called me. By then, he was all too happy to split from Loretta.

The problem was the kids. She was demanding full custody, but he had been the primary parent for some time, and he was not about to hand his kids over to a whackjob. Through her lawyer, Loretta claimed that he had an alcohol problem and that he was a pothead and cocaine addict besides.

That is to say: the war was on.

Harry assured me the addiction charges were crazy, but I had him tested all the same. Trust but verify.

He was clean.

A few weeks later, Harry called me, all excited. "I settled the case!" he shouted.

"What do you mean you settled the case?" I asked him.

"I got her to give up all claims to primary custody."

"Well, that's great," I said, kind of surprised. "But how the hell did you do that?"

"I offered to buy her a little place around here so she'd have somewhere to see the kids."

"Okay." I made a note on a sheet of paper: *House.*

"Nothing big," he went on. "Just enough for her and the kids."

"So, like four bedrooms?"

"Yeah, something like that."

On the sheet, beside *House*, I made a line and then wrote *$1MM.*

"Anything else?"

"I agreed we'd keep the place in Naples jointly."

"Okay, joint title." I put down *1/2 Naples condo. $750,000.* "That's not so bad," I told him. "That it?"

"Oh, and I agreed to give her three million."

"*What?*"

"Three million."

"Why?"

"For the kids. I need to protect the kids, Jerry."

Well, yeah, I wanted to say as I wrote down *$3MM,* but there are a lot cheaper ways to go about it. Add up all the figures, and you get almost five million altogether, which is more than $1.6 million per kid, which is a lot. This wasn't a negotiation, this was ransom.

What I said was, "Fine. It's your money. Congratulations."

Every once in a while I can see the future. Like I'm reading tarot cards. I just know exactly what is going to happen next. So here, I could see it: Loretta was going to take extensive absences from the darling little Winchester house and spend the time in Naples, which had been such a happy hunting ground for her—and would be even more of one if she was in a big condo, living it up on her three mill. She could easily trade up for a new guy with a zero or two more than Harry and climb the ladder to serious cash.

And that's exactly what she did.

ભળજ

IN CHILD CUSTODY CASES, THE KIDS AREN'T KIDS. NOT REALLY. THEY'RE not little Julie in her rumpled tutu in ballet class, or Nathan Jr. in his pin-striped pj's with Lil' Slugger across the front. For one side or the other, and often both, they're little bags of money—either the cash that comes with them for child support, or the dough a loving parent like Loretta can get for selling them back to the richer spouse. But then, the money isn't really money either. Lots of times it's just an instrument of torture, a way to stick it in the eye of the ex who dumped them or who committed the crime of having more money. Face it: in a divorce, it can be fun to hook the other party up to jumper cables.

The thing is, there is only one of each kid. You can't split a child down the middle so that she takes half and he takes half, the way you do everything else. Okay, maybe there's only one primary residence in Beverly Farms, or one twelve-million-dollar Matisse over the fireplace, or one Piper Cub at Hanscom Airfield. When there is heavy sentiment attached, a couple can do a tug-of-war over such things, but most of the time even the most crazed spouse will just sell them and split the cash, or have them appraised so one side can buy the other out.

Not so with the kids. If you can't agree on joint custody, one side will end up getting sole physical custody of the kids, and the other side won't. All or nothing.

In this regard, the Bible had it right, in the famous story of King Solomon and how he had to choose between two warring moms, each of whom furiously insisted a newborn baby was hers. Solomon thought about it and thought about it, and then—wise man that he was—he said he couldn't decide between them, so it seemed only fair to split the baby in two and award half of the child to each. One mom nodded and said terrific! Great idea! She was fine with that. The other was horrified, and said, God no, she could never do that to her child. Give her to the other woman if you must, but don't slice the baby in two. Please! Solomon decided she must be the true mother. No true mother would ever think of slicing her child in half.

Which sounds obvious. But as in the case of Harry versus Loretta, I haven't found too many true mothers. Or true fathers, for that matter. Otherwise, they'd do everything they could to skip the custody fight, because it's so ruinously expensive, endless, mindless, and emotionally devastating—to say nothing of the open-heart surgery without anesthesia it performs on the kids.

℘

STILL, SINCE THE BEGINNING OF TIME, EVERY PARENT WHO HAS EVER pushed the custody fight insists he or she is doing it out of love.

Hate is more like it. Divorce is never pretty, but custody fights define ugly. Parents throw everything they have at the other side, the more disgusting, horrendous, and despicable the better. They'll claim a spouse posted dirty pictures of the kid on the Internet, or spread around explicit e-mails of depraved sexual activities, or videotaped himself receiving oral sex from the babysitter (but never produce a video), or insisted the wife have sex with the family dog on camera, or beat the kids with a riding crop, or locked them in a closet, or sent them naked into the snow, or broke the law in other ways, like theft, tax evasion, fraud, or any number of things that may or may not have happened. You name it, they throw it.

Those are the hand grenades each side is lobbing into the other bunker. Meanwhile, they're offering the kids an endless Valentine's Day of sweets. One divorced dad, Leonard, built a brand new house with a pool and a suite of rooms for his fifteen-year-old daughter, Penny. And he bought her a horse. I told the ex-wife, Jean, there was no way she was going to top that, so just let her daughter go—for now. It was a fight she'd lose even if she won. So keep your money, and just wait for Penny to come back, as I was sure she would. Well, Jean waited and waited, and Penny never did come back. That was a first for me. Every other bribed child had come back. Just not this time. Jean was devastated. Cried and cried. I felt like shit. Time for another set of nonexistent tarot cards for me. Thing was, Jean had remarried and had three young children. And Penny may have figured there was no room for her in her mother's life anymore. Or maybe she genuinely preferred Dad. Or maybe she really loved that horse.

Worse, though, is when the kid ping-pongs between the parents, trying to get a better deal. I had one client Ralph, a stockbroker, who had moved from Massachusetts to New York. He wanted custody of his two teenage boys, but the judge gave it to Ann, his wife here in Massachusetts, instead. That pissed Ralph off pretty badly. The arrangement lasted only a few months before the kids showed up at Dad's apartment door. The boys had been hellions, supposedly selling drugs and doing all sorts of crazy things, and Ann had cracked down on them, and she'd been able to make it stick because her father was chief of police in the little town where they lived. The kids thought, to hell with that.

So now they wanted to try Dad, and he was thrilled to have them.

For about two months. Then Ralph came to believe that the younger one, Pete, was selling dope in the boys' locker room at the local public school rather than going to physics class. He told Pete to cut it out, but he didn't. Things deteriorated from there, and eventually Pete said to hell with Dad, and they ran back to Mom.

That is not the end of the story, alas. Ralph remarried, had another child, but then the second wife wanted a divorce before the baby was even a year old. He called me because he wanted to get custody. I told him, "Ralph, cut the shit, would you? She's the one home all day with the kids, not you. No judge is going to give you the baby. And besides, haven't we seen this movie already?" He'd stopped paying his bills, so I wouldn't represent him, but he stayed in touch. I told him I could put him in touch with a great New York custody lawyer. He said he wasn't ready for that yet. He sounded spacier and spacier with each conversation. Finally, I got a call from him from LaGuardia Airport about six months later. He had his oldest son, Eddie, with him, and he was sending him back to Ann.

Here we go again, I thought. "Fine," I said. "That makes sense." He wanted me to ask Ann to pick him up at Logan.

I was thinking, why don't you just call her yourself? But I was also thinking, you don't sound so good.

So I said, "Ralph, what's going on? You okay?"

"Jerry, I've just shot and killed my wife."

"Cut the shit." He had to be joking, right?

"Jerry, I did it. I shot her."

"Oh my God. When?"

"About two hours ago."

"Where?"

"At our apartment. Down in Soho. She wanted me out, Jerry. She wanted to take my baby away."

"Ralph—God!"

Nothing.

"And the baby? Ralph, where's the baby?"

"Don't worry. I have the baby. She's right here in my arms."

"Does Eddie know about this?"

"No."

This was all too terrible. "Do you want me to hang up and call the police now, Ralph?" As his lawyer, I couldn't call them without his permission.

Ralph remained strangely calm, or maybe he was just exhausted. "Just wait ten minutes until Eddie boards, okay? I'll stay right here, I promise."

"Now, Ralph, one more time—is this a joke? Tell me it is."

"It's no joke, Jerry."

"Can I tell the cops where you are?"

"Fine."

Silence again.

"I don't know what else to say, Ralph."

"You don't have to say anything. Just call my ex's lawyer, okay? Get him to have Ann pick up Eddie at Logan. Can you do that for me?" I told him I could. He thanked me, told me good-bye, and hung up. I immediately called Ann's lawyer and asked him to have her pick up Eddie at Logan in about an hour.

"Why?" he wanted to know. "What's up?"

"I can't tell you right now. Just do it, okay?"

When the ten minutes were up, I called LaGuardia security and explained the situation. They picked Ralph up right there in the Delta Shuttle area of the Marine Terminal. He was sitting on a bench, waiting. He's in prison for murder now, and will be for some time. The mom's sister has the baby.

ॐ

LOTS OF TIMES, A PARENT WILL JUST GRAB THE KIDS AND TAKE OFF, like Loretta tried to do. By now, I've had abductions to or from about half the other states. Usually, if it's the mom who makes a mad dash to what she thinks will be freedom, she'll head for a small town or an obscure part of some city. If she's smart, she takes another name, pays for everything in cash, and alters her social security number. It works best if she claims she's fleeing an abusive husband. That way she can hook up with a women's protection network that will, no questions asked, place her and the kids in a safe house where the dad will be unable to find her. Dads, by contrast, tend to go overseas, even though the laws against that are pretty severe. It's kidnapping, after all. Still, I've had abductions to or from Brazil, England, Israel, Hungary, Ireland, Egypt, and Singapore, along with several other countries.

One abduction sticks out in my mind because it didn't happen. It involved Ali, a major in the Israel Defense Forces and a man who specialized in the very spooky stuff that is the Israeli military's forte—like kidnapping Arafat's number two and smuggling him out of Palestine and into an Israeli army base. Ali organized that little project, led it, grabbed the man, and hustled him back to Israel for weeks of rather intense discussions about Arafat's ambitions. Ali had an American wife and a five-year-old son in Tel Aviv, but the marriage fell apart when she got involved with an American businessman. After the divorce, she took their son back with her and her boyfriend to Massachusetts, which is when I got into it. The major flew to Boston to meet me. Tough, leathery, he could have snapped me in two.

I felt a chill when he looked me dead in the eye and said, "I want my son back, Mr. Nissenbaum."

"Given what you do," I said, "I've got to ask. Why didn't you just grab him?"

"If I wanted to, I could do that," he told me with a slow nod of the head. "It would be very easy to arrange. Very. No problem at all. But it would hurt my son."

Right away, I loved that man. I so rarely hear such words. So few of my clients put their children's interests first. So we went to court and negotiated an agreement with his ex-wife whereby their son would stay in this country until he was ten, and then he would return to his father in Israel. The "out" parent would have the boy for all vacations. And that's what happened. The mother married her boyfriend, and she gave birth again, this time to a baby girl. So she had a daughter, and the father had a son. It seemed fair.

197

Then again, there are abductions and there are abductions. The following wasn't a literal snatch and go, but rather a matter of a mother, Jackie, winning custody and then enclosing her infant son in the heroin den she had made of her apartment. I was pretty sure that Jackie wasn't just using but selling too. To prove it, and thus spring the child, I turned to an ex-CIA agent with the unlikely name of Ernie Botchco to get the goods on her. This was the seventies, and in those days we didn't have hair or blood testing like today. You pretty much had to catch someone in the act. Ernie threw himself into it, and he tailed Jackie down from Boston to New York, where she got what had all the earmarks of being her weekly supply of heroin—plenty for her, and plenty more to deal. But he never saw her sell or shoot up. She was very crafty.

Ernie was patient. One night my client, Jackie's soon-to-be ex-husband, Roger, got a call that all hell had broken loose at Jackie's apartment. Roger dashed over there and found police cars and ambulances everywhere, his son in the arms of a police matron, and Jackie being led away in handcuffs. What the hell happened? Apparently, after making a buy, one of Jackie's customers had shot up in her bathroom and OD'd in there. Frantic, Jackie called 911 to report a possible drug overdose. Well, in Boston, if you call EMTs for drugs, the cops come too, and they're allowed to look around at anything in the open. I doubt Jackie knew that. But that was the sort of thing that Ernie knew.

Plenty of drugs were found. Enough to charge Jackie for possession with intent to distribute, and for Roger to get his kid back. He was as happy as happy could be. He had no further questions, but I did. Like, whatever happened to that guy who'd OD'd? He was taken by ambulance to the hospital, but the hospital had no record of treating him. Either that guy made an incredibly fast recovery, or he was never in trouble in the first place. Either way, the guy just walked out. Never even gave his name. Weird.

It had to be Ernie. He could easily have faked the OD—the spacing out, the gagging, the shakes. For him, it was no problem. And the scheme was perfect: the wife was outed as a junkie and a dealer, the cops took her away, and the kid was restored to the parent who would take proper care of him. A job well done, and no tracks.

ༀ

ANOTHER THING SPOUSES DO MOST OFTEN IS BADMOUTH THE OTHER parent to the children, to try to prejudice the kids against their mom or their dad. They'll talk about the other spouse as an incompetent, a loser, a misfit, an embarrassment. In these cases, it's almost as though the kid has become the judge, and the two parents are trying to win some favorable judgment. But of course none of this takes place in a courtroom, with evidence and precedent and law and all that. It's anything goes. And if it works to sway the kid, it works. The witnesses here are not available for cross-examination, and they are not under oath. All of this makes for a terrible tangle, and it can take forever to straighten it out. But that's my job.

Like with Zelda. She had inherited fifty-three million dollars. She was married to a guy, Phil, she did everything for. He was a seven-handicap golfer, but his father had been a circuit pro, and Phil dreamed of being another Arnold Palmer and showing up his dad. So she built him a five-hole golf course on their estate in western Massachusetts and hired a golf pro to work on his game practically full-time, and even travel about the country with him to try out all the courses in the pro tour, so Phil would be ready. A couple of years went by, and Phil never got much better, just more frustrated. His golf game, his life—everything sucked. But he decided the real problem was Zelda, and he demanded eight million dollars to walk away from her. She was sick of him too, and she figured it was worth the money just to get this loser out of her life. He pocketed the cash.

Actually, I thought $1.6 million a year for being married to Zelda wasn't bad pay. Zelda was intelligent and beautiful. But Phil wanted more. When Zelda refused, he worked on their kid as a way to get deeper into Zelda's pocketbook. He became Superdad, spending every minute with Jasper he could, and he had lots of minutes available because he wasn't working on his golf game anymore, or on anything else. He used much of that time to pour this anti-Mom venom into Jasper's ear. He complained that Zelda mistreated him, made him beg for money, and never let him feel like a man.

It came to a head, finally, when Zelda was having a party on a day that the court order said Jasper should have been at Phil's. Zelda ignored that it was Phil's day and kept Jasper overnight so he could attend her party. Zelda shouldn't have done that, but it wasn't a huge deal. Still, Phil made a big scene, and had his lawyer charged into court for sanctions. I countered with a motion to get Phil to stop bad-mouthing Zelda to Jasper. I knew perfectly well that there was no way to shut him up, but I wanted Phil to know that we knew what was going on. And I wanted to plant the notion in the judge's ear too, because he was the one who would hear the case. That case is still going on. I know this much: Phil will lose in court. No more time with Jasper and no more money. Zelda will pay all the same. And Jasper will be hurt.

Sadly, lies are the coin of the realm in the land of divorce. With some of my potential clients, I rely on a polygraph test to separate the truth from their fictions. With the other side, I am a demon on cross-examination, to catch the lie that blows the other side's case apart. It's always best to nail people with their own words. The parent said this to the cops, but is saying the opposite to the guardian ad litem. So my question: "Well, tell me: were you lying to the cops, or to the GAL?" Hard to answer that one.

But the thing is, there is always something big behind the lies, or people wouldn't work so hard to hide the truth. And some of the lies that families are built on can be explosive. Everything is in a fine balance, but when the truth comes out, the whole house of cards comes crashing down. Like with Alicia, the sweet-tempered mom who came to me sobbing because she'd found the diary of her daughter Janie, fifteen, the second-oldest of her four girls (tousled blondes, all of them). Alicia's hand shook as she handed me Janie's diary, bound in pink leather. "There," she said, pointing to where she'd placed a strip of paper as a bookmark. "Read that part." I flipped the book open. The page was covered with little-girl printing in blobby ballpoint pen.

"Dear Diary, I hope Daddy doesn't come tonight," I read out haltingly, because it was a little hard to make out all the words. "I'm going to tie the sheets in knots so he can't get at me. If he does, I'm going to pretend to be asleep. I hate it when he licks me, and puts his fingers up inside, and then climbs on top of me and pushes and pushes. I hate it! Hate it! Hate it! I tell him, No! Daddy! Don't! Please don't. But he does it anyway. Why does he do it? WHY?"

"That's your husband she's writing about?" I asked.

She nodded. A few tears started to fall.

"How long has this been going on?"

She shook her head. "But—"

She couldn't continue. She reached for a tissue to wipe her eyes.

"But what?" I prompted, gently. "Did your husband do something else?"

She nodded. Tears poured down her face.

"What, Alicia? What did he do?"

"Lauren."

"The oldest sister?"

"He did that to her too?"

She nodded. She swiped at her eyes again. "From—"

I waited.

"From behind."

I just looked at her, stunned. Then she grabbed more tissues, covered her face with her hands, and sobbed.

I copied the pages, and went straight to the judge here in Middlesex County, which includes Belmont, where Alicia lived. Horrified, the judge ordered the father out of the house. Now, how to keep the family going financially, since the mother didn't work? We were still working on that a few weeks later, when Alicia told me her husband, Travis, had come to the house with a big bouquet of flowers for her. She'd let him in, and he'd dropped down on his knees in front of her and begged her to please, please forgive him. He'd never do that again. Ever. Travis hugged her around the legs. He wept. He carried on. He pleaded with her. He couldn't stop crying.

Alicia took pity on him. And she took him back.

When she called to tell me that, I was appalled. "Alicia, listen to me," I said. "Anybody who does what this guy did is a monster, and I don't want him back in the house to prey on his daughters again, and I can't believe you do. I just can't."

"Jerry, I'm sorry, but I have made up my mind."

"Okay, go ahead," I told her. "But I'm not going to be a party to it. I'm not going to prepare any motion to lift the restraining order, as if everything is hunky-dory. It isn't okay. Not with me. Your husband's saying he's going to be a good boy isn't going to make him one. You get me?"

She didn't answer, which just made me more upset.

"If you're going to dismiss the case against him, you'll have to get another lawyer to do it. I'm done."

As a last word of advice, I told her to go into therapy, and send the girls too. Because if this ever goes back to trial, Travis was going to claim that she knew all about his behavior, and she did nothing about it. And that would make her just as guilty as he was. Then I hung up, hoping I was exaggerating.

For years, I never heard another word about it. But then, maybe eight years later, I heard that Dad was back at it. The older two daughters had gone off to college, but the younger ones were still in the house, and Travis had victimized them like the other girls before. This time, Alicia divorced him. The therapy did indeed establish that she knew about, but did not condone, what was going on.

Still, it was not a happy ending. By then, all four girls had all kinds of problems—bulimia, alcoholism, depression. They were all in intense therapy, and I couldn't imagine it would ever go right for them.

~

A SAD STORY, BUT A COMMON ONE, THAT TALE OF ALICIA AND TRAVIS. The wives may get restraining orders against their husbands one week, but as soon as the order is up, the husbands promise they'll change, they send flowers, they tell the kids they can have the dog they always wanted. They're back in the house, and next thing you know, they're abusers again. It's love—hate—love—hate, and lots of times it doesn't end until the kids are finally grown, and the wife finally realizes she doesn't need to protect the kids from the guy anymore, and she's out of there. She'll leave everything behind, she's so happy to be out. All the property, all the money. Good-bye. She's free, but just a few inches above the poverty line, and too often without much of a work history to fall back on.

With all the charges going back and forth, it's inevitable that the kids will get wind of the acrimony, even if unlike Alicia's kids they are not directly affected by the awful behavior themselves. Children know when divorce is in the air. Often they'll pick up on it before the parents do, the way certain animals can smell trouble from miles away. After all, their lives depend on their parents getting along. Once the breakup occurs, it's hell for them. Each side tries to win them over—being nicer than ever, while painting the other side as evil incarnate. It's wrenching for the kids to be in a tug-of-war like this, since each side is forcing them to choose which parent they love most. It's *Sophie's Choice* in reverse.

~

THESE CASES ARE OFTEN SO INVOLVED, I HAVE TO PULL IN ALMOST ALL the troops. Not just Stanley, Wendy, and Mindy, but my polygraph guy, Victor Lee; the former CIA operative, Ernie Botchco; and the private investigator I like to use, Ted McCallum. While not directly involved, Madeleine stays fully informed about all our cases and offers key opinions that I have learned it's wise to follow. I am usually up against quite an array as well—the opposing team of attorneys and their investigators in the *Spy vs. Spy* atmosphere of these cases of Mom versus Dad. Then there is that court-appointed in-home investigator, the guardian ad litem, and, once a trial starts, a range of expert witnesses on either side to back up one claim or another. Of course, the more professionals involved, the more complicated a case can become, as the professionals themselves can get sucked into the vortex of strong feelings that comes with a high-stakes custody fight.

I learned this early on, in late 1969, when I started representing Dr. Christine Francis, a nervous, wiry, late-thirties ophthalmologist with two kids, one just a toddler, when we first met. Her husband, Dr. Gregory Francis, was an engineer at MIT's Lincoln Laboratory. Nearly fifty, that Dr. Francis was brusque, confident, and celebrated for his work in the Apollo space program that had, just months before, placed an American on the moon. Totally mismatched in age, temperament, and status, the Francises had never gotten along, and were ready to murder each other by the time I came on the scene.

The moment I laid eyes on Gregory, I could see he was a problem. He had a tone of superiority that just naturally pissed you off. Then again, Christine was no day at the beach. Oversensitive to the point of lunacy, she might cry if you looked at her wrong. Still, she was the mom, and she'd spent a lot more time taking care of the kids than Gregory had, especially now that he was so preoccupied with the space program. I thought she should get the kids just on those merits. It also seemed clear to me that Gregory didn't really want them. He just wanted to keep Christine from getting them. He was mad that Christine had stood up to him by splitting. Well, he'd fix her.

Gregory was represented by Cameron Durant, a talented divorce lawyer who was also a big believer in men's rights. He was counsel for an organization called Fathers United Against Injustice that pushed to get better treatment for men in divorce cases just like this one. As I've said, I don't agree with the idea that men routinely get screwed in divorce, although a lot of men think so these days. Not if you look at it from the kids' point of view, which should be the only one that counts. Kids have an interest in keeping things even between the parents, even if that means one parent paying a lot of child support to the other. And it makes sense that mothers usually end up as the primary guardians, because that was usually their role in the marriage. So for continuity's sake, that arrangement should continue during and after the divorce.

To help sort out the situation with the Francises' kids, the judge appointed a GAL to investigate the kids' home life and see how the kids were treated by each parent—who spent more time with them, what the emotional atmosphere was, and all of that. It took a few months, but the GAL finally came back with a long report, and the short of it was that Christine was too frail emotionally to handle the kids. I was floored. That was way off, and even if it wasn't, it wasn't like the father would be any better. It troubled me that the GAL was not a psychologist—he was a lawyer, like many GALs—yet he was offering this psychological evaluation that was very damaging to my client. Even worse, when that report was introduced as evidence at trial, the judge did not allow me to cross-examine the guardian who'd produced it. That was ridiculous.

I told the judge it was unconstitutional not to allow my client to confront her accuser, which is really what the GAL was. It's right there in the Bill of Rights. But the judge said no soap. "Take it upstairs," he told me, which is lawyer talk for pursuing it in the appeals court, which would be costly and time-consuming and, at best, would win us only the right to go through this whole circus before the very same judge again, and in the meantime Christine wouldn't have the kids. So that was bad. Christine was starting to get nervous, and so was I.

In April 1970, in the middle of the trial, the *Apollo 13* moon shot went up—the one that inspired the movie of that name. Disaster nearly struck when an oxygen tank blew out, and Commander Lovell radioed the famous words, "Houston, we've had a problem." Well, we had a problem down on earth too. Gregory had to rush back to Lincoln Lab to do what he could to rescue the astronauts. Supposedly, it was Gregory's idea to use the space module's thrusters to swing the main capsule once around the moon and then slingshot it back to earth. Other people were probably in on that decision, but Gregory wasn't the kind of guy to share credit. The judge bought it, which was all that mattered. To him, Gregory was a big American hero. And that was big trouble for us.

Still, even given all that, I'm pretty sure I could have won the case if it wasn't for the expert witness that Durant, the opposing counsel, hired to back up the GAL and testify to my client's deficiencies as a parent. The man's name was Dr. Jason Gill, and he was the chief of psychiatry at Ross Sanitarium in nearby Winchester. Stocky and assertive, he got up on the witness stand and, in tones of utter authority, questioned my client's sanity, suggesting she was a paranoid schizophrenic. It didn't seem to matter that he'd never even met Christine, let alone sat her down for a proper psychiatric interview. Instead, he'd relied solely on a transcript of her deposition, which is a little like diagnosing me on the basis of this book. This was worse than the GAL nonsense. The deck was totally stacked against my client. "Maybe you could diagnose me on that basis," I joked, trying to take the edge off my irritation, "but not her."

He didn't laugh. Nor did the judge.

When I first learned that Gill would testify, something started to bother me. His name sounded familiar. Jason Gill. I rolled the name around in my head. Something to do with a divorce maybe? *His* divorce—could that be it? How could I know anything about his divorce? Was it in the newspapers? It wasn't much to go on, but I've learned to trust these recollections. Bad as I am at other things, I still have a sharp memory.

This was long before a Google search would have given me the answer in a nanosecond. Back then, you had to hunt. Physically hunt.

On a hunch the next morning, I drove to Salem and paid a visit to the probate court, where I checked the divorce files in the second floor office. They're public records, open to all, unless one of the parties of the divorce has them sealed. (Which is why I usually counsel my prominent clients to do just that—no point leaving them open for just anyone to rifle through.)

Bingo! The Gill file was right there. And it filled a whole box.

It turned out that Dr. Jason Gill had indeed been divorced—from the former Barbara Neal, his wife of fourteen years, back in March of 1964. Each side had demanded primary custody of their seven-year-old son, Peter, and twelve-year-old daughter, Suzanne, known as Susie. It all came back to me as I read, all the grisly details. Gill had lost the custody case, but a related file told the rest of the story. Two years later, in 1966, Susie was coming out of a local store, where she'd picked up some milk for her mother. She gaily dashed back across the street to her mother's car. She hadn't seen the sedan speeding toward her through the red light. It struck her just as she reached the car, knocked her twenty feet down the street. An ambulance rushed her to the hospital. As soon as he got word, Gill raced to her bedside, where his ex-wife and son were waiting, terrified. The impact had cracked Susie's skull, broken a leg, and demolished several ribs; it had crushed several organs and caused other massive internal injuries and severe hemorrhaging. She was in terrible, terrible shape, but there was nothing the doctors could do. Gill pulled the child up off the hospital bed to comfort her one last time. She died in his arms.

Gill couldn't bear it, and I can't blame him. He took six months off work to pull himself together. After he returned to his practice, he went back to court to seek a modification of the original order in his divorce case, trying to gain custody of Peter, because he was convinced that Barbara was patently unfit as a mother. She had to be if she could let such a thing happen to Susie, he insisted. The court ruled against him. She was not to blame for the accident. In his anger and his grief, he stopped paying child support.

When Barbara brought the matter to the attention of the court, the judge said he'd find Gill in contempt if he didn't pay within a month.

He didn't.

Back in court again, the judge gave Gill one more chance.

He still didn't pay.

So Gill was sentenced to six months in jail. "The key to your freedom is in your pocket," the judge told Gill at the sentencing. "If you pay what you owe, you'll go free. If you don't, you'll stay there."

Gill still didn't pay. After five months in jail, the judge relented and released Gill after all, figuring he'd never give in.

Gill never got over his outrage—at his wife, the court system regarding the divorce, the justice system regarding custody and child support. All if it. He became an expert witness for Fathers United Against Injustice, testifying for aggrieved men all over the country in their custody fights, pretty much regardless of the particulars of the cases. That's how Durant found him.

So this was the guy who was killing us.

The afternoon that Gill was due to resume his trial testimony, I spotted him chatting with Durant in the hall outside the courtroom. So I approached them and asked Durant if I could ask Dr. Gill a question.

"Why not," Durant replied genially.

I turned to his client. "So, Dr. Gill," I began. "By any chance did you ever have a daughter named Susie?"

It was like I'd shot him. He went white, and I thought he'd collapse. "Don't talk to me!" he shouted, and put his arms up as if to shield himself from me. "Don't you fucking talk to me." Then he retreated into the courtroom.

Durant immediately went to the judge and asked him to meet with us for a conference in the judge's chambers. There, Durant complained that I'd asked Gill "an improper question."

"But that's silly," I shot back. "You were right there! And besides, there was nothing improper about my question. Under the circumstances, it was completely germane, and totally reasonable."

The judge, of course, had no idea what we were talking about. I quickly filled him in on Gill, explaining how the family tragedy in his background might lie behind his attitudes. "This is about his possible prejudice," I said. "It is completely relevant to this case."

The judge thought for a bit and decided he had no problem with my question. The trial resumed, and Durant put Gill back on the stand. When I had him on cross, I produced material that I'd previously shown the judge in his chambers—the full record of his own court case and of all the cases in which Gill had served as an expert witness. That established, I asked him the question he must have feared more than any other.

"Are you the father of a girl named Susie?"

He reared up and screamed, "You dirty rotten son of a bitch!"

The judge whipped his head around, and the stenographer stared.

Then Gill started to sob. Just broke down, his shoulders heaving. He could scarcely draw breath. I'd never seen anything like it. So the judge called a recess. When we picked up again, I figured I'd made my point about his daughter and that anything more from me would seem cruel.

Instead, I led Gill through his history as an expert witness for the last couple of years and asked him if he had ever found that, in his professional opinion, the woman was qualified to be the sole custodial parent.

"No," he admitted. "I haven't."

"Not once?" I asked. "Not a single time?"

"Not that I recall."

I left it there, and let the judge draw his own conclusions. I thought I had done a good job discrediting him, which was big, since Dr. Gregory Francis's whole case rested on it, but Christine wasn't convinced. "You don't know Gregory," she kept telling me. "He always gets his way."

And she was right. There was no way that the judge was going to deprive an authentic American hero of his kids.

Within two hours of the judgment, Gregory was pounding at Christine's door with a constable and several cops, demanding she hand over the kids. Right now. When she refused to open the door, Gregory said the house was still half his, and directed the constable to retrieve an ax from his car, which he had brought along for just such a contingency. Then Gregory laid waste to the door, reached in, and unlocked it while Christine cowered in an upstairs bedroom, the children huddled around her. Gregory ordered the children to come to him, which they did reluctantly, terrified of what might happen if they didn't. He put a hand on the back of the older girl, scooped up the toddler, and marched them both back to the constable's van.

I was flabbergasted when I heard that. Why the constable? Why the *ax*? It took a judge to order that, and I couldn't believe our judge did that in this case.

It turned out that it was all Durant's doing. He was still smarting from my confrontation with Gill and figured I was still smoldering too. When he saw me leave the courthouse looking angry about the judge's decision, he assumed I was going to tell my client to flee with the kids, or she'd never see them again. He told the judge of his suspicions, and the judge ordered this preemptive strike.

I was furious, but there was nothing I could do. The judge overruled my emergency motion to return the children to Christine, and he didn't appreciate the rather earnest tone I used with him when we discussed it.

With that, Christine lost all confidence in me, and I don't blame her. I'd failed. She turned to Monroe Inker to handle the appeal. I was still the new kid coming up, and he was much more established, so he didn't have any compunctions about taking all my work on the case—my briefs, my records, my everything—to get the judgment reversed and win the kids back for Christine, without ever giving me a drop of credit. That was not Monroe's way. Once again, anything good that happened, he was responsible. Anything bad, it was on somebody else. Well, that reversal was only good until there was a new trial. In the meantime, the judge left custody as it was, not wanting to disrupt the children's lives any more than he had to. Now Gregory was the primary caretaker, so the consistency factor cut his way, and Christine saw her kids only on alternate weekends, just like before. So it wasn't that much of a win for Monroe. And this time, when Monroe waged the real case, he used his own strategy, his own evidence—and he lost just like I did. Because now the status quo argument worked for Gregory. Christine was devastated. Monroe wasn't one to let on about his feelings. Few lawyers are. But I am sure that he was plenty upset too.

Coda: Flash forward three more years, and I was in the judge's courthouse on another case, and this time he summoned me back into his chambers. He sat me down in a chair by his desk, and he told me something had been nagging him for a while now.

"What's that, Judge?" I asked.

"That Francis case. I need to apologize to you for what I did."

I let that sit there for a bit. Judges rarely apologize, because they almost never think they've made a mistake. "And why's that?"

"It bothers me," he went on.

"What does, Your Honor?" Quite honestly, there were plenty of possibilities to choose from. The decision regarding the GAL, the weight given to that crazy doctor's testimony, the order allowing the seizure of the kids—those were three that popped immediately to mind.

I could tell he was wrestling with something even now.

"I was too enamored of the husband in the case. I cut him too much slack."

"Dr. Gregory Francis, you mean?"

"Yes, Dr. Francis." He sighed. "He got those astronauts down."

"That he did," I said. "Or people say he did. But then, they're not sworn in."

He chuckled softly. "She was crazy. Paranoid."

"Maybe."

"But he was even crazier! I shouldn't have let that Dr. Gill persuade me otherwise. I saw how Dr. Francis was in the courtroom. Crazy. Totally high-handed, imperious. He was the worse parent. The children belonged with her."

"Well, thank you, Your Honor. I think you are right about that. The case has bothered me too. I keep wondering what I could have done to get a different outcome."

"You could have pulled a different judge." He had a twinkle in his eye as he said it.

That was gratifying, but it didn't change anything.

I still lost the case, and Christine never did get her kids back.

CHAPTER
TEN

PERSONALLY, I THINK CHILDREN SHOULD BE RAISED BY BOTH parents, if at all possible. I was raised that way, and it was a good thing to have my mother there as something of an antidote to my father, and vice versa. I am glad that Madeline and I are together to raise our two sons and our daughter, and I regret I couldn't hang in with my first wife to fully raise the first two boys together in the same house. Just as it takes a couple to conceive a child, I think it takes a couple to raise one, whether they are living together or not. I'm a big believer in joint custody, which is the rule in most of the Western world. But sadly that doesn't stop the fighting over which parent has physical custody over them. Wherever they occur, custody fights for mercenary reasons are an embarrassment. It is not just what I call the monetization of the child, but it's all the lies, the blatant disregard of the child's interests, and the pollution of the family atmosphere with the broadcasting of perversions that go along with it.

It makes for some gruesome stories, no question. Nobody ever shies away from hearing them. In all the time that I have been doing this work, nobody has ever said to me, don't tell me what happened in that custody case. Please, change the subject. No, these tales have a grotesque allure, probably because they're so human. They can be soap operas for sure. But they can also be the real opera I love in New York, with the thick, meaty chords from the orchestra, and the baritones and divas all singing their hearts out about love and betrayal, as the audience listens in rapture.

By now, I've handled hundreds of custody fights. Most of them demonstrate just one or two aspects of the full range of issues involved—the money aspect, the bad-mouthing of one spouse or the other, or the threat of kidnapping, to name just a few. Or if they do have more, they just touch on them; they don't really sound the note with full brass. A few custody fights, however, strike all the chords, and one that did in full, thundering fortissimo, was the Weber case. For my client, Hans, it was the perfect storm. His wife, Delores, was trying to bankrupt him, steal his children, destroy his business, wreck his reputation, and ruin his life. Can't get much more extreme than that.

I didn't come into the Weber case until the story had already played out on three continents—in Hong Kong, Berlin, and the quiet, inland town of Hopkinton, Rhode Island. Its near-global scope, and its pivot point here in Little Rhodey, the smallest state in the union, were apt. For all custody fights amount to a world war over a tiny prize—although, of course, the prize is anything but tiny to the combatants. In this case, it was a couple of freckle-faced towheads, Wolfgang and Jacob, who were ten and seven by the time I met them. By then, they seemed much older than their ages, like the doughboys who go off to war fresh faced and enthusiastic and come back with their faces lined with worry and fatigue, their shoulders slumped. The two boys didn't have the energy I expected of kids, they rarely smiled, they had trouble sleeping, and they had both developed nervous twitches around their eyes.

From the moment I got into the case, I was pretty sure the mother, the former Delores Sanchez, was nuts. But it was a canny sort of nuts that to the uninitiated could easily be mistaken for rationality. She was a Rhode Islander by birth, a child of Spanish immigrants, and she had the wild emotional intensity that I associate with Spaniards. She'd moved to Berlin to marry Hans, and it was there that their sons were born and raised. By January of 2007, when I came to the case, she'd scooped up the kids and fled to Rhode Island. That was after she found out that Hans had done something she considered unspeakably awful, something she had to protect the boys from at all costs. He'd taken graphic, close-up pictures of their genitals. More than that, Delores claimed Hans had woken the boys up to take such pictures, and then put the pictures up on the Internet.

People talk about the fog of war—that heavy cloud that descends over battle scenes and keeps everybody from seeing what is going on. A similar fog settles over custody fights. There are so many charges and counter-charges going back and forth that, after a while, it gets hard to figure out the truth of the matter. People will say just about anything to keep their kids or to get them back. Some of it may be true, or all of it, or none of it. But in this case there were pictures, and some were pretty explicit.

I didn't meet Hans Weber until he'd taken a leave from his job and moved into a Holiday Inn in Providence to deal with the court case over the fate of his boys. I had experience with international cases of this sort, as he could see from my Web site, and he decided that I was the best lawyer for him. To persuade me to take the case, he drove up to see me in my office in Boston.

I had no idea what to expect. I had never represented a client I knew to be a child abuser, and never would, but I have seen plenty of them on the other side, enough to know that most are surprisingly mild and pleasant. It's usually only when you touch on what they've done that they reveal themselves, either by turning defensive or unnaturally withdrawn. This made it difficult to evaluate Hans. If he seemed normal, did that mean he was? He was obviously under enormous stress, having just flown in from Germany under the darkest imaginable suspicions for a parent, and was now forbidden to see his kids except under close supervision by court-sanctioned personnel. Plus, he was stuck in the same dreary hotel for days on end. Still, I was relieved when Mindy reported from the reception desk that he'd greeted her good-naturedly and was now idly flipping through magazines in the reception area.

"He seems fine," Mindy whispered into the phone.

"I hope you're right."

"I'm always right," Mindy replied, matter-of-factly.

When I came out to greet him, I found a tall, thickset man in his late thirties, with a full head of hair and a broad smile, although the strain was visible around his eyes.

"It is very good to meet you, Mr. Nissenbaum." His English was clear, but accented.

"Please—call me Jerry." I shook his hand.

"Then you must call me Hans."

"Happy to." I smiled. "Hans."

At the risk of cultural stereotyping, I'll say that I've generally found Germans to be a precise, logical, orderly people. And Hans had the manner of the cool executive, one who is accustomed to maintaining order amid chaos. But there was also a hardness to him, and I had to wonder what was contained inside. I ushered him into my conference room, where I had him sit beside me, so I could observe all his body language.

He handed me the narrative I always ask for. His version laid out the story chronologically, incident by incident, each one with a date, like a medical history or a time line. I flipped through it quickly, and would return to it later. The account proved to be quite dry, as if it had all happened to somebody else. In fact, Hans referred to himself in the third person throughout, except when he slipped up and used I. Most innocent men, under such circumstances, express outrage that they should be so abused by their wives. Hans wasn't the least bit emotional about it. He never once expressed pity for himself or anger at Delores. Rather, he was fatalistic. He later told me with a shrug, "Delores simply does what she does, Jerry. I don't know why." It wasn't much of a defense.

I thanked him for the narrative and set it down on the table.

"So how can I help you?" I asked.

"I'm here to get my boys back," he began. He started to offer some of the details of the court case that he was facing, but I asked him to start at the beginning. For the next two or three hours, he told me the story of the marriage that had led him to me. It was a bright afternoon when he started, and the evening sky was streaked by a rose sunset by the time he left. Hans scarcely moved the whole time, except to sweep his hair back off his forehead.

He was a senior executive at a company based in Berlin, which sold high-quality optical equipment; the firm had been started by his grandfather and passed down through the family. He handled the North American operations and was frequently in Atlanta, Georgia, the site of the company's U.S. headquarters. That's where he had perfected his English. "Delores always thought I was some kind of German aristocrat," he said with a quiet laugh. "I think she found that appealing. Sadly for her, I am not."

Delores's mother was an elementary school teacher, her father a postal clerk, and she had a number of brothers and sisters. It was a big step for her to go to a fashion institute in New York and become a fashion designer. She had a nice figure, and wore clothes that showed it off.

They met in Hong Kong in 1988. Hans was in his early thirties, and Delores was six years younger. Both were single. She was there for a fashion convention, he for a scientific conference. But they were staying at the same hotel, and they bumped into each other one morning over the breakfast buffet. She spilled some orange juice, and he helped her mop it up. They sat together that morning, and the rest of the mornings, and they spent the last night together in his room. Delores found him fascinating, all the more so once a girlfriend filled her in on the Webers' family business. "She told me later that the friend told her that if she could land me, she'd be set for life. Delores was very matter-of-fact about it." From that point on, the relationship came on like a whirlwind. When the conference was over a week later, Delores invited Hans to go back with her to her place in New York on the Upper East Side.

The differences in their backgrounds were stark—in class, nationality, and profession. So the sex must have been pretty hot, although I never asked Hans about it. Still, there were warning signs. "When we were in New York, she had another boyfriend besides me," Hans told me. "And she spent nights with him sometimes. I should have left, right then. I'd never be here now." Delores had problems developing a career. She'd managed to talk her way into design jobs largely on the strength of her physique, but they never lasted. I asked why. "Because she had a temper. Anyone who knows her would tell you that. I should have paid attention to that too." Twice she got fired for blowing up at her boss, just losing it.

Meanwhile, Hans was diligently bringing the family optics business into the American market. He created the U.S. headquarters in Atlanta, and Delores moved in with him. She landed a design job there, then lost it after making another scene.

"That didn't scare you off?" I asked, amazed that he could have just let all this go.

"I loved her, Jerry. We had some great times together. And I always figured she didn't really mean it. She just couldn't control herself sometimes."

After that, Delores gave up on gainful employment and devoted herself to studying German. Hans was flattered. She was committing herself to a life with him.

"But why would you commit to *her*?" I couldn't get over it. As he described her, Delores had warning labels all over her.

"I like Americans. I like how confident they are. They're brassy."

And he still liked her even when her behavior turned what I would call criminal. Like when she'd sneak into fashion shows with phony press credentials to illegally photograph some new fashion and then send pictures of the patterns to some American clients who had even fewer scruples than she did. It wasn't really a business, more like organized crime. But Hans didn't mind. Brassy. Besides, she wasn't stealing from him.

A year after they moved to Berlin, he asked her to marry him. They were in a restaurant, and he gave her a ring. She squealed with excitement, disturbing the other diners. Before any marriage, though, Hans insisted she sign a premarital agreement that would waive all her claims to Hans's portion of the value of his family's business. With the firm worth well over fifty million dollars, it was his only significant holding. "Of course, it's not really mine," he told me. "I won't get it until my father and two of my uncles die." For legal purposes, that made the value of his future interest too speculative to value. If Hans were to die before his father and his uncles, he would never get his share. Besides, they'd never allow him to put any possible share of the firm at risk by letting Delores take it in a divorce. "They were very insistent I get a premarital agreement," he said.

That didn't sit well with Delores. "She felt I was holding out on her." She hired some lawyers in Germany and in Rhode Island to bang away at the agreement, trying to win her a chunk. Hans had to hire lawyers in Berlin to keep her from getting anything. Documents flew back and forth, translated from German to English and back again. Delores pushed and pushed, but she was up against a deadline—the wedding date itself—which was fast approaching.

"I worried, yes," he said, anticipating my question. "But I thought that if we could just push this issue behind us, we would be okay. We would have children; we could begin a nice life."

Finally, Delores relented. Just a week before she was to march down the aisle, she realized her cause was hopeless. She signed off on the document, surrendering all claim to his family business. Hans sensed she was not very happy at their wedding.

A year later, Wolfgang—known as Wolfie—was born, and Jacob

followed three years after that. Forceful as she might have been with her bosses, Delores proved to be a nervous, flighty mother. "It started to get absurd," Hans said. "Even if I was in Atlanta, she'd call me up all hysterical because one of the boys had scratched a shin or something. It might be three in the morning for me. Didn't matter." And when he was home, she'd hand the boys over to Hans for much of the weekend so she could go shopping with her girlfriends, get her nails done, and have a few drinks.

He'd been talking for almost two hours, and I thought he might like to take a break for some tea or coffee, but he waved that off and, after a couple of deep breaths, continued on with his tale. His portrait of Delores continued to darken. If before there had been some bright spots, now a blackness pervaded. People can get consumed with some dark emotion—anger, bitterness—and that becomes all they are. At this point I knew her only through Hans, and the real Delores might be very different. His version seemed pretty awful.

Hans skipped ahead a few years to when the boys were five and two. It can be hard to handle two toddlers, especially when one of them is in the terrible twos, alternately fussing and raging, and the other is trying to start acting grown up. But as Hans told it, Delores was the only one who was acting childish. "I started to be afraid sometimes," he said.

"Of?"

"Of her. Of what she might do."

"What do you mean?"

"I was afraid she might hurt them. I really was. She could be very mean, Jerry. You have no idea. The smallest thing, she'd be on them, almost screaming, and she'd slap them, hard, till they cried. Not Jacob so much. He was still in diapers. With Wolfie, she'd yank down his trousers and smack him. He'd try to bite down, but he'd soon start to wail, and that would set Jacob off, and that made Delores all the angrier. Wolfie took it hard, poor guy. He thought it was all his fault, something he'd done. I once found him banging his chest with his fist and saying he was 'bad, bad, bad.'

"She was hard on me too. She complained about everything—the dirty dishes, the street noise, anything. But I just assumed she was depressed, lonely. She was overwhelmed being a mother of two little boys that were always getting into everything. It was just a bad time for her. I figured if I could just wait it out, she'd calm down."

Well, she didn't. Her anger only built—at the boys, at Hans, at Germany, everything. Hans and Delores retreated to separate rooms in the big house they rented, hoping the distance would do them good, but it just made things worse. They stopped having sex, which didn't help either. They tried seeing a marriage counselor, only to resume the same fights in front of her, so they quit after a few sessions. The conflict was starting to eat at Hans, and he knew it was hard on the children too. The boys had started developing some of the nervous tics that would become more pronounced later. Delores's behavior was rough even on her friends. She'd driven most of them away. Now when she went shopping, she went alone.

"I could not take it anymore. And I knew the boys couldn't either."

In most states, here in the United States, you can get an uncontested divorce in a matter of months if everything breaks right for you. In Germany, the first step is to give the other party formal written notice of your intent to file for divorce. Then have to wait a full year before you can do the actual filing. Such a cooldown period may sound like a good idea, since a lot of people get divorced in a burst of anger and then regret it later. But it can also drag out a marriage that has gone terribly and permanently bad.

When Hans delivered the formal notice of his intent to divorce Delores, he did it in person, handing her a letter. She just lost it, and, done with him and his household, she packed up in a screaming fury. "I was sure she was going to hit me," he said. But she didn't, just shrieked at him while the boys cowered in the corner. She rented a place in a big apartment building a full hour away from the boys' school. Hans found a nice little house with a garden that was just a fifteen-minute walk away.

☙

THINGS WERE OKAY AT FIRST. HANS AND DELORES WORKED OUT A deal whereby the boys would live with Delores when Hans was in the United States, overseeing operations there, which was about half the time. Otherwise, they'd be with Hans. It was all surprisingly smooth and reasonable—until Delores started brooding about money, chiefly about how much money Hans had, and how much more she wanted. That prenup started driving her crazy. She should never have signed it. It was going to ruin her! It was outrageous! She hired a succession of lawyers to look into it. Each of them tried to persuade her that she had no case, so she fired them all, one after another.

She decided to take matters into her own hands. One day, she paid Hans a surprise visit at his little house. Just saying hello, she said. But she'd concealed a miniature tape recorder in her purse. She hoped to lure Hans into saying something, anything, that would weaken the prenup. But Hans could see the recorder's little microphone poking out of her bag. As soon as she worked the conversation around to the prenup, Hans leaned down and spoke directly into the mike.

"You know, Delores, tapes like this aren't admissible in court," he said. "So you might as well stop trying to be James Bond."

She stalked off, furious. Then she seized a twenty-thousand-euro investment fund—worth about twenty-five thousand dollars at the time—that had been set up for the children and placed it under her name. To get even more, she'd call Hans up and threaten to take the boys to the United States forever if he didn't pay. "She was acting so crazy," he told me. "I was really afraid she might do that." So he started writing checks. Ten thousand euros, fifteen thousand, whatever it took to assuage her, month after month. I'd have told him: for God's sake, don't. Don't pay anything, or you'll just have to pay more. It was ransom to a potential kidnapper; he felt he had no choice but to write those checks. By the time he finally stopped, six months later, he'd shelled out one hundred fifty thousand euros—all the money he'd set aside to buy a house someday. Now he was tapped out.

In October, Delores went with one of her few remaining girlfriends to a raunchy bar outside Berlin and got so hammered she could hardly drive home. Seeing her weaving all over the road, cops pulled her over and gave her a Breathalyzer test. Her blood was practically all booze. She lost her driver's license for seven months, which was lucky. It could have been a lot longer.

"But you know what?" Hans said. "She blamed *me*! She said I'd followed her, had the waitress give her too much booze, and then called the police when she left for her car. They'd never have caught her otherwise."

"Are you saying she was paranoid?" I asked.

"That's one word for it, yes."

After Delores lost her license, Hans pleaded with her to economize by taking the train. But no, she took taxis everywhere, despite the cost. She was sure Hans was good for it. "And if I wasn't—so much the better, since she figured the court would force me to pay it anyway. She figured I was—what do you say? Made of money? Yes, that is what she thought. And if all else failed, she could always threaten to cut back on my time with the boys. She knew I would do anything to avoid that."

Even here, when discussing his boys, I was expecting at least a flicker of emotion, but Hans remained a rock. In such a situation, it is nearly impossible to maintain complete emotional control. It is too trying. It is your children, which means it's your heart, your lineage, your future. As he gazed at me from his chair, every word he spoke was to the point, and none of them revealed how the story affected him.

"She was determined to get some dirt on me," he went on. "She needed leverage."

She broke into Hans's apartment and found a Geneva hotel bill showing that he had spent a night there with a woman. "I was entitled," Hans explained. "This was well after we'd separated." But no matter. When she got home, Delores waved the receipt in the kids' faces, telling them to look, *look* at what a bastard their father was. He was leaving them for another woman! "She said they'd definitely move back to the States now," Hans said in a monotone. "Their father obviously didn't care about them anymore." She also found a pornographic DVD, which she waved in the boys' faces too, to show them how depraved their father was. "Look what he watches," she'd hissed. "It's disgusting."

It is a tradition in Germany for well-to-do parents to take their school-age children off to the Alps for a midwinter holiday called Ski Week. Hans had spent months planning a trip with the boys to three different Austrian resorts. On the day of their departure, he arrived at Delores's to pick up the boys as planned. "There was no sign of them." He let himself in and looked around. "To be honest, I was afraid of what I might find there. At this point, I really did not know what Delores might do."

"You thought she might harm them?"

He shrugged. "I just didn't know."

Delores was not a tidy housekeeper, and the house was a mess. He sat down in the living room and flipped on the television to wait. Finally, at eight or nine o'clock in the evening, he heard the rumble of an engine coming into the parking lot. Hans rushed outside just as Delores and the kids emerged from the car in the driveway. Delores looked astonished to see him. "What are you doing here?" she asked, drawing the boys near her to keep Hans from taking them.

"We need to stick to my vacation plan, Delores," Hans said evenly. "I have all the hotel reservations. I'm going to take the boys with me for Ski Week, and that's all there is to it."

Delores did not back down. "No, you're not." She clamped down on the kids, who squirmed at being squeezed so hard.

"Yes, I am," Hans insisted, and he reached for Wolfie's hand.

I could easily picture this scene. The parents might as well be a pair of dogs pulling on a bone, each trying to wrest it from the other. This was a custody fight. This was all custody fights. One child, and two parents pulling him apart.

"Fuck you!" Delores screamed. She finally let go of Wolfie and then grabbed onto Hans's hair and tugged it hard.

"Delores!" Hans screamed, from surprise and pain.

The two of them glared at each other, Hans from a strange angle as she pulled him down.

It was young Jacob, just four, who broke the impasse. "Stop that, Mummy! Please. You shouldn't do that. You'll hurt him." He tried to reach up to her arm, but he was too short to do anything more than slap his hand against her chest. "Daddy's right. His plan is fair. Ski Week is for him. Easter is for you."

Delores turned to the boy and froze for a moment.

"It was like she couldn't believe that little Jacob had said that," Hans said. "She let go of my hair and ran into the house to call her lawyer. That was her usual response to a situation like that. That was my opportunity."

Seeing her go, Hans grabbed the boys' jackets, packed their things into his car, and started it up. But he couldn't get away before Delores ran into his path, all lit up in his headlights. Then she charged at him, and slapped a piece of paper down on the windshield.

"Sign it!" she shouted.

"What is it?" Hans asked.

She peeled it back off the windshield and held it like a rag. "It's a promise to return the boys by this Sunday."

"Okay, fine." Hans rolled down the window; took it from her, along with a pen; scribbled his assent; and handed it back. And they were finally off.

"My pulse was really racing," Hans told me. "To do all that in front of the children. I mean—can you imagine?" He just shook his head.

The ski trip was great. The hotels all had fabulous views of the Alps, the sun shone every day, and the skiing was sensational. The only problem was that Delores bombarded Hans's cell a half-dozen times a day for updates on the boys' condition, demanding to talk to them to make sure everything was all right.

"They're fine, Delores," Hans would reassure her. "I'm here. I'm their father. I'm looking out for them. Please remember, they're my sons too." That did not mollify her, and as the days went along, the calls increased. Eight, ten, twelve times a day. Sometimes more. He answered fewer and fewer of them, and passed the cell on to the boys even less.

He was driving back from the slopes on a narrow, twisting road through the mountains when his cell rang again.

Before me now, Hans tensed and clasped his hands, then ground them together as if he might crush a walnut between them. Then he continued. "I figured this was another call from Delores. But it was from my lawyer, Katrina Menzner. This was strange. She almost never called. She said, 'Hans, we received a letter from Delores's attorney.'

"I didn't like the sound of her voice," he told me. "I said, 'Okay,' and she said there were two photographs clipped to it. She sounded very disturbed. 'They're of your children, Hans. They're horrible. One of them is of the boys eating off the floor, and their hands are tied behind their backs.'"

Speaking to me now, Hans paused.

"How did you react?" I asked him.

"Why, I—I felt sick."

"Did you know what she was talking about?"

"Well, yes. I did, sure."

"Did you take the picture?"

He didn't hesitate. "Yes, I took it. But I never imagined that anyone could use such a picture against me. It was innocent. Playful."

"Eating off the floor?"

"Okay, it might sound strange." He ran his hand through his hair. "But they were just pretending to be dogs. It was no big deal. Really."

"Okay, so what did you tell the lawyer?"

"I had to pull off the road. Truly, I was afraid I might faint. Then she told me about the other one."

"And what was that?"

"The other one is of the boys—" He paused. "Naked, showing off their—their genitals for the camera."

The scene reminded me of all the other scenes just like it that I had encountered through the years. Not the scene depicted in the photograph. The scene in which one or more parties to a divorce case are forced to defend themselves. It's the time when the air war has begun, and the bombs are going off everywhere, and shrapnel is flying, and you don't know who or what is going to be blasted next.

Hans continued his story. In the car on that mountain pass, he felt like he was having trouble breathing. He cracked the window open, tried to take deep breaths.

"The claim is that these were taken with your camera," the divorce lawyer asked. "Is that true?"

"Yes."

"Well, I don't have to tell you that these pictures will cause us some difficulties."

"What is it, Papa?" Wolfgang asked from the passenger seat. "What's wrong?"

"Nothing. I'm just going to get a little air." He stepped out of the car to continue the conversation with his lawyer, pacing along the side of the road.

"She sent that?" Hans asked.

His lawyer said that she had.

"I can't believe it. I can't believe she did that. How could she do that? What a *bitch*!"

"You need to focus, Hans."

He could scarcely hear over the sound of his own breathing.

"There's one more thing."

"And what's that?"

"She's going to the police with these. Or threatening to, anyway."

"Fuck!"

"And—"

"And what?"

"She has filed for sole custody."

"But she can't do that!"

"Actually, she can. She is within her rights. We can fight it, Hans, and we will. But she can."

෨෦

IN GERMANY, AS IN MOST COUNTRIES, THE PRESUMPTION IS THAT A divorcing couple will receive joint custody. Sole custody is reserved for cases of extreme danger to the children, with abuse as the standard charge. And that's what Delores was alleging: emotional abuse.

Hans's heart was pounding when he closed out the call, and he had to walk a bit more along the roadside before he could bring himself to climb back into the car.

Still, the boys could tell that something had happened.

"What's the matter, Papa? Is everything all right?"

"It's fine. Everything is fine." He reached back and rubbed their tousled heads. He wondered how often he'd be able to do that in the future.

෨෦

SO THAT WAS THE CRUX OF IT—THE PICTURES. CUSTODY CASES CAN be like murder cases, in that they turn on a single piece of evidence. Yes, there is often a welter of supporting detail, but a single act can be definitive. Did the mother strike her toddler with a hairbrush? Did the father allow his daughter to drive on the highway when she was eleven? Here, though, there was a complication, for the issue wasn't about whether the act had occurred. There was no doubt it had. The question was what it meant. Was it a case of perversion, as Delores alleged, or just a bunch of harmless fun, as Hans insisted?

It turned out that there were several dozen photographs, with the offending ones intermixed with the usual kid stuff of Wolfie and Jacob playing or goofing around for a birthday photo. Delores, in fact, had only known about them because Hans had sent them to her months ago when, in a rare bit of mutual civility, they agreed to swap photographs of the kids.

He'd sent the questionable ones along with all the others. Again, he'd thought that they were all just fun and games, but Delores had found them weird. They were grouped under the title, "Naked boys at home." Most of them were pictures Hans had taken of the two boys cavorting about the living room buck naked the previous fall. Six of them were "significantly more graphic in nature," as one court finally summarized it, and to many eyes, they were definitely not okay.

Before I saw the pictures, I doubted this was kiddie porn. Nissenbaum's Fourth Law states that, in a custody fight, charges inflate to the size necessary to win the case. And, indeed, when I first took a look at the digital images on Hans's computer screen, my impression was that Delores was making a lot out of nothing. For the most part, they just showed a couple of boys goofing around and flashing their bums for the camera. But then I hit a few that made me wonder, where Hans had really zoomed in on one of the boys' little penis, rumpled balls, and puckered anus with an intent that seemed to go beyond the playful and into the troublesome. There was a cultural element operating here. To Germans, nudity is nowhere near the big deal it tends to be here. There are parks in cities in Germany where its citizens strip off their clothes to sunbathe in the buff. We don't do that on Boston Common. But these were children, and at the very least, didn't Hans, as a father, worry about what might happen if those photgraphs fell into the wrong hands? Digital images, after all, can spread anywhere in the world.

There were four that especially got to me. In one of them, Wolfie was bent over, looking back through his legs at the camera, everything hanging out for all to see. This was the one that Hans's lawyer had described to him. Another one zeroes right in on little Jacob's private parts. And in another, one of the boys is shown facedown on a couch with his legs spread apart, seemingly unaware that he is being photographed naked from behind. That one troubled me. The camera seemed to scrutinize the boy with a leering glance. And the last image showed Wolfie bent over the couch, with his face in the crook of one arm and his ass up in the air, like he was waggling it for the camera.

Whatever Hans's intent was in taking such photographs, they definitely cost him. About a million dollars when you tallied up all the legal costs. A million-dollar mistake. Or was it a crime?

If Hans was trying to make all this seem purely innocent, his case was not improved by the assertions of the nineteen-year-old American nanny, Karinne Thomas, that he'd hired to take care of the boys during this period. In a statement to the court, Karinne said that when she arrived at his house the first morning, Hans had greeted her in a skimpy bathrobe, which struck her as "suggestive." And she claimed that a few weeks later Hans had propositioned her. He'd come home one night and found her on the couch, sobbing from homesickness. He asked her what was wrong, and she said that she was desperately lonely. In her account to the court, she stated that Hans replied that he "got lonely too" and that he gently and, to her, provocatively put his arm around her shoulder.

To Karinne, this was an unwanted advance, and she was frightened. That night, she barricaded herself in her room. Early the next morning, she packed up her things and left. She placed a note for Hans inside the door, saying that what he had done was "inappropriate" and that she had returned to the United States in search of another position.

"It's all nonsense," Hans told me.

I wondered about that too.

 ☙

As soon as Hans returned from vacation, Delores's lawyer took the pictures to the German court, which took no chances. It immediately suspended Hans's visitation rights, and ordered an investigation by a kind of psychological SWAT team known as the GWG. The court also referred Hans's case to the Department of Youth and Family, or DYF, which is like our old DSS. And it handed off the photographs to the German FBI to see if they had been released on the Internet, and whether the pictures themselves warranted criminal charges.

The first of the interrogators was DYF social worker Johanna Hurtweiler, a large, serious woman whom the Germans called a "social pedagogue." Hans was trying to go on offense now, and he collected an affidavit from Delores's maid, saying that Delores seemed to have a drinking problem and that her house was a stinking mess. But Frau Hurtweiler concentrated her attention on "matters pertaining to August 17, 2004," the day that the nude photographs were taken. She interviewed Hans about them for more than two hours, jotting his answers down in a spiral notebook. He was not allowed to have a lawyer present.

∞

DELORES TOOK UP THE ASSAULT FROM ANOTHER ANGLE AND HAULED the kids into Hans's office early one morning. He found her sitting in his executive chair when he came to work, the kids playing on his computer.

"What the hell are you doing here?" he demanded. "The children should be in school."

"We need money, Hans. And we're not leaving until you give me ten thousand euros. We'll sleep on the floor if we have to."

"Not in front of the boys," Hans told her. "Please, Delores."

"I have nothing to hide."

He tried to move her into the tea kitchen, a kind of small dining room German businesses have, where they could talk privately by themselves, but she wouldn't budge. "I need the ten thousand euros, Hans. Or the boys will starve."

"That's ridiculous. You already have twenty thousand. You can always use that." He was referring to the children's trust fund she took over.

"*We need ten thousand euros, Hans,*" Delores repeated, her face ice cold.

Hans could see the boys were getting upset at witnessing such a fight. "Your parents are just being silly," he told them. "It's nothing." Then he ducked into another office to call his lawyer and asked her if he should give Delores the money.

"Don't," the lawyer told him. "It's a bad idea."

"Okay, Delores," he told her jauntily when he returned to the office. "If you really want to, why don't you spend the night here tonight. I'll get you a pillow. You can stay the week if you like. But I'm not going to give you any money."

She turned to the boys. "Tell him."

"Don't let us starve, Papa," Jacob pleaded. "Please. We need food to eat."

"Jacob, no one is going to starve," Hans assured him, sickened that Delores would draw the boys in.

"I'm frightened," Jacob continued. Then he started to cry.

Hans moved to comfort his son, but Delores warded him off with her arm.

"Don't touch him," she barked. Then she took the boy in her arms. "I'm so sorry, sweetheart," she cooed. "I don't know why your father acts the way he does."

"Delores," Hans said. "*Do not do this*. It's cruel."

"It's crueler to let them starve."

Then, taking Jacob and Wolfie by the hand, she marched off to the common area, where she told everyone that Hans was letting his little boys starve.

Hans had an assistant, Maria Schinden, who had always been on good terms with Delores, and he asked her if she could possibly talk sense into his wife. She went off to do what she could. Hans then called his lawyer back to ask how he could possibly get his wife out of the office. The lawyer recommended that he call the police.

"I can't make a scene like that. It is crazy enough as it is. I don't want the boys to see their mother getting taken away by policemen."

Instead, they decided that Hans should just grab the boys and hurry them off to his car. So he hung up the phone and steadied himself for the attempt. He snatched up their coats and planned to grab the boys by their arms to hustle them down the hall to the front doors. But the partitions between the offices were made of glass, and Delores saw Hans coming well ahead of time. She held on to the boys so that Hans could not get to them.

Hans called his lawyer back. "That didn't work," he explained. So his lawyer called Delores's lawyer, Victor Bech, and with the three parties on speakerphone, Bech persuaded her to quit the whole operation. "You can't just stay there," Bech told her. "The police will have to be called eventually, and no one wants that."

With that, Delores took the boys' hands and marched out of the building.

That didn't soften her any. The next day, when Hans came by the house to pick up the boys for one of the rare visits the court still allowed him, he saw that the house was a horror. Delores had gotten a German shepherd puppy for the boys, and the dog had proved uncontrollable, chewing things and having accidents on the rugs and in the hall. It was disgusting. Delores had been reasonably pleasant when Hans arrived, but she snapped when she saw him sitting on the living room couch and talking to the boys, and she started raging at him: "If you won't give me more money, you don't deserve to be in this house. Get out! Get out!" Hans said okay, he'd leave.

The house was a split-level, with the living quarters on the second floor. He started down the stairs. He was about halfway down when Delores came charging down the steps and shoved him from behind.

He just managed to grab onto the banister and avoid sprawling head-first toward the floor below. Before he'd fully regained his balance, she rammed him again with a scream, knocking him down another stair or two. By now, the kids were watching from the top of the stairs. "No, Mommy, stop it!" they begged her. But again she shoved him, scream-ing, "Get out!" at the top of her lungs. Then she slammed him once more. Finally, Hans managed to right himself, grab Delores's hands, and force her to sit down on a stair. "Now, stay there," he told her. Then he went down. The boys followed after, stepping around their mother without a word.

ତ୍ତ

MEANWHILE, THE PSYCHOLOGIST, FRAU HURTWEILER, KEPT AT IT. IN the second interview, Hans was able to steer the investigation around to Delores, zeroing in on the dog, the mess in the house, and her drinking. She'd gotten so bombed at a local disco that a girlfriend had to drag her over to her house, since she was unable to walk back to her own. Hurtweiler listened. She'd spoken to Delores by now, but she didn't let Hans in on any of her own conclusions. The tension was starting to get to him. He'd stopped eating, and he was not sleeping well.

But it was worse on the boys. They were both starting to wet their beds, something new for them, and unusual for boys their age; the edges of their eyes twitched nervously, and the eyes themselves sometimes rolled weirdly in their sockets. They both had terrible trouble sleeping; they often sobbed, or even screamed, at night. And they had started playing with their penises, pulling at their foreskins and engaging in what they called "pee-pee dances," as they paraded around in the nude, swinging their little penises this way and that as if they were tiny gui-tars. Was this their response to the conflict over the nude photographs? To Hans's provocations? Or was this just the acting out that often ac-companies high-conflict divorces?

These questions preoccupied the many psychologists on the case, and probably their endless probing only made things worse. On top of everything else, Wolfie had developed a chronic ear infection that pained him endlessly. Delores was sure that he required surgery, but after consulting with three of the leading ear, nose, and throat specialists in the country, Hans was convinced that antibiotics would be enough, and that surgery might well be harmful. This produced more fights.

Meanwhile, the DYF filed an interim report recommending that Hans be allowed to visit with the boys as before. Delores objected fiercely but the court agreed and made the order.

Hans's uncle Arthur had a place in Palm Springs, California, and Hans and Delores always used to take the boys there for spring holiday. This time, Hans took them there by himself for a week while Delores went to her parents' place in Rhode Island. When the week was up, Hans packed the kids off onto the flight to Providence for a week with their mother while he returned to Berlin. Delores was supposed to bring the kids home a week later.

But the week passed and—no kids. Not on that day, or on the next, or on the one after that. Not knowing where else to turn, Hans hired a private investigator over the Internet to track down his boys. He was still looking when Delores finally flew the boys home four days later. She seemed almost amused that Hans was so worried. "We just got delayed, that's all," she said airily, when he met them at the airport, slapping him gently on the cheek.

ELEVEN

Before she'd left for Rhode Island, Delores had taken Wolfie to see one last ear specialist. Like his colleagues before him, he declared that surgery was out of the question. Delores blew up. "You're a total incompetent," she screamed at him in what German she knew, and she stormed out of the examination room. That made it four specialists who agreed that surgery was not needed.

Now Delores called Hans to say that she had booked Wolfie for surgery after all. To keep Hans from stopping her, she wouldn't tell him which surgeon or which hospital. He hung up the phone in a panic, knowing that the surgery was completely unnecessary and possibly dangerous to his son. But how to stop it? As the parent who paid the medical bills, Hans had kept all the specialists' invoices, and he called all the clinics Delores had consulted and found that one of the doctors had indeed made the appointment—for later that very day. This was about ten thirty in the morning. Hans jumped in his car, drove straight there, and tore into the office, where he filled out a form stating that, as Wolfgang's father, he was withholding his consent for the planned surgery. He made sure that the hospital and the doctor's office had copies. "There was no way I was going to let Delores do that to Wolfie," Hans told me. Delores was furious when she found out what Hans had done.

❧

WORRIED THAT DELORES WOULD TAKE THE KIDS BACK TO THE UNITED States, as she often threatened to do, Hans persuaded the court to order her to surrender their passports and confine the boys to Germany. Initially, Delores refused to give up the passports, so, with the court's approval, Hans took the boys out of school and had them stay with him.

Despite the decision of the court to resume Hans's visitation, the matter of the photographs was still unresolved. It was as if the court found them so distressing, it needed to do something to purge them from its consciousness. That is, it needed someone to blame. Like Hans. Johanna Hurtweiler came around to meet with Hans yet again. The questioning was relentless, dizzying. It seemed to him that she was going over old ground, again and again. She said she was simply being thorough.

"Why did you take the pictures?" she asked Hans, for what seemed like the hundredth time.

"Just for fun."

"Have you ever had lustful feelings toward the children?"

"Absolutely not."

"Have you engaged in any irregular sexual activities with your wife?"

"No."

"Do you harbor any unusual fantasies?"

"Define unusual."

"Involving children."

"Absolutely not."

"Do you ever find the image of naked boys erotic?"

"No."

"Do you ever masturbate?"

"Sometimes."

"What thoughts come to your mind?"

"Normal ones with women."

"Fantasies?"

"Yes."

"Of?"

"Heterosexual sex."

"What age are the females?"

"Adult."

"How adult?"

"Over thirty."

"None younger?"

"No."

It was exhausting and humiliating. Hans resented the implication that he was guilty, and that all this questioning was designed to get him to confess to a crime that Frau Hurtweiler was certain he had committed. Meanwhile, of course, his wife had attempted to subject their son to unnecessary surgery. Had kidnapped the boys for four days. Had become an alcoholic. And had spiraled completely out of control.

Yet Delores didn't have to submit to any questions.

And she had primary custody, while he had to beg to see his kids.

It was verdict first, evidence later, just like in *Alice in Wonderland*.

It took three more months, but in July the Department of Youth and Family was finally set to issue its report. Hans was extremely apprehensive. He was sure it would go against him. Sure that Frau Hurtweiler had decided that he was a pervert and that only Delores, since she was the mother, was fit to raise their children.

In fact, the court decided to reaffirm the old setup, declaring that each parent was qualified to take care of the two boys. Given Delores's erratic behavior, I was surprised the court did that. But it occurred to me that the court was troubled by the nude photos that Hans had taken of his boys. It didn't feel safe entrusting the boys exclusively to him but didn't want to give them solely to Delores either.

Seeking an advantage, Delores had her lawyer send all the photographs to the Department of Youth and Family, along with a request to the court for permission to remove the boys to America permanently. Evidently, her hope was once the DYF, GWG, and the court saw all the pictures, they'd see how unfit Hans was as a parent. For good measure, Delores spread vicious rumors about Hans in the boys' school, just as she had in his office. She declared that Hans had taught the boys the "pee-pee dance," by stripping naked himself and actually leading them through it, and that the red welts and dark bruises that appeared in a few of the pictures on the insides of Wolfgang's thighs had come from whipping. The boys themselves never made such claims, or agreed with them. Hans believed the bruises occurred during one of the many soccer games that both boys played in. None of that mattered to Delores.

Regardless of the merits, the request to take the boys to America to escape the supposed perversions of the father provoked yet another inquisition from the dogged Johanna Hurtweiler, with a new emphasis on the full array of photographs that Delores had provided.

Hurtweiler watched Hans look through each one while she fired questions at him. "It was the longest two hours of my life," Hans told me. "She was relentless. We'd gone over this any number of times, but each time she bored into me as though I might finally tell her the truth." It wasn't an interview; it was an interrogation.

"Have you ever touched your sons' genitals?"

"No."

"Do you want to?"

"No."

"Have you ever thought of putting your mouth on them?"

"Absolutely not."

"Are you certain?"

"Completely."

"Why are you so angry?"

"Because you don't seem to believe me."

"Should I?"

"Yes."

"What about their buttocks? Have you ever touched them?"

"No."

"Not with either of the boys?"

"No."

"The anus?"

"What about it?"

"Have you ever touched one of them there?"

"Of course not."

"Not even when you wiped them?"

"Well, perhaps then."

"How old were they then?"

"One, two. I don't recall."

"Nothing more recent?"

"No."

"Now, the 'pee-pee dances'—did you teach them that?"

"Absolutely not."

"Did you lead those dances?"

"No."

"How did they think to do them?"

"I don't know."

∽

THREE WEEKS LATER, HANS MET WITH A COURT-APPOINTED PSYCHOL-ogist from the GWG. There was scarcely any warning. The man called, and Hans had to be in his office within an hour. This time, Hans was required to bring his laptop, and he and the psychologist went through each of the forty-nine pictures he had stored there. Hans flipped open the computer lid and brought up the photos.

"How did this one come to be?" the psychiatrist asked, pointing.

"I don't know, the boys were just there."

"What did you feel when you took this one?"

"I don't know, happiness."

"Happiness? Why happiness?"

"Because the boys were having such a good time."

"Did you wish you could join them?"

"No."

"Why not?"

"I don't know. Do you?"

"I'll ask the questions, okay, Herr Weber? Now, what part of the boy's body were you thinking about when you took this one?"

"No part, except the face maybe."

"But he's nude."

"That's my answer."

"Any part you want to touch?"

"No."

After an hour of questioning, the psychologist wanted Hans to describe the history of his relationship with Delores. Hans blew out a long sigh. "Where to begin?" he asked.

"How about at the beginning," the psychologist said drily.

Hans went through the relationship from their Hong Kong meeting on, and then, once he reached the part about the kids, the psychologist veered off to try to understand each boy individually, their relationship to each other, to their mother, to their father, and even to the family collectively. Even after all that, the GWG was not done with Hans. He had to take the German version of the Minnesota Multiphasic Personality Inventory test, with more than six hundred questions, all intended to reveal Hans's true nature. A week later, Hans was seen by yet another GWG psychologist, Talia Helkorn, to go over the whole thing again. Then it was back to Frau Hurtweiler for still another round.

Near the end of September, the Department of Youth and Family issued another letter, saying that despite the new photographs and Delores's claims about them, it would make no claim against Hans. But to be on the safe side, the court insisted that a team of psychologists observe Hans playing with his sons in a special laboratory that was outfitted with video cameras and two-way mirrors. The psychologists also came to Hans's home one day when the boys were there with him to see how he played with his children. At one point, Hans and the boys played hide-and-seek—but now that the psychologists were in the room, the boys refused to come out from their hiding places.

Meanwhile, Delores refused to participate in any of the testing at all. She declared that, since she was fluent only in English, she would cooperate only with professionals from DYF or GWG who likewise spoke "good" English. Of course, only she would determine what good English was.

∽

IT WAS ONE THING FOR THE GERMANS TO DO THEIR INVESTIGATION. I had to do mine. An informal one, to be sure. But one that would be no less decisive. I had to determine whether I could trust Hans, and whether I could believe him when he claimed he was not into child pornography and that the shots were merely playful, both for him and for the boys.

We were almost two hours into our conversation when I asked him to tell me how he happened to take all those pictures. With something explosive like that, I try to keep it conversational. You get accusatory, or edgy, and it's hard to tell what someone's really saying because they get so defensive. Most people automatically get a little evasive or defiant if they are going to lie about something, either deflecting the question or pushing it back in your face. To my relief, Hans did neither. He still had that coolness, but this time he seemed calm and relaxed. I got a feeling of tremendous warmth when he thought about his kids, even under these circumstances.

"I came downstairs one night into the big playroom which is next to the boys' bedroom," Hans began. "They'd just gotten out of the bath, and hadn't put their pajamas on, and they were goofing around naked. Dashing around, jumping on the furniture, throwing pillows around and at each other. They were having such a grand time, laughing and having such fun. The camera was right there on the table, so I picked it up and started shooting. It really was very innocent, Jerry. It was nothing. No big deal. Really."

"But the close-ups," I said. "Why'd you take those?"

"I didn't. The boys did. They called them 'butt shorts!'" It was their fractured English. "Butt shorts!" He nearly shouted it, there in my office. I had to smile, and that's when I realized that I was going to do whatever I could for Hans Weber.

"Why didn't you tell that to Hurtweiler and the others?"

"I did. Of course I did. I'm just not sure they ever believed me. Once they get an idea about you, Jerry—" He didn't complete the thought, nor did he need to.

There's usually a moment when you decide whether you are going to represent someone. That was my moment with Hans. When he said "butt shorts."

It was all in fun after all.

∽

Delores continued to intrude relentlessly in Hans's life, in every way. Day or night, she'd call him up out of the blue and start screaming obscenities at him. She made five of these calls in a single hour one September day. The boys were with her, and she accused him of running off with the kids' notebooks, which of course he hadn't done. Then she said he'd failed to put their textbooks in their knapsacks, although he had carefully included them. The next time she simply screamed—an earsplitting, banshee screech. He told her to stop screaming, or move to another phone, where the kids couldn't hear. After that, the next call was from Jacob, and he repeated Delores's line that he'd run off with the notebooks. "Daddy, can you please take the notebooks to school?" It was a stilted, forced way of speaking that reminded him of Delores, as if she was coaching him on exactly what to say. Indeed, he could hear Delores whispering in the background, "I also miss the reading books, Daddy." Jacob repeated it word for word. Then the whispering again: "Daddy, you also have the Spider-Man lunch box." This he repeated too.

Telling me all this in my office, Hans looked agonized. "I can't tell you how tense, hatred-filled, and terrified the atmosphere was in my wife's house, Jerry. My wife had turned into a mean and hateful woman. And my sons had changed from cheerful and relaxed little boys to frightened and defenseless animals. Jerry, I am not exaggerating."

Hans sent Delores a text message: "I am shattered after these phone calls. Fine, Delores—you broke me. Tell me what it will take for you to end the war and stop using our innocent little boys. I give up—state your terms."

Hans looked up at me again. "I couldn't fight or defeat a woman who abused our children without restraint. This war was not going to be won by the stronger person but by the more unscrupulous one."

༄

WHEN HANS SHOWED UP AT SCHOOL ONE AFTERNOON TO TAKE THE kids home, he found Delores already there. She claimed that, since Hans had supposedly been late dropping them off after the previous weekend, she had a right to keep them. Hans reminded Delores that this was his day to take them, but Delores was insistent. Since there were other parents around, and the boys were right there, Hans tried to control his temper, but Delores didn't bother, and lit into him for being an irresponsible father, a porn freak who'd taken pictures of his kids in the nude. "Yes, in the nude!" she shouted to anyone who would listen. "This man is a pervert!" Hans tried to quiet her, but she would not shut up. As the disagreement deepened, the headmistress tried to quell the ruckus, but made no progress. So Hans called his attorney, who faxed the most recent reports by the DYF to the headmistress's office so she could see that the court had dismissed the charges. Still, Delores was not going to budge, and, knowing she would never give in, Hans figured he had no choice. When he went back outside, he let the boys know there had been a change of plans. Both boys started to sob, even Wolfie, who was normally stoical. Hans told his sons they'd see him plenty over the holiday next month, but it did no good. When Hans left, the boys raced after him and clung to him, defying their mother's efforts to peel them away. "Just one more day, Mother," Jacob pleaded with his mother, tears streaming down his face. "Please?"

"That's out of the question," Delores snapped.

When the boys continued to wail, Hans offered to take them aside for a moment to calm them down. But Delores wouldn't hear of it.

"No, Hans. We have to go now."

Delores scooped Jacob into her arms, but he squirmed so much, it was hard to hold him. Before she turned to carry him back to the car, she shot Hans one last look.

"It was ice-cold," Hans told me as he sat in my office during that first meeting. "It put a lot of fear in me. The way she dealt with the children—it was scary. I knew she emotionally brutalized them. They'd told me, and I'd seen the effects. I was so afraid that after they left she would do more of the same. But there was nothing I could do."

Frightened by the depth of Delores's rage, Hans pleaded with the court to force her to comply with its order to surrender their passports. But Delores's lawyer argued that United States passports could only be deposited at a U.S. embassy. He insisted that would be plenty secure, and respected international law besides.

That's what the court ordered.

Three weeks later, on January 24, 2007, Delores took the boys and somehow disappeared from the country.

‿◌‿

Hans had not had a court-sanctioned visit with the boys for several days. When he called Delores to set up a time for the next pickup, he couldn't reach her on her cell, or on her home phone. That was odd. He tried the boys' school and learned that Delores had called to say that they had both fallen sick and probably wouldn't be well enough to return for several days. Increasingly distressed, Hans drove over to Delores's apartment, but no one answered the buzzer. Since he'd signed the lease for Delores, he had a key, and he used it now to enter. The place reeked from the food that had been left out in the kitchen with flies hovering around it, the overstuffed trash can, and the soiled carpets. There was a mess everywhere he looked. The couch was heaped with old magazines and catalogs. A small mountain of rubbish was piled up in a corner. Cushions were scattered about on the floor. Rumpled clothes littered the stairs.

Hans gave a shout as he glanced about, but no one answered. He went upstairs to peer into all the bedrooms, at their unmade beds and open drawers, and even into the bathroom, where the medicine cabinet door hung open, the contents half-emptied. The toilet was unflushed and clogged with toilet paper. When Hans opened the basement door to check downstairs, he heard a mewing sort of bark. He flipped on the light and found the German shepherd leashed to a pipe in the far corner, his dish empty, his water bowl tipped over. Hans freed him and brought him upstairs, gave him some water, and found some food for him in the pantry, which the dog nibbled at, too spent to eat.

It looked like Delores had hurriedly packed up for the kids and rushed off. Hans called the police, who arrived quickly, sirens blaring. After Hans explained the situation, they searched the house for clues to the whereabouts of the three, and then went outside to interview the neighbors. One recalled that a cab had pulled up at the house a few days before and picked up a woman and two young boys with a large number of bags. From the neighbor's description of the car's markings, the police were able to identify the taxi company. When they called the company, they discovered that the ride had ended at Berlin International Airport.

And all three of them had passports. A clerk at the U.S. embassy admitted that, despite the order of the German court, he had given Delores the passports for her sons. He had required her simply to sign a statement acknowledging that it would be illegal for her to take the boys out of the country without their father's consent. Then she did just that.

But where did she take them? Hans had no idea. The first thought, of course, was that she had taken them to Rhode Island, but that seemed so obvious that he couldn't believe she'd actually do it. She had to have taken them somewhere else, right? She could have taken them anywhere in the world. After 9/11, airlines made it a policy not to release information about their passenger lists. Delores had grown up speaking fluent Spanish, so she could have gone to live with relatives in Spain or to Mexico, where she would be even harder to track. She could have gone to any English-speaking country, or she could have fallen in with pockets of English-speaking expats in just about any big city around the world. Since she and the boys also spoke German, they could also have gone to any German-speaking country: Austria, Switzerland . . . The list of possibilities was endless.

In his worst moments, Hans pictured Delores dragging the boys about some desolate corner of the world where he could never find them. Distressed, Hans hired detectives to develop any leads they could, but they turned up nothing. Two days later, in some frustration he went back to Delores's place with the police to search again for leads. Amid the wreckage, he found a lot of correspondence strewn across the dining table, including a lot of letters to and from various Rhode Island politicians about the possibility of relocating there.

He tried calling Delores's cell phone at least thirty times a day for the next couple of days, but no answer.

Finally, about a week into the ordeal, Hans got word from an administrator at the boys' school that a woman had just called to say the Weber boys would be out sick for a few more days. The woman refused to identify herself. Unlike normal residential telephones in Germany, an institutional phone like the one at the school was able to record incoming telephone numbers. This call came from a U.S. area code. Hans tried the number. He had dialed enough numbers around the world that he could tell just by the ringtone that the receiving cell phone was indeed in the United States.

So was its owner. A woman answered. "Hello?"

Just one word, but it was enough for Hans. "Hello, Delores," Hans replied.

Delores hung up. Not much, but it was enough. Delores had brought the kids to the United States.

To Rhode Island, Hans figured, based on the correspondence. And probably to her parents' house in Hopkinton. He tried that number next. His father-in-law, Tito, came to the phone. Hans identified himself and said he was looking for his boys. "Are they there?" he asked. "Did Delores bring them to your house?"

"I got no idea where they are," Tito replied, a note of defiance in his voice. "I thought they were in Germany," he said. Then he changed his tack. "Why don't you come to Rhode Island and, I don't know, maybe we can work out a financial settlement. You do that, and maybe you'll see your kids again. You follow me?"

Hans was not going to be distracted by him. "Is Delores there now?"

"Maybe," Tito replied.

"Maybe?" Hans challenged him. "What do you mean, maybe?"

"Maybe she is. Maybe she isn't."

Most likely she was. But how to nail that down? For that, Hans turned to his corporate attorney in Atlanta, Nick Bradley, a versatile lawyer who had done some family law earlier in his career. Nick agreed that the boys were almost certainly with Delores at her parents' place. To make sure, Nick recommended looping in a well-connected Rhode Island attorney named Ceslay Svoboda, known to all as Bodie, who'd been an assistant U.S. attorney. Bodie quickly put together a crew of private detectives to watch Tito Sanchez's house around the clock in eight-hour shifts. If Delores was there, they had her, and if she'd holed up anywhere else, they'd try to follow her back.

The Sanchez place in Hopkinton was way out in the sticks, which did not make it the most hospitable place for a squadron of private eyes out on a job. With so few people about, neighbors are likely to get suspicious about any car they don't recognize. For a PI to park a car anywhere near the Sanchez's—well, it would be like pulling a Sherman tank up to the curb. So Bodie had to get a fleet of different cars for his guys and then have all of them drive slowly by to keep an eye on the house without being noticed, none of them going by more than a few times.

Just in case, Bodie paid a call to the Hopkinton police chief to let him know what was up. Right away, the chief started chuckling: "I've been fielding calls all morning from the Sanchez's neighbors, saying that there were a lot of strange cars passing by their house."

"This is a case of international abduction," Bodie told him. "We'd appreciate your help." He gave a few details, but not many.

"Well then, I'll tell my guys to cut you a little slack."

"We'd be grateful, sir."

Early one morning, a few days later, the detectives who were coming on the shift saw a beige Mercury Marquis start up in the driveway of Delores's parents' house. They hadn't ID'd everyone in the car, but it looked like the driver was a female, maybe forty, blond and slender. They followed the car down the street, and then down a few side streets, before it turned onto a highway ramp and sped off. The detectives couldn't keep up for fear of causing an accident or being spotted, but just before the last turn, they got enough of a look at the car to know they had seen Delores and the boys—plus an older, yellow-haired woman who was probably Delores's mother, Gracia.

That sighting was enough for Bradley to fly into Providence and file a petition in federal district court. It called for a return of the Weber boys to their father in Berlin under the terms of an international law that governs such kidnappings, the Hague Convention. He had a summons to that effect served on Delores.

Now, I'd have handled that whole situation differently. I would have asked the judge for a writ of habeas corpus to permit the county sheriffs, local police, and U.S. marshall to take possession of the kids and bring them into court. I would have assured the judge that Hans was flying in to join the arrest team so he could be reunited with his boys right away. That would have immediately freed them from Delores's clutches, and it would have forced her to explain why she had violated the German court's order not to flee. She'd be on defense, not offense.

But Nick went the summons route, and Hans paid for it.

In the district court in Providence, the presiding judge held a preliminary chamber conference, and Nick quickly got snared in the brambles of the Hague Convention, which can be forbiddingly complex to the uninitiated. Delores had landed a former federal prosecutor named Stanley Minsk, who agreed to represent her pro bono. (Good news for Delores; bad news for Stanley. I always say: if you've got the client's money, you've got her attention. Otherwise, you don't.) Minsk had done several Hague cases, and he boasted to the judge that he'd never lost a single one.

"It looked like the judge wanted to bed down with Stanley and really snuggle up," Nick told me, irked. Hans couldn't follow all the details of the discussion, but he got the body language. He was afraid he'd never see his kids again.

Nick knew he needed to go Stanley Minsk one better and find someone with even more experience with Hague Convention cases than he did. That's when he found me—on the Web. When he reached my site, he could see all my international work, and my stint as president of the International Academy of Matrimonial Lawyers, and a lot more.

Nick called me up, laid out the facts of the case, then came right out with it: "So, Jerry, do you want to try the case?"

"Well, when is it?" I asked.

"Thursday."

"Wait—*this* Thursday?" This was on Monday.

"That's right. Three days from today."

I'm a fiend for preparation, spending weeks to lay out a single cross-examination, and I had a lot of other cases on my desk. "I'd love to help you, Nick, but I need more time."

"Sorry. This is all the time we have."

Even if I pushed all my other cases aside, this one would be a bear, demanding all my attention, going late into the night, starting very early, and taking over my weekends. What about my obligations to other clients? It made no sense to get involved. But I was intrigued. The case had all the angles. Plus, I sometimes get righteous about these things, and I didn't think that Delores should be able to pull this stuff and get away with it.

"Well?" Nick asked.

"You're really squeezing me."

"Well?" he repeated.

"Okay. I'll do it. *But.*"

"But what?"

"I've got to be sure the money is there." I made a quick calculation. "This case could run a half million, easy."

"Not a problem."

"I've got to meet Hans first. If we get along, fine. I'll do it. If we don't, no go."

"You got a deal. He'll be there this afternoon at two. Now—want to know the latest?"

He didn't wait for me to answer.

"Delores called the Hopkinton Police yesterday. She's claiming that Hans has physically abused her and the children. That the kids were covered with bruises and wounds whenever she picked them up from his house. That he gets off on seeing naked pictures of them. And that she has an affidavit from the kids' nanny, a woman called"—he paused for a second, looking through his notes—"Karinne Thomas, confirming all of this." So she's asked that a restraining order be taken out against *him*, to keep him from grabbing the kids and flying them back to Germany. How's that for a nice little greeting card from your wife to get at the airport?"

"But he has the summons on her, right?"

"Right. She didn't take it too well." Nick chuckled. "When she answered the door, and Bodie's guy handed her the paperwork, she started screaming, just screaming. Top-of-the-lungs screaming. Totally hysterical, the guy said. He couldn't believe it. She called him every filthy name you can think of and lots more. And then she crumpled up all the papers, threw them in our guy's face, and slammed the door."

"Nice," I said.

℞

As soon as I signed on, I knew that this was not a conventional case. It wasn't about who ends up with the kids. It was a Hague Convention case, which is different. The whole point of the Hague Convention is to keep a parent from grabbing the kids and "forum shopping"— hunting up a court somewhere in the world that they think is likely to see the case more favorably than a judge would at home. That was what Delores was doing. She thought that she had a better chance of winning in Rhode Island than in Germany. She'd researched it a bit when she was in Rhode Island over Easter, that time she was late bringing the kids back. Along with the letters to various politicians, Hans found some notes Delores had left scattered across her desk at her apartment in Berlin. On a sheet of paper, she'd typed out a number of questions, with a few answers added in curly ballpoint. They showed her state of mind.

Under "lawyer questions," she wanted to know if the court could "force" Hans to "release all his income, shares, and net worth." How long would that take? And could she get child support and alimony out

252

of a "nonresident." And finally, in pen, "What about just fighting the contract [as] invalid now?"

It was all about the money—canceling the prenup and boosting the payments she could get out of him. She didn't mention the kids by name, or refer to Hans's possibly being a threat to them.

To Dolores, the kids had turned into little bags of money.

The purpose of the Hague Convention's 1980 decree "The Civil Aspects of International Child Abduction" is to return children who have been removed by a parent from their place of "habitual residence" to another country. Since Delores had obviously done just that, you might think this would be an open-and-shut case. The boys had always lived in Berlin; the mother had taken them to Rhode Island. She should return them. Down comes the gavel. Next case.

Except for one thing—Article 13b. It's the briefest of the forty-five articles, but it's the most potent. For it allows a parent to prevent the return of the kids if they'd be placed in "grave risk of harm" in their home country. And *harm* in this case meant the possibility of sexual exploitation by my client. Those nude photographs, in other words.

ॐ

THE FEDERAL DISTRICT COURTHOUSE IN PROVIDENCE IS A SQUARE building that takes up almost a full city block. With its high ceilings and fans going everywhere, the building stayed cool even through the height of summer. I got to court right at eight thirty, pulled open the heavy front door, and passed through security. I wanted to go over some last details with Nick Bradley, who would be presenting the case with me, and with Bodie Svoboda, the former U.S. attorney who'd serve as the obligatory local counsel. I was pleased to see the portly, mustachioed Werner von Schmidt, whom we had flown in from Germany as one of the many world-class experts we'd bring into the case. His résumé ran thirty-five pages, and his list of publications fifty more. He greeted me warmly, stating the obvious, that he'd been able to find his way to the second floor courtroom just fine.

As I was chatting with von Schmidt, I caught sight of a slender woman, heavily made up, who was wearing a light and flowery dress under her mink coat. She was sitting on a wooden bench by the wall, and she seemed fidgety, crossing and recrossing her legs as she talked with a lot of hand gestures to a balding, thickset man. It had to be Delores Weber. The man was her lawyer, Stanley Minsk, the one who prided himself on his knowledge of Hague cases. I always try to exchange a few pleasantries with opposing counsel before the trial starts. It helps to get things going on an amicable basis, and Minsk responded warmly, with a bright smile. He introduced Delores, who all but hissed at me and refused to shake hands.

The courtroom itself was large and ornate, with a carved mahogany bench raised in front for the judge and another lower bench for the court clerks, tables for the petitioner, in this case Hans, and the respondent, Delores, and their respective counsel, which made for quite an assemblage of lawyers, with three on each side. I'd had our paralegal, Mindy, lay out copies of our exhibit books for everyone, with each document carefully numbered in sequence and indexed. At nine o'clock, as the bailiff announced the arrival of Judge Hubert Browning, and we all stood up while the tall, white-haired, black-robed justice swept in and took his seat at the bench.

Civil Action *Hans Weber v. Delores Weber* was under way.

After the judge bid us all good morning, Minsk immediately started complaining about von Schmidt, claiming that he was qualified only to offer opinions on the Hague Convention, and not on the custody issues in German law that we had planned to ask him about. The judge dismissed the objection, but the notion that von Schmidt might not be qualified to testify on such an aspect of the law did not sit well with him, and once on the stand, von Schmidt retaliated by revealing himself to be a pompous ass. I'd used von Schmidt before, and even spent a pleasant evening with him over a few glasses of choice Riesling once in

Frankfurt. I had not thought him capable of being such a windbag, but windbag he was. And this was a big problem, because he was a pillar of our case, establishing, first, that German courts conventionally award joint custody in cases like this and, second, that a German court is, as the Weber case has demonstrated, no less capable of ensuring the boys' safety than one of ours. Not such a hard assignment, but the trick was communicating this to the judge in a neat, convincing, and therefore unassailable fashion.

American courts do not favor the long-winded. They encourage little bursts of expert opinion that can be assembled neatly into a forceful argument. In such a setting, yes and no are plenty eloquent answers. I had spent several hours coaching the eminent von Schmidt on the virtue of brevity. Several times, I'd marched him through his testimony, so he could get the rhythm of it.

"I'll ask you your name," I told him. "You say—" I turned to him.

"Werner von Schmidt," the great man replied.

"Yes. Perfect. Now, I ask, 'Where is your professional office?' You say—"

"Frankfurt, Germany."

"Marvelous! Exactly! I ask you about your education and training and experience." He looked up at me, uncertain how to answer. "You sum it up," I told him. "Just the important points."

"Yes, yes."

The eminent legal theorist assured me that he had it. And, indeed, it was so simple that a third grader could have managed it. So I put him up on the stand, and got to the part about his professional qualifications, and a glow of savage pride came over his face, and, my God, he went through every point on his lengthy résumé in extravagant detail, with numerous asides, all pointless, and all conveyed with the passionate fervor accorded to Holy Writ as declaimed from the pulpit of St. Peter's. He filled more than twenty pages of transcript. After finally pulling von Schmidt through his direct testimony Minsk started in on a cross-examination, but when, in his first answer, von Schmidt went on and on in his first answer about some obscure point of German legal theory, Judge Browning cut him off, which is never a good sign for the home team. Happily, though, before opposing counsel was done with von Schmidt, Browning thumbed through one of our exhibits, a key treatise of German law. Browning noted that in Germany there was a presumption of joint custody from birth, which means one parent simply cannot snatch a kid without the permission of the other. This was key. Still, I wanted to strangle von Schmidt as he stepped, beaming, off the witness stand.

So it was a rocky start for us, but at least some of the key evidence got in. Then a bizarre thing happened. Delores declared that the proceedings would have to be interrupted because she had to take Wolfgang to the Massachusetts Eye and Ear Infirmary in Boston for an emergency ear appointment. She said the boy had been suffering from agonizing earaches, and that he'd already suffered some hearing loss. She was sure Wolfgang would need an operation. The judge had little choice but to let her go, although he ordered, at our request, that Hans be allowed to go too.

Jaws dropped all around the room. Here were five high-priced lawyers, two paralegals, and a federal district court judge all left to twiddle their thumbs while Delores took her son for a checkup. As theater it was a big win for her, since it allowed her to play the conscientious mom who sacrifices everything for her son—and made Hans the clueless dad who had no idea his son's health needs were so dire. What she didn't know was that Judge Browning didn't enjoy theater.

And there was another catch. For this gambit to work, the specialist had to agree that Delores's fears were warranted. But he didn't. He conducted an extensive battery of tests and didn't find any sign of loss of hearing or any need for surgery. Hans was there, and he had to smile. But Delores stormed out of the doctor's office, grabbed Wolfie, who was being watched over by his grandfather, and dragged him back into the specialist's office to use him as a prop while she launched into the child pornography allegations against her husband. The doctor listened, perplexed. Hans was furious, but could do nothing except plead with his wife to stop. She did not.

To show that Wolfie really was seriously ill, and Hans too out of it to acknowledge it, Delores demanded a sleep test. Wolfgang's sleep cycle was off, she declared. And it appeared to be true that Wolfgang was still waking up several times a night, sometimes with a shout, and sometimes in tears. (She never accepted the more likely explanation that the stress of the abduction and the endless court cases might have played a role.) The test cost four grand, which Hans's German health plan wouldn't pay for. Of course, Delores didn't have the money. Once again, Hans stepped up and put the charge on his credit card. That test took a while; it meant attaching a myriad of wires to Wolfie's cranium to monitor his sleep overnight. He was fine.

By the time that bit of evidence came in, the trial had taken an unexpected turn. Delores's charges against Hans seemed almost tailor-made to win her a Hague Article 13b exception, allowing her to keep the boys in the United States and fight the custody case through Rhode Island courts. Among them: that Hans posed a danger to the boys because he had taken those naked pictures of them, been lax in attending to their medical needs, been preoccupied by sex videos, and had beaten the children. She also argued that his native country, Germany, felt foreign to the boys and was either unable or unwilling to protect the children from their father.

With such claims, Hague law is designed to place the burden of proof on Delores to demonstrate their legitimacy. But Judge Browning had never tried a Hague case before, and, in effect, he forced us to prove Hans's innocence. We had to show that Hans never did any of these things, no, no, no, without a shadow of a doubt, no, sir. That's tough. It's always harder to prove a negative, which is one reason why the legal standard in America is what it is. Now, Hans was assumed to be guilty until we could prove him innocent.

Nick and I spent a lot of time trying to figure out how to win that game, and we decided that the best way was not to play it. Instead, we'd play the game we could win. Since Delores was the one who was bringing all the charges, we'd dispute them by disputing her. She was hardly the most credible or reliable accuser. If we could show that she was not to be believed, then her charges were not to be believed either.

Hans was our next witness. Given the stakes, he was remarkably composed and polite, never once raising his voice or showing any temper, no matter how outrageous the questions. We had his testimony very tightly choreographed, actually scripting long swatches of it for him to memorize, and that went off without a hitch. Despite Minsk's efforts to shake him, Hans came across as the man he is—a sensible, devoted father whose patience has been worn thin by an out-of-control wife. At least, I thought so, and the judge seemed to agree, based on the way he looked at Hans, his features soft, as if he was more receptive.

I spend a lot of time reading judges. I never know for sure, but I felt good about the way this was playing out. More importantly, we made sure that Hans told the truth, even if it reflected badly on him. He admitted straight out to watching the porn DVDs, and agreed with Minsk's salacious descriptions of them. He didn't sound defensive, but comfortable that the truth wouldn't hurt him. He described the naked photographs as the product of a big goof, just as he had told me. We established that if Karinne was to be believed, why wasn't she here to testify? We'd tracked her to a small town in California where she was working as a waitress and served her with a federal subpoena, but she never showed up for the deposition.

He went through the medical issues with Wolfie, patiently describing what each specialist had told him, and when, and making clear that he had done his best to appraise the medical opinions conscientiously and act on them appropriately. All of this was supported by reports from each doctor, dutifully translated into English. Altogether, a winning performance.

Delores's wasn't. She got through her direct testimony, in which Stanley Minsk did his best to establish her as a loving, competent mother who was doing her best for her boys—even if it meant removing them from the company of the father they loved. Then I went at her in a quiet and slow but calculated and relentless cross-examination designed to get the judge angry at and frustrated with her answers. Slim anyway, she looked all the tinier on the witness stand in a demure, gray dress. As I approached her, I could see a hollowness in her eyes that I hadn't noticed before. She looked troubled, frightened. I remembered the raccoon I'd once found in the corner of our garage. It was the same look of savagery and fear. This was a woman who was cornered, and would do anything.

One point I bore in on right away: from the beginning, Minsk had worked hard at establishing that Delores and the kids primarily spoke English. It was their mother tongue, she kept saying. To her this meant that they were better off in America. But it wasn't true. Delores spoke fine German. She was great with foreign languages, and she'd been in Germany for almost a decade, and now Delores spoke English with a marked German accent. And the boys certainly spoke German as fluently as they did English.

So, how to establish this? I went back to the prenuptial agreement that Delores had fussed over for months. It was written entirely in German, a language Delores professed hardly to know, and pertained to a matter that mattered to her absolutely. When I asked her if she'd read it, she was noncommittal, saying she couldn't remember. I let that sit there for the judge. Couldn't remember? I pulled out a photocopy of the document—and pointed to the five places where she'd signed it. If she'd signed a document of such significance, she had to have read it. "Isn't that your signature?" I asked.

That's when I thought of the raccoon. She was cornered, and she couldn't decide whether to flee or strike. She froze, refusing to concede the obvious fact that it was her signature. Who else's would it be?

"It's a photocopy," she said, "so I can't be sure." She said this with a note of satisfaction on her face, as if she'd won. But I had the original too. I pulled that one out, festooned with ribbons since it was German and that's the way they do things—and showed her the signatures again.

"I don't know," she said. I could hear the judge sigh. That didn't help her cause any.

Later, I asked her about the Easter when she was in Rhode Island, that time when she'd held on to the boys a few more days than Hans had expected. She'd spent the time researching United States divorce laws and sending off letters to various congressmen and state legislators to persuade them to pass a special law to allow her to get divorced here immediately, rather than wait for a year as Rhode Island law required. It was an unlikely quest, since politicians would have little incentive to bend the rules for her. She had left a list of all the recipients in her apartment in Germany. Hans gave it to me and I went right down the names. "Who's this one? Who's that one?" Like that, all the way down. Delores kept claiming that she couldn't remember, she wasn't sure, in a way that was very dismissive.

She was trying to evade the Hague rules, which dictated that you can't take your children from a country just to forum shop. So she needed to distance herself from these letters by claiming she had no idea who the heck she was sending them to. Not the best defense, since she must have known at one point, or she wouldn't have sent the letters to these particular Rhode Island legislators and administrators. But it was all the worse because of the judge involved. For Judge Browning had himself been a Rhode Island state senator for more than twenty years before he mounted the bench. He knew every single one of the politicians personally, and he looked more than a little riled that Delores, herself a native Rhode Islander, was claiming such ignorance. I could see his jaw tighten.

In the course of Delores's testimony, she had repeated her claim that Hans had posted his kids' naked pictures on the Internet. I got her to admit that she had spent "hours and hours" searching for those photos on the Internet. "But you never even found one?"

"Not yet."

"Yet you still made those claims about Hans?"

"Yes, I did. And I'll find those pictures. I know he put them there. I just know it."

"But if they were there—and I'm not saying they are—how would you know that Hans had put them there? Anyone could have done it, couldn't they? Even you."

Minsk objected to that, but the point was made. Her entire claim was pulled out of the air, with no evidence, to embarrass Hans and make him seem hazardous as a parent.

The judge didn't want the matter to rest so ambiguously. He referred the question to the FBI and the National Center for Missing and Exploited Children, which could search both its own extensive database and the Internet for nude photographs of Wolfie and Jacob. It was a matter of developing a computer model of their forms and faces to check against the millions and millions of images of child pornography in cyberspace. It took several days. It produced no matches.

ॐ

WE WEREN'T DONE WITH DELORES, BUT WE'D DAMAGED HER CREDibility enough that I could tell her lawyers were getting nervous by the way they whispered and scribbled frantic notes to each other. This behavior became all the more feverish when I called up to the stand the Webers' Polish housekeeper, Wera Czajkowski, who, after the separation, had worked for Delores before becoming disgusted and switching to Hans. Through an interpreter, Wera described what a pigsty Delores's place was, and she'd seen Delores smack the boys as a matter of routine. And not light slaps either, but real stingers that made Wera consider reporting her to the police. And another fact, Wera only spoke German with Delores and the children.

Before, whenever she'd felt most threatened, Delores had scooped up the kids and run, and I wanted to make sure this didn't happen again here. I mentioned my concern to the judge, who shared it but said there wasn't much more that law enforcement could do. After the initial location of Delores and the boys, we'd let our own team of detectives go. But I thought it might be a good idea to bring them back now in case Delores tried to bolt. The group was taken over by Ted McCallum. Because this was Rhode Island, he had to get a local guy involved too. We ended up having four investigators altogether, working around the clock, at serious expense.

A few days later, Delores brought the boys home from their private school in the afternoon as usual and, as an investigator watched, fed them dinner. Maybe an hour passed, and then the front door burst open and she hustled the kids into the back of her rental car, threw some things in the trunk, and took off. The investigator jumped on the radio to alert the others and gave chase. Delores wound through the rural byways of Hopkinton and the surrounding towns and, passing a cluster of small stores, finally pulled into an Avis rental place in the university town of Kingston. There she dropped off her car, that Mercury Marquis. Just as the investigator was trying to figure out how she was going to get home, she came barreling out of the lot in a white Impala. After a few turns down some Kingston side streets, she made her way south on Route 108, a two-lane highway that runs through the center of town. We had two guys on her by now, but traffic was heavy, and Delores alternately sped up and slowed to a crawl so the tails would have trouble keeping pace with her. It was a strange piece of surveillance, since she knew full well they were there. Once she had them both in front of her, she pulled off the road into a fast-food joint that, her luck, had a second entrance from the street behind. McCallum's guys kept flying along while she U-turned back to God knows where.

Where to this time? The court had impounded her passports—securely, I hoped—so she had to stay in the United States, but that still left a lot of places to hide. Panicked, the two investigators called in for reinforcements, and we got four detectives out there as quick as we could. Since it was almost ten o'clock at night, McCallum figured that she'd need to find someplace to crash. So he had the guys cruise all the motels in the area, checking for a white Impala with the license plate 508-AYR, which one of the investigators had thought to memorize. The four kept going farther and farther out in a widening circle. But Mc-

Callum thought he should track back to the spot where the investigator lost her. By midnight, McCallum had spotted her rented white Impala outside the Oceanview Motel. He went in to have a talk with the manager and discovered that Delores had registered under an assumed name. McCallum had a man stay on the car for the night, to make sure Delores didn't go anywhere.

First thing the next morning, I called Bodie Svoboda, who got an emergency motion to Judge Browning, formally requesting that Delores bring back the kids immediately. Browning obliged, and in a matter of hours Delores returned the kids to her parents' house. This time, we parked an investigator right outside the front door, with orders to follow her everywhere she went. The store, hairdresser, doughnut shop. Didn't matter. We wanted Delores to know she was being watched.

ভ

THE FINAL QUESTION THAT WE HAD TO ADDRESS IN COURT WAS THE central one. Were the pictures pornographic? In this, we argued that there was no absolute standard. The issue wasn't whether they were pornographic here in the United States, but whether they were in Germany, where the shots were taken. Cultural standards, after all, are very different in the two places. To determine this, after consulting widely with some of the leading experts in the field, we turned to a man named Michael Kimmelfarb, a professor of cultural anthropology at New York University, who was widely considered qualified to make such an analysis. A bearded gentleman of German descent, he was fully immersed in the languages and cultures of both countries.

After a series of failed attempts, I finally reached him on a Friday afternoon, and told him exactly what I needed and when I needed it—by six o'clock in the morning on Monday, so that I could familiarize myself with his report before we entered it into evidence after the court session opened at nine. We settled on a generous fee that Hans had approved for such an important rush job. I dispatched a young paralegal, Lara, to drive down to New York and hand-deliver a full set of the forty-nine images to Kimmelfarb at his apartment in Greenwich Village.

The first part of her mission complete, Lara went on to spend the weekend at her cousin's in Brooklyn. The plan was that she would drive the photographs and his report back very late Sunday night to hand-deliver them to me by six o'clock Monday morning. We set a deadline of midnight for Kimmelfarb, so that Lara would have plenty of time.

Well, whatever other skills he might possess, Kimmelfarb had very little sense of time, or perhaps of his own capacities, because he had opera tickets on Friday night, a faculty brunch on Saturday, and then something with a nephew later that evening. Lara reported all this to me with some anxiety after she called on Sunday morning to check in on him and discovered that he hadn't even started. I got Kimmelfarb on the phone and barked at him about the urgency of the undertaking. He got cracking a little before noon. But then his academic conscientiousness kicked in, and he didn't feel that he could say anything about German cultural standards without at least three footnotes per sentence. With mounting exasperation, Lara kept reporting to me about his inchworm progress across each line of each page. I kept Lara right there to keep him on task, with orders for regular injections of caffeine from the Starbucks across the street. It wasn't until three in the morning that a weary Kimmelfarb pulled the final pages from his printer. Lara grabbed them, dashed to her car in an all-night parking lot, sped up the FDR Drive, over the George Washington Bridge, and up Route 95 to Rhode Island. I was waiting for her on the steps of the Providence courthouse when she pulled up and delivered the precious text to me at a little after seven. I quickly ran my eyes over it—twenty pages of the densest prose I'd encountered since law school. It wasn't until I hit the final paragraph that I finally saw what I needed, as the mighty Kimmelfarb asserted that, in his professional opinion, not a single one of the forty-nine pictures would be considered pornographic in Germany.

That was big. At that point, it was pretty clear to me that things were going our way. You can always tell how you're doing by taking a close look at the opposite counsel, and when the trial resumed, Minsk was getting downright nasty. Once before, in hopes of getting an agreement, Judge Browning had put us before a magistrate judge whose job was to try to settle the case. The magistrate acted a bit like the host of *Let's Make a Deal*, and neither Minsk nor I felt like obliging. Minsk was mad about the way I was cutting up his client on cross-examination, and when Browning suggested that we appear before the magistrate again, Minsk agreed, but refused to be in the same room with me. He said he would negotiate only with Bodie. Alone.

"You can't tell us who you're going to negotiate with," I told him sharply. "I'm lead counsel. I'm the guy you'll be talking to if you're talking to anyone."

Now, before the magistrate, Minsk revealed that he was authorized by his client to make an offer for a financial settlement that would allow Mr. Weber to return immediately to Germany with the two Weber boys, never to deal with Mrs. Weber's interference again. Not now or ever.

"She would give up all claim to her sons?" I asked, dumbfounded.

"Yes."

"Well then," I said.

So it was not about the kids after all. It was about money. Or rather, it was about converting the kids to money. A marriage that had begun in conflict over money would end in conflict over money. "What's the tab?" I asked.

"Mrs. Weber has authorized me to demand a figure of five million dollars."

I was astounded. "Five million dollars?" I repeated.

"Yes, that's right."

It was quiet in the room. The magistrate asked me if I had any response.

"That's ridiculous," I said. "As Attorney Minsk well knows, this is a Hague Convention case. It is not a marital property case. It's not a custody case. There is nothing to buy here. You know that, Mr. Minsk. You're an expert in this area. My client is not going to pay ransom for his children. We are not going to pay five million dollars or five cents. And frankly, I would have thought you'd know better than to ask."

That infuriated him. "You just don't want to settle!" he shouted at me.

"Mr. Minsk," I replied. "You are acting like a fool."

"Don't call me a fool!" We were in the playground now.

"I didn't call you a fool. I said you were *acting* like a fool. There is a difference."

Minsk was furious. "I'm going to tell the judge what you said."

"Tell the judge whatever you want."

So Minsk roared back into the courtroom and rushed up to the judge's bench and said, breathlessly, "Mr. Nissenbaum just called me a fool."

Judge Browning just looked at him, and I thought I saw a little flicker of amusement cross his gray features. "Mr. Minsk, in my experience, this sort of name-calling is never a one-way street. For your sake, and for mine, let's not pursue this, okay?"

Poor Minsk didn't realize that he was standing on a trapdoor that was about to be opened. Delores was not pleased. Shortly after the session started in again the next morning, she told him to make another demand, and this time Minsk said no, he wouldn't. I could hear them arguing about it. I never found out what it was, but it must have been pretty off-the-wall for Minsk to refuse to pass it along. So she fired him. Right there in the courtroom. Boom!

Unfortunately for Minsk, he served at the pleasure of the judge, and Browning would not let him withdraw from the case. So he was stuck until he could be replaced. That made for a very unhappy member of the bar. I hated the way Minsk had acted, but I felt for him there, roped to this losing proposition, more of his money flying out the window every day. Still, I felt a lot worse for Hans.

All that remained was the report of the child psychiatrist that Judge Browning had retained to evaluate the analysis of the photographs done in Germany. She had reviewed the photographs, analytical procedures, and reports produced by each of the evaluators in Germany. Now she'd offer her expert opinion on the issues before the court, and in making his ruling the judge was likely to rely heavily on what she said. Browning had appointed Carol Coco, a well-known expert in child abuse and child pornography who was also a professor at Brown University. At first, I was worried. I'd seen her reports in several other cases, and it seemed she always sided with the accuser, regardless of the merits.

Coco was certainly brisk. Even though she was loaded down with tons of material from both sides of the case, she still managed to take just two weeks to issue her final report. She hand-delivered it to the judge at his home late on Wednesday, before the court was to be adjourned for two days. If I'd known that she was going to do that, I wouldn't have planned on heading to New York the next morning with Madeline and our three children—to see Beethoven's *Fidelio*, an appropriate opera for a divorce lawyer, surely. I was driving through Connecticut when Mindy called on my cell, saying the judge wanted all the lawyers on the Weber case to meet him in his chambers at noon. Well, this was eleven, and there was no way I could get back by twelve. So we decided that I would join the meeting by conference call. At noon, I pulled over to the side of the road and called in.

Judge Browning himself ran the meeting. Just from the sound of his voice, I could tell that he had come to some important conclusions about the case.

"Counsel," he began. "I have read Dr. Coco's report, along with the many others in the case, and I have weighed the testimony. And I have decided that, based on Mrs. Weber's attempted abduction of Wolfgang Weber and Jacob Weber a very short time ago, it is imperative that I not wait any longer before issuing a preliminary ruling in this case. So I want you all to know I have decided to award Hans Weber temporary sole legal and physical custody of the two boys, Wolfgang and Jacob." He paused for a moment. I expected some reaction from Delores's side of the case, but heard none. There were five lawyers in on the call, but there was nothing but silence, which must be a first in the annals of jurisprudence. "I'm directing Hans Weber to go directly to the Matthews School"—this is where his sons were temporarily enrolled—"and pick up the children immediately. I assume they are there today. Isn't that right, Mr. Minsk?"

"I have no reason to think they aren't."

"Good. Now, Mr. Minsk, I must ask that you and your two associates remain here in my office until that is accomplished. A bailiff will secure the door."

"Wait, I'm your prisoner, Your Honor?" Minsk asked. It was an attempt at levity, but I could hear the irritation in his voice.

"I'm simply taking some necessary precautions. I would appreciate it if all of you would also take out your cell phones and place them on my desk."

"Your Honor, don't you think this is a little excessive?"

"Normally, yes," Judge Browning replied. "In this case, no."

Browning instructed the clerk to fax a copy of his order to the headmistress at the school the boys had been attending in Rhode Island. The meeting went on a little longer, but there wasn't much more to say. We won. They lost. For now.

When I let Hans know what happened during the judge's conference, he thanked me. But any thought of me quickly paled beside the thought of his boys. He immediately drove to the school, and after explaining the situation to the headmistress who by then had the judge's order, he took his kids outside, where he gave them each a big hug and lifted them into the air.

Once the trial was officially concluded, Delores tried for a stay, but it didn't work. Hans was free to go with his boys back to Germany. He left for Berlin with the boys the next afternoon.

I wasn't there to see them off. I'd spent some time with Hans and the boys a few days before. They had all been staying at my house in Boxford while we waited for the judge to issue his findings and judgment. The visit confirmed what I had already amply sensed: that the boys loved Hans, and he loved them, and they deserved to be together. I was really happy that things worked out for them. When they returned to Germany, the Webers sent me three of the warmest and most heartfelt thank-you notes I've ever received from clients.

∞

THE KIDS ALL COME FROM SOMEWHERE, YES. AND THESE HAD THEIR origins at a breakfast buffet in Hong Kong. But then, what really matters is where they go. And in this case, they went back to Berlin with their father, back to their private school there with all their friends, and back to the domestic peace that all kids are entitled to.

And away from their mother.

∞

THE MATTER DID NOT END THERE.

After the case was over, Delores fell apart. Although all the detectives had been removed, she continued to believe she was being stalked by strange men in cars or on foot. When her parents couldn't bear such paranoid behavior any more, she moved to a small apartment across town. With her money running low, she used the last of it to fly to Berlin to see the children. Unable to afford a hotel, and not presentable enough for a shelter, she lived on the street, panhandling, for several weeks, until a childhood friend named Anna took pity on her and invited Delores into her home. But Delores was sure the stalkers were pursuing her there, and Hans was among them now, and he'd slashed her tires, tampered with her car, and encouraged strange men to proposition her.

Late one fall night several months later, Hans's front doorbell rang.

When he opened the door, he was shocked to find Delores. It was pouring out, and she had no umbrella or even much of a coat, and she was dripping wet. Hans had thought she was still in the United States.

"Let me in, Hans," she said. "Please. I want to see the boys."

"That is out of the question," Hans replied. "You must leave right now."

"I need to see the boys."

He shut the door, and bolted it. He could see through the glass that she was still there. So he went to call the police. That's when Dolores slipped around the outside of the house, trying to find a loose window or an unlocked door where she could get in. The boys were still up, watching TV, when they saw this bedraggled woman loom up in the window. Delores banged on the glass with her fist. "Open up," she yelled. "Please! I want to see you!"

Terrified, Wolfie and Jacob ran for their father, who sent the boys down into the finished basement while he raced around making sure the windows were all locked. Delores watched the boys disappear into the basement; then she went around to the far wall, where she got down on her knees on the wet ground by a low cellar window, and banged on the glass so hard with her shoe that the kids were afraid she'd break it open. She beckoned to the boys to come outside, come outside, now. Frightened, the boys raced back up the stairs to look for their father—only to find their mother blocking their path, a pool of rainwater around her feet. The back door had been left unlocked.

"Dad!" Wolfie screamed.

"Come children," Delores said quietly.

"No," Wolfie said, shielding the younger Jacob behind him.

"You should be with me. I'm your mother."

"We don't want to, Mamma. We don't want to go. We want to stay here. Don't make us go!" Wolfie yelled. Behind him, Jacob started to whimper, then cry. Delores stepped toward the boys, and was reaching a hand out to Jacob when a voice rang out: "Stop right there, right where you are. Don't move."

It was the police. They'd arrived while the boys were in the basement. Hans had gone to open the door for them.

"But these are my children," Delores told the men. "They should be with me." She reached for them and started to tug Wolfie toward the back door. But the boys stayed rooted where they were.

"Delores, I have custody, remember?" Hans told her. "You don't." While the police kept watch, he hurried to retrieve the court order. He brought back the documents and handed them to the police.

The policeman read it, and handed it back to Hans. "You will have to go now," he told Delores. "I'm afraid you have no choice."

With that, Delores left Hans's house.

She has not returned since.

ॐ

HANS DID NOT EMERGE UNSCATHED. AS THE CASE WENT ALONG, HE revealed to me flashes of anger that he had previously been at pains to conceal. I can't say I blame him. Delores had put him in a maddening situation. But he had styled himself as a man who was above such feelings. Emotionalism of that sort was for his wife—and I wondered if he had inadvertently encouraged such fits in his wife by being so measured and controlled. I'll never know, but I do know that in marriage it is rarely so simple as he is this way and she is that way. Plenty of times, he is this way *because* she is that way. And vice versa.

And while he came across as highly principled, there was one principle he overlooked. Paying up. After I knocked myself out to see justice served and get him his kids back, Hans stiffed me on the final portion of my bill, leaving me out more than three hundred grand, or half my fee.

So I got burned there. He promises to pay eventually. And if anyone will ever keep a promise like that, it is Hans.

All of this may be an apt conclusion for divorce work, where right and wrong don't necessarily move to separate addresses. Instead, they stay together, warring within the souls of my clients, as within the souls of me and you. My work isn't surgery, where the bad part can be neatly excised with a slice of the scalpel. No, this is law, where the best you can do is make a bad situation better. In my profession, I take a life that has been broken by divorce, and I try to make it less broken. I like to think I did that for Hans Weber.

Part Five

A PIECE OF
ADVICE

CHAPTER
TWELVE

IVORCE IS NOT ALWAYS THIS CRAZY. YOUR WIFE WON'T NEC-essarily run off with your children and accuse you of taking and distributing pornographic shots of them in order to extort money from you. Your husband is not likely to co-opt the top personnel of his company into cheating you out of your fair share of the marital assets. You probably won't marry a hooker who will rob you blind while trying to kill you.

While those situations are nearly unique, bad stuff can certainly happen. The hazard is out there. It walks into my office every day. While I make my living off it, I think it wouldn't be fair to let you return to your marriage, or enter into a fresh one, without a few tips to keep the relationship you now prize from turning into the kind of vicious, over-the-top divorce that could be featured in a volume like this. So let me turn avuncular.

First of all, to avoid a bad divorce, avoid a bad marriage. Unlike with stocks, in marriage past performance is indeed predictive of future results. If the man you are dating now is a heavy drinker with a mean streak, he is likely to remain so after you stroll down the aisle with him.

Sure, there are interventions like AA and exceptions like your uncle Herbie, but not that many. The fact is, there is nothing about marriage that is likely to improve serious character flaws. Rather, the stresses of a shared life are more likely to make them worse. Like arrows in flight, people tend to stay on a line.

And the greatest sex in the world won't save a bad marriage, if that's what you're thinking. Good sex can make a good marriage. But good sex will not save a bad one.

Nor will a baby.

Okay, let's assume it's too late for such wisdom, and you're stuck in a bad marriage that's getting worse by the day, and you want out. How can you and your spouse get divorced in a reasonable and dignified way, without ripping your children apart, bankrupting you, or ruining your reputation? First off, recognize that it takes time for a divorcing couple to accept the death of a marriage, and the longer the marriage lasted, the longer the mourning period will be, and neither spouse will be any good at divorce until that's done. So wait. And remember that the spouse who has decided to end the marriage is likely to be ready sooner—and so should, out of decency, give the other spouse time to catch up. Otherwise, any negotiations are likely to get ensnared in the anger and spitefulness that comes with grief.

Once divorce is in play, play fair. Don't try to hide marital assets. Instead, make everything available for a full accounting. Do not call the cops claiming your husband (or wife, for that matter) is physically abusing you unless he (or she) actually is. It's a charge that is all too easy to make, and a lie bears few legal consequences. No cop is going to dare question a wife (as is most often the case) who is screaming that she has been abused by her husband, even if the husband is yelling right back that he did no such thing. In this game of she said, he said, if there has been no sign of violence, the better actor will win every time. If you genuinely have been hurt, seek immediate protection. Even in the middle of the night, there is always a judge available to take calls from cops so protective orders can be issued. But if this is just a trick to get your husband out, you are simply lying, and you'll never be forgiven. This is no way to begin the delicate business of a divorce. And you absolutely shouldn't do this if it is all a plot to bring a new partner in. If you do that, your ex and your kids will hate you until the end of time.

Face facts. If the marriage has gone on for more than a decade, the marital assets—all the money that has been made during that period—will likely be divided fifty-fifty. There really aren't many exceptions to this rule, unless, that is, you have signed a premarital agreement. So don't waste your money on lawyers who won't be able to do any better for you or who want to rile up both parties in an attempt to earn their pay. It is more sensible to spend money on obtaining a fair appraisal of those assets, so both sides can agree on what a 50 percent share is. Only about 5 percent of divorce cases go to trial. Half of those cases are folks fighting over the value and division of assets. The other half are fighting over custody and visitation. Some fight over everything. It is far more expensive to fight things out in court than out of it. If you can avoid it, do. It will dramatically cut costs and reduce antagonism.

The children come first. That means an effort should be made to maintain the continuity of the children's lives as much as possible, even if that doesn't sit so well with the noncustodial parent. If the kids have been raised primarily by their mother, because their father has been jetting around the world as a corporate lawyer or working long hours at the office to support the family, then the mother should probably retain physical custody and the children should stay mostly with her, sleeping over at their father's only on alternate weekends. This may be hard on the father, but it would be harder on the children to do otherwise, if they are to maintain as much as possible the life they knew. For the father, this can be ameliorated by getting a house within walking distance of the mother's house, so that the kids can come and go more easily.

Given the antagonism that is often involved in adversarial divorce, with two highly paid lawyers going at it hammer and tongs, people sometimes wonder if it might be wiser to try mediation instead. Well, I am a professional mediator, and I know it can be—if the case is fairly simple, and all the financial information is out in the open. Are we dealing only with W-2s or 1099s, an IRA or 401(k), and an easily appraised house? Go for it. Mediation is cheaper and may be calmer too.

But mediation is not so good when everything is not out on the table. Mediators are not masters of discovery; they'll never find anything that is not laid out for them. It is not their job to look, or to force everyone to reveal all their information. So if one side is hiding assets, or lying, the other side has no way of knowing or proving otherwise. Mediators who are not lawyers are less likely to know the intricacies of the law. The mediator's goal is, simply, to get two parties to agree. It is not to ensure fairness. From the mediator's point of view, any settlement—even a bad one—is better than going to court to fight it out. So you should protect your interests by having a lawyer advise you at the start, in the middle, and at the end of the mediation process. And be sure to have a lawyer review the proposed settlement with you and prepare the agreement. Even lawyer-mediators prepare incomplete and internally inconsistent agreements. These don't settle things, but merely defer the fight to a later date.

☙❧

MY CLIENTS TURN TO ME IN HOPES THAT I CAN BRING ABOUT THE best result for them. Well, do I? How do things turn out once my work is done? Good question. The truth is, I don't know. I rarely hear from them again, except in the most oblique ways. A woman came up to me recently at a holiday party, and hissed at me, "I know who you are. You're Jerry Nissenbaum."

"Yes," I said. "That's right."

"You ruined my life! I hate you!" And then she called me a lot of rude names. I had no idea who she was. I excused myself and made my way to the bar, where she pursued me with more invective. This time she identified herself, and I remembered her case, even though it had been almost ten years. She and her husband had been warring over their two children, and I managed to get the husband joint legal and equal physical custody, so the kids spent half their time with him.

It wasn't until later that I understood why she was so upset. A friend of hers clued me in, and said that six months after the case was over the children had moved in with her ex full-time. And that's why she was mad at me now.

Another time, I heard from an appraiser who worked for a guy my client had divorced many years ago. We figured out he'd been cheating on his taxes for years, and the judge sent the information on to the IRS, who nailed him, imposing nasty penalties and auditing him every year. "My guy swears at you and about you every day," the auditor told me. "He says, 'I'm going to get that fucking Nissenbaum!'"

I get that kind of thing, but aside from Emily Worthington and a few others, I almost never hear from my clients again, even when the cases come out beautifully. And I understand. These people have come to me at the absolute worst time in their lives, and they tell me all about it, all the grimy details. They don't want to think, when they're talking to me, about how I know all their secrets. When they're done with the case, they're done with me. It's the same reason why a big law firm, one that does everything, almost never does divorce. No client wants to have to worry that the paralegals are gossiping about the intimate details of his or her life.

There's a client who sends me a big box of oranges and grapefruits every Christmas, and another one, of Turkish descent, who sends Madeline some Turkish delight. But that's about it. I'm fine with it. I was paid for what I did, the work is done, and that's the end of it.

But I know my clients have a hard time letting go. I call it Jerry Decompression. When we're all hot and heavy on a case, a client is probably thinking about it around the clock, and sometimes I am too. She may send me half a dozen e-mails, and add a phone call or two, and maybe even a piece of mail. It's not about me. It's about the case, and it shows how all-consuming cases are. It seems like her life is on the line. Or he's at a place where his past is over there, and his future is over here, and he is trying to cross the bridge between them. They've all got so much on their minds! Jerry, how much is it going to cost? Jerry, how long will it take? Jerry, how's it going to come out? Jerry, did you think of this thing, or that thing, or the other thing? Jerry, Jerry, Jerry. It can go on like that for months, sometimes years.

And then the gavel comes down, and the case is finally over. There is a bit of a wind-down, when we tidy things up. But soon that ends too. And then comes Jerry Decompression. All that Jerry, Jerry, Jerry has nowhere to go. The clients have no more questions for me, because all the questions have been answered, and all the issues resolved. The case is done. That's it. They need to get on with their lives, but they aren't ready. I am still on their minds, because I have been on their minds for so long. I warn my clients about this. I tell them they will still want to e-mail me, and call me, and send me things, even when they have nothing to say or send. I've seen it over and over. It's like a compulsion. Jerry, Jerry, Jerry.

I tell my clients that they have to ride it out. It's like a craving, and they simply have to resist the urge. It will subside. After a couple of months they won't feel the need to be in touch nearly so much. They'll wake up one morning, and they'll be amazed that they got through the previous day without thinking of me. And maybe three, four months after that, they'll go weeks without wanting to e-mail me. And then maybe a couple of months after that, they won't even be able to remember when they last thought of me. I'm gone from their lives completely. And you know what? That's when the divorce is over.

ACKNOWLEDGMENTS

We'd like to begin by thanking the many good people at Hudson Street Press who have worked so hard to create the book you now hold in your hands. Special gratitude goes to Luke Dempsey, who first took up the project and thrilled us with his infectious enthusiasm; and to the very capable Meghan Stevenson who has seen it through. Our agent Dan Conaway of Writers House has worked tirelessly and brilliantly to bring out the best from his two authors—and to bring the best to them as the manuscript underwent that magical transformation into a published book.

—G.N. and J.S.

All I am I owe to others. The debt goes back through countless generations, but I'll limit myself to the ancestors I best know and have most loved: my parents, Nettie Leah Nissenbaum and David Benjamin Nissenbaum, and to their parents, Rebecca Sugarman and Mendel Sugarman and Bessie and Joseph Nissenbaum. I can't resist including my wife's parents, John and Maria Celletti, whom I love as dearly as my own. And I am proud also to be the link to another generation—my five spectacular children, Marleah Rose, Nicholas Joseph, Benjamin John Celletti-Nissenbaum, Dion David Nissenbaum, and Kent Allan Grayson. The first three with my wife Madeline, and the other two with another extraordinary woman, Barbara Vincent.

Curiously, it was John Sedgwick's ancestor Theodore Sedgwick, a Revolutionary War–era lawyer and politician, who brought us together. I read John's remarkable family memoir, *In My Blood*, in which he recounts Theodore Sedgwick's tenacious and daring legal work to win the freedom of the now-celebrated Mumbet in 1781. She was the first slave in Massachusetts to win her freedom. I was so moved by the story, and John's telling of it, I knew I wanted to work with him. I had accumulated a basketful of amazing stories over the years, but it has taken John to make such a captivating book out of them. He has turned my legal style into something far more compelling, created a structure that pulls together the many different elements of my practice, and has brought a wonderful vitality to the writing, which animates the many characters of my tales. John, you and I have made a great team, and I can't thank you enough.

I am indebted to my many clients over the years, all of whom have trusted me with the secrets of their past and with their hopes for the future. In telling their stories, I have concealed their identities. Even so, I know that they would want a book like this to be written, both as a record of their own travails and as a caution to others about what can happen and what to be prepared for.

I can't say enough about the many partners, associates, law clerks, paralegals, secretarial staff, and bookkeepers I have had through the many years of my practice. But I am especially grateful to my present colleagues— my wife Madeline, Wendy Hickey, Stanley Cohen, Mindy Markvon, and Marie Trinagale. This work cannot be done alone. It is all of you who make it possible.

—G.N.

As a coauthor, my role was fairly simple. Listen to Jerry. Sharp-eyed and hilarious, blessed with total recall and a storyteller's gift, Jerry enthralled me with hour after hour of his reminiscences and observations about law and life, which seemed increasingly inextricable the longer he talked. Jerry gave me complete access to case files, investigative reports, client narratives, court testimony, and lots more. And he was endlessly patient as he answered yet another layman's question about the form UCC-1, the meaning of *pro se,* and the difference between a guardian and a Guardian ad Litem. With me, Jerry handled all of it with a degree of merriment I would have thought unimaginable, as if divorce law was actually the cheeriest possible occupation—as for him it is. In short, he proved the perfect colleague and companion for what has proved to be an astonishing journey across the little-charted, often spooky, always astonishing landscape that is divorce. Thank you, Jerry, for bringing me along on this wild ride.

—J.S.